D1593811

Confronting Ecological Crisis in Appalachia and the South

CONFRONTING ECOLOGICAL CRISIS IN APPALACHIA AND THE SOUTH

University and Community Partnerships

Edited by
Stephanie McSpirit,
Lynne Faltraco, and
Conner Bailey

UNIVERSITY PRESS OF KENTUCKY

Scholarly publisher for the Commonwealth,
serving Bellarmine University, Berea College, Centre College of Kentucky, Eastern
Kentucky University, The Filson Historical Society, Georgetown College, Kentucky
Historical Society, Kentucky State University, Morehead State University, Murray
State University, Northern Kentucky University, Transylvania University, University of
Kentucky, University of Louisville, and Western Kentucky University.
All rights reserved.

Editorial and Sales Offices: The University Press of Kentucky
663 South Limestone Street, Lexington, Kentucky 40508-4008
www.kentuckypress.com

16 15 14 13 12   5 4 3 2 1

Library of Congress Cataloging-in-Publication Data

Confronting ecological crisis in Appalachia and the South : university and community
partnerships / edited by Stephanie McSpirit, Lynne Faltraco, and Conner Bailey.
      p. cm.
   Includes bibliographical references and index.
   ISBN 978-0-8131-3619-6 (hbk. : alk. paper) — ISBN 978-0-8131-3661-5 (pdf) —
   ISBN 978-0-8131-3972-2 (epub)
   1. Environmentalism—Appalachian Region. 2. Environmentalism—Southern States.
3. Environmental protection—Appalachian Region—Citizen participation.
4. Environmental protection—Southern States—Citizen participation. 5. Environmental
policy—Appalachian Region—Citizen participation. 6. Environmental policy—
Southern States—Citizen participation. 7. Community and college—Appalachian
Region. 8. Community and college—Southern States. 9. Industries—Environmental
aspects—Appalachian Region. 10. Industries—Environmental aspects—Southern States.
I. McSpirit, Stephanie, 1962-   II. Faltraco, Lynne, 1947- III. Bailey, Conner.
   GE198.A33C66 2012
   363.7'060974—dc23   2012013775

This book is printed on acid-free paper meeting the requirements of the American National
Standard for Permanence in Paper for Printed Library Materials.

Manufactured in the United States of America.

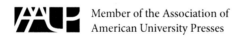 Member of the Association of
American University Presses

Contents

Foreword
Work That Is Real

Marge Piercy tells us in one of her poems,

> The pitcher cries for water to carry
> and a person for work that is real.[1]

These lines came to mind while I was reading the stories in this book. As I read them I could *feel* the truth Piercy was trying to communicate in her poem. But I felt and learned a lot more. That's because the stories in *Confronting Ecological Crisis in Appalachia and the South* aren't about people who merely cry or yearn for real work. They're about people who jump in and do it.

The realness of the work in the stories of community-university partnerships you'll read about in this book stands in stark contrast to the artificiality of so much of what we do and experience in both our communities and our universities. Carefully staged public meetings, hearings, and forums in communities; scripted role plays; case studies; and lectures in university classrooms—whatever value such activities may sometimes have, they often feel like meaningless rituals without consequence. And they rarely, it so often seems and feels, involve much work that is real.

So what makes work real? Simply put, work is real when it matters. When it makes a difference. When it calls for and enables individual and collective initiative, improvisation, innovation, spontaneity, and creativity. When its steps and outcomes aren't fixed or predetermined by a set of "best practices," an "evidence-based program," or a cookie-cutter recipe or blueprint. And not least, when people who are engaged in it are honest with each other about what they feel and think and believe.

This probably sounds like a mere truism, something everyone already knows. And of course, it is. But the real work you'll read about in this book has a provocative edge to it that's simultaneously refreshing and troubling. The edge has to do with the ways students and faculty members engage with their community partners. They do so not only as scholars and scientists but also as activists and advocates who openly take sides in real-time, on-the-ground battles that pit one set of interests against another. Battles that have real consequences for real people and communities. Battles that hold in the balance the integrity of a region's environment and the physical, economic, cultural, and political health and well-being of its people. Battles, in other words, that matter.[2]

For those who have long called on universities to be on the side of "the people" instead of corporations and other powerful interests, all this is refreshing.[3] So why and how would some see it as troubling? In short, because it violates a widely held principle about the university: that it should be neutral, unbiased, and detached.

For a pointed description and defense of this principle, listen to John Taylor, a professor of philosophy from Michigan State University who wrote a book that was published in 1981 under the title *The Public Commission of the University.* In his book Taylor claimed that the modern university was established as "a neutral ground beyond politics or ideology, upon which questions of public importance might be debated." According to him, the university is supposed to be "a neutral assembly of scholars gathered for the critical exchange of ideas." He declared that it "must enact the role of an impartial observer, set apart from all of the estranging contests that divide us, in action or passion, in the neighborhood, the market and the forum." In order for the university "to perform its public office, to do its proper work," he wrote, it "must preserve itself beyond partisanship and beyond advocacy."[4]

While Taylor's conception of the neutrality of the university included a negative function of refusing partisanship and advocacy, it also included a "positive" function of criticism. "By the neutrality of the university I understand the obligatory refusal of the corporation to identify itself with any of the partisan positions that are contested in theory within it or that are agitated in fact beyond it," he wrote. "But I intend also, besides this bare obligation of detachment, a positive commission. The positive exercise of neutrality in the university is what ordinarily we entitle the function of criticism." With respect to criticism, Taylor made an astonishing claim: "All the university can offer in any of its functions is criticism." He acknowledged that the function of criticism from a position of neutrality "is unavoidably a political role. The problem of a neutral is not how to be out of the world but how to be in it—how to be in it without being of it."[5]

According to Taylor, the neutrality of a university "is the price of its freedom. Let its neutrality be doubted, all of its acts will be thought suspect. . . . Let its neutrality be assured, a democratic society will license it to discuss all matters, to enter unprohibited into every avenue of rational inquiry, to pursue truth critically by demanding for every belief evidence." Maintaining neutrality, Taylor argued, benefits both the scholarly enterprise and democracy. "What the scholar wants, what a democracy needs," he wrote, "is precisely what the university affords—not silence, not unanimity, not even agreement, but the civilization of argument. What the university distinctively affords is the unspoken condition of all rational inquiry, a neutral ground upon which divided partisans may meet, listening as well as speaking."[6]

Taylor's claim that "the function of criticism" is the "positive exercise of neutrality" is incoherent. Since when are critics ever neutral? Doesn't criticism arise from a particular view or bias? More importantly, Taylor's ideal conception of the university as a "neutral assembly of scholars" is hard to square with its many non-neutral relationships and activities. Universities serve particular interests through their research, teaching, and "service" missions. They aren't neutral. To be fair, Taylor recognized this. And he wrote his book in protest. Whatever truths there may be in what he wrote, his view of the possibility and desirability of neutrality in academic work has increasingly been thrown into question.[7] To many today (including me) it's both mistaken and out of date. Despite this, his main position is still held and espoused.

Here's a striking example that happens to be directly relevant to *Confronting Ecological Crisis in Appalachia and the South*. In 1999 the Kellogg Commission on the Future of State and Land-Grant Universities issued a report on the theme of engagement. In making its plea for scholars and universities to become actively and directly engaged in civic life, the commission was careful to say that engagement must meet the test of "academic neutrality." By necessity, it noted, engagement will sometimes involve contentious civic issues, and the way such issues are addressed have profound social, economic, environmental, and political consequences. Therefore, the commission stated, the question that must be asked is "whether outreach maintains the university in the role of neutral facilitator and source of information when public policy issues, particularly contentious ones, are at stake."[8]

What are we to make of the fact that the stories of community-university partnerships in *Confronting Ecological Crisis in Appalachia and the South* violate the neutrality principle that Taylor and the Kellogg Commission describe and defend? Or do they really violate it? Wasn't Taylor speaking of the neutrality of the university as an institution rather than the neutrality of faculty and staff as individuals? And wasn't the commission speaking of formal public policies that are being considered by legislatures rather than public issues and problems that are being faced by communities? Maybe so. But do these distinctions matter? And can the operating principles and behavior of the university as an institution really be separated out from the principles and behavior of its faculty and staff? After all, it's not "the university" that does outreach or engagement. It's faculty, staff, and students.

I don't have the space to take these questions up in detail here. What I want to do is simply say that one of the reasons why this book is valuable is because it troubles long-standing claims and convictions about the principle of neutrality in American higher education. And it does so in ways that provoke debate, discussion, and reflection about an extraordinarily important set of questions:

What is the university's "public office"? What are its core public purposes in a democracy? What do citizens want and need from their universities? What do scholars want and need to perform their work? How should students, professors, and other academic staff work with citizens and communities in addressing pressing social and environmental problems and struggles? What roles should they play? What should—and what can—they contribute? How can they avoid the exploitative and parasitic patterns of relationships that have been all too common in academic history? How might they build and sustain public relationships that are respectful and mutually beneficial? What do they need to do—and not do—in order to advance the larger interests of the public instead of the smaller and narrower self-interests of corporations and other powerful groups?

These are not easy questions to raise, let alone answer. But we need to do both. And we need to do so in ways that are open to different and sometimes conflicting answers that are contextually and culturally sensitive rather than universally true or correct.

I'd like to end with another question and a related suggestion.

One of the most important questions we need to be able to answer better than we currently do is this: What kind of knowledge does a democratic society need? The short answer to that question is, knowledge people can trust. Given this, instead of worrying and arguing about neutrality, we'd be better off if we spent our time thinking about the issue of trustworthiness.[9] To do so, we'll have to ask and consider even more questions.

How trustworthy are our universities today? What does a university have to do—and not do—to be worthy of people's trust? How, where, and by whom is trustworthy knowledge discovered or constructed? Is knowledge that is produced by academics who strive to be neutral inherently more trustworthy than knowledge that is produced by activist scholars who choose to support particular interests, causes, and values? How do activist scholars avoid the danger of producing propaganda to advance their preferred interests and agendas instead of knowledge that can be trusted?

The people who are engaged in the partnerships we read about in this book have taken these questions seriously. But they haven't been paralyzed by them. I admire them for that. They've plunged into complex, controversial, and difficult work headfirst, contradictions, uncertainties, and unresolved tensions and theoretical fine points be damned. By engaging in work that is real, they're like the people Marge Piercy says she loves best—people who

> jump into work head first
> without dallying in the shadows
> and swim off with sure strokes almost out of sight.
> They seem to become natives of that element,
> the black sleek heads of seals
> bouncing like half-submerged balls.

Having been given their stories, having admired their sure if not also sometimes awkward or mistaken strokes and their efforts to become natives of the elements of civic life, we as readers have some real work of our own to do. Not only the work of learning from their stories but also of living and telling our own.

Scott J. Peters
Author of *Democracy and Higher Education:
Traditions and Stories of Civic Engagement*

Notes

1. Marge Piercy, "To Be of Use," in *Circles on the Water* (New York: Alfred A. Knopf, 1982).

2. For an important study of this kind of real work in Appalachia, see John Gaventa, *Power and Powerlessness: Quiescence and Rebellion in an Appalachian Valley* (Urbana: University of Illinois Press, 1982).

3. On the theme of the university siding with "the people," see Leonard Fink, *Progressive Intellectuals and the Dilemmas of Democratic Commitment* (Cambridge, MA: Harvard University Press, 1997); John L. Recchiuti, *Civic Engagement: Social Science and Progressive-Era Reform in New York City* (Philadelphia: University of Pennsylvania Press, 2007); Davydd J. Greenwood and Morten Levin, *Introduction to Action Research: Social Research for Social Change*, 2nd ed. (Thousand Oaks, CA: Sage, 2007); Charles F. Hale, ed., *Engaging Contradictions: Theory, Politics, and Methods of Activist Scholarship* (Berkeley: University of California Press, 2008); and Scott M. Gelber, *The University and the People: Envisioning American Higher Education in an Era of Populist Protest* (Madison: University of Wisconsin Press, 2011). For an exceptionally articulate case against activist scholarship of all kinds, see Martyn Hammersley, *The Politics of Social Research* (Thousand Oaks, CA: Sage, 1995).

4. John F. A. Taylor, *The Public Commission of the University: The Role of the Community of Scholars in an Industrial, Urban, and Corporate Society* (New York: New York University Press, 1981), 12, 14, 17.

5. Taylor, *Public Commission*, 7, 25–26, 29. Taylor's point is similar to one made by Frederick Jackson Turner in his 1910 essay "Pioneer Ideals and the State University," in *The Frontier in American History* (1920; reprint, New York: Dover, 1996). In that essay Turner wrote that the state university has "a peculiar power in the directness of its influence upon the whole people and a peculiar limitation in its dependence upon the people. The ideals of the people constitute the atmosphere in which it moves, though it can itself affect this atmosphere. Herein is the source of its strength and the direction of its difficulties. For to fulfill its mission of uplifting the state to continuously higher levels the University must, in the words of Mr. Bryce, 'serve the time without yielding to it'; it must recognize new needs without becoming subordinate to the immediately practical, to the short-sightedly expedient" (283–84).

6. Taylor, *Public Commission*, 15, 18–19.

7. On the theme of neutrality, see Sandra Harding, "After the Neutrality Ideal: Science, Politics, and 'Strong Objectivity,'" *Social Research* 59, no. 3 (1992): 567–87. It's important not to confuse neutrality with objectivity. They're not the same. See Thomas Haskell, *Objectivity Is Not Neutrality: Explanatory Schemes in History* (Baltimore, MD: Johns Hopkins University Press, 1998).

8. Kellogg Commission on the Future of State and Land-Grant Institutions, *Returning to Our Roots: The Engaged Institution* (Washington, D.C.: National Association of State Universities and Land-Grant Colleges, 1999), 12.

9. On trustworthiness, see Naomi Scheman, "Epistemology Resuscitated: Objectivity as Trustworthiness," in *Engendering Rationalities,* ed. Nancy Tuana and Sandra Morgen (Albany, NY: SUNY Press, 2001), 23–52.

Introduction

Forging Partnerships between Communities and Academic Activists

Stephanie McSpirit, Lynne Faltraco, and Conner Bailey

There are places in Appalachia and parts of the South that are characterized by widespread ecological degradation and community crises. These phenomena of environmental and community conflict are closely linked and have their origins in a history where the power to make decisions that affect people's quality of life often is held by people living elsewhere. Recurring patterns of corporate control over local economies and absentee ownership of land and resources historically have made it difficult for communities in Appalachia and the South to protect the purity of their waterways, the sanctity and beauty of their mountains and forests, and the health and safety of their families and communities. Over the past several decades academic observers have documented the political and economic causes of the social and ecological problems that have afflicted Appalachia and the South, and these academic works as well as many others start to provide social and historical context for this book.[1]

However, this litany of woe may falsely portray Appalachian and southern residents as victims and invariable pawns in structures of production and resource extraction over which they seemingly have little control. The authors of the following chapters would definitely see this as a misreading of the Appalachian and southern experience. Shaunna Scott makes this point in chapter 2 by reviewing the Appalachian Land Ownership Study, which involved more than sixty activists, citizens, and academics between 1979 and 1980. Taskforce members were involved in collecting county data on landownership and property taxes across the states of Kentucky, West Virginia, Tennessee, Virginia, North Carolina, and Alabama. Shaunna explores the recollections and reflections of some key taskforce members and makes clear that the study became a vehicle for discussion, organization, and political action throughout the Appalachian region. As Shaunna recounts, soon after the study's release citizens throughout the region began meeting about tax and property laws that exempted coal owners and that allowed the strip-mining of another property owner's land. Not just Shaunna but all of the authors of each of the chapters that follow write lucidly about emerging new partnerships and alliances that have formed between community residents, activists, and others, and how, through these alliances, people have begun working together to challenge powerful internal structures and outside global forces to protect local ecosystems and the human communities that are part of these living systems.

The chapters in this book address a wide range of cases that have presented challenges to local environments, public health, and social justice faced by the people of Appalachia and the South. Readers will encounter political systems based on patronage and paternalism from the coalfields of eastern Kentucky (chapters 4, 5, and 10) to the chemical weapons demilitarization program of the U.S. Army (chapters 8 and 9). Yet standing in front of these looming and powerful structures are committed citizens who have organized themselves to confront both external power holders and, often, their own local, state, and federal representatives. Out of these alliances new environmental groups and organizations have emerged across Appalachia and the South over the past several decades.[2]

Citizen activists and organizations have demanded the end of the wholesale destruction of mountains, forests, and waterways and the contamination of their communities. Many of their valiant efforts have been documented by academic researchers and scholars. Two included here, Conner Bailey (chapter 6) and Robert Futrell (chapter 9), explore academic and community partnerships in combating environmental harms. Conner coauthors chapter 6 with Lynne Faltraco, a founding member of Concerned Citizens of Rutherford County (CCRC). Together they describe a struggle to protect native hardwood forests of Appalachia from being clear-cut, chipped, and made into paper products. Chip mills are highly automated facilities that grind whole trees into woodchips for making paper, particleboard, and other wood-based materials. Between the late 1980s and the mid-1990s more than 140 large-scale chipping operations were established in the region. In the mid-1990s

CCRC emerged to challenge one particular chip mill facility in Rutherford County. Citizens challenged the local ordinances that allowed for unconstrained clear-cutting of local woodlands to feed this mill. In chapter 9 Robert and his coauthor describe how the Kentucky Environmental Foundation (KEF) coordinated local activism, tied local activists into wider political networks, and built political strategies, work that has since redirected the U.S. Army's efforts away from incineration of chemical weapons at one storage site toward more environmentally sound, closed-loop disposal systems.[3]

Rising academic and public consciousness about environmental, public health, and social justice issues in Appalachia and the South are by no means isolated phenomena. But based on our reading and review of other materials, little attention has been devoted to interactions between college faculty and students with community activists and the community-based organizations that are emerging across Appalachia and the South. Most of what we know is related to the historic role of the Tennessee Highlander Research and Education Center as a meeting place for activists and university people committed to social justice and social change. Having institutional resources on the side of communities is of vital importance. Highlander has been a model example of such a resource, providing meeting space for people to come together and think through their problems and providing small grants to communities. Universities and colleges can be another important institutional resource, as demonstrated in the pages ahead. Our own personal experiences suggest to us that interaction between community and academic activists is becoming more common, more accepted, and more important. This volume attempts to highlight some of the partnerships that have emerged throughout Appalachia and the South between community activists and university people and how they have worked together to confront threats to local environments and communities.[4]

This volume has been written to be useful to people both inside and outside of academe. It is important that this book speak not only to faculty but also to students and community leaders to encourage greater collaboration between communities and colleges and universities. A growing number of academic institutions, in the name of service and regional stewardship, are encouraging faculty and students to work within local communities and with community groups on environmental, educational, and development initiatives. In chapter 1 Sherry Cable addresses this shift in focus among universities from purely research and teaching toward civic engagement. As she notes in her final pages, this kind of engagement with local communities and community groups has become a core mission for some universities. In other words, it has become increasingly evident that while some academics still choose to ignore community problems, even in their home communities, others have ventured forth, often with teams of students, to meet, talk, and work with community leaders and residents. As a result, many university faculty and students have become more and more engaged in local community issues and community struggles.

This book focuses on environmental problems and struggles. The chapters share with readers the conversations, interactions, and actions that various university researchers, university students, and community residents have had together in confronting challenges to the local ecosystem, public safety, and public health. Many of these chapters have been cowritten by community and academic partners, which makes this volume all the more unique in providing insight into the perspectives of both community and academic partners and partnerships. Through these cases readers will learn not only about partnerships and collaborations between university and community people but also about several important cases of environmental struggle and conflict not reported elsewhere that have occurred in Appalachia and the South over the past decades.

As the chapters ahead will reveal, when academic activists and students enter the field to assist local residents in collecting interviews and conducting surveys or in analyzing regulatory and scientific documentation, they help broaden the tools that are available to a community fighting against powerful interests. Likewise, community residents and local activists bring their own skills, knowledge, and expertise that are grounded in a sense of place and rooted in the context of the immediate struggle. The powerful and convincing contributions that community residents can make to a partnership and collaboration can help in gaining a fuller and deeper understanding of the problems at hand and can help set the course of action. However, the local knowledge, insights, and abilities that community activists possess have typically been discounted and even dismissed by corporate and governmental power brokers. By contrast, many college and university faculty have come to recognize and appreciate the local expertise and holistic knowledge that community residents can provide in understanding local environmental conflicts and struggles. Subsequently, there has been growing recognition within universities and community colleges that there are mutual benefits when working with community activists on an environmental issue.[5]

In each chapter of this book readers will see the connection and benefits of working in partnership in the search for democratic and sustainable alternatives. Readers will see citizen activists and their university partners poring over regulatory documents and scientific, technical, and legal papers to challenge the causes of continued ecological degradation and other threats to people's ability to enjoy life free from environmental risks and pollution. In chapter 8, for example, Suzanne Marshall provides a historical overview of the two major environmental justice issues facing Anniston, Alabama: PCB (polychlorinated biphenyl) contamination and the U.S. Army's incineration plans for the chemical weapons stockpile there. As a historian, Suzanne committed her time outside of work to collecting oral histories with residents and collecting and compiling other records and information to document historical trends between race and pollution in Anniston. As Suzanne and her coauthors, Rufus Kinney and Antoinnette Hudson, explain, although these two problems initially were seen as separate issues, they were soon seen as part of a larger environmental injustice facing Anniston citizens.[6]

For many concerned citizens, scientific, technical, and legal arguments by corporations and governments assuring the safety of a new technology or corporate plan have not added up. Let's face it, governments, corporations, and the military lie. They have institutional interests, and they hire people to carry out and promote those interests. Such people have no connection or loyalty to the communities being harmed or at risk of being harmed by government, corporate, and military decisions. Moreover, people representing institutional interests have little or no respect for the communities in which they operate, where they often take the approach of mushroom growers—keep them (local residents) in the dark and feed them bullshit.

Because of this, some citizen activists have started to look to colleges and universities for some sympathetic help in effectively countering the legal and scientific claims brought forward by timber companies (chapter 6), coal companies (chapters 4 and 5), industrial hog farms (chapter 7), or the government (chapters 7, 8, and 9). The kind of university-community engagement represented in these chapters can result in outreach being transformed into something else, which is described in chapter 11 as "inreach." This is the growing recognition that colleges and universities are not the sole repositories of knowledge in society and that faculty and their students have much to learn and understand from community activists. This learning and sharing, through a mutual meeting place of conversations, interviews, and deep discussions such as those that Suzanne was a part of in Anniston, can produce a richer understanding of the ecological and economic problems that local communities face.

Empowerment through Participatory Research

Partnerships between academics and citizen activists have become increasingly important in Appalachia and the South, but they are certainly not limited to these regions. Such participatory research, where community residents and academics have both been involved in local causes, has been well established in the field of international development and has found its way into the general fields of environmental sociology, natural resource management, and public and environmental health. There also has been a small proliferation of literature that documents participatory approaches and citizen involvement in the reconstitution of environmental risk assessments and impact statements so that they better capture the perspective and position of local communities. Within the field of risk assessment, participatory types of research have addressed the impacts of industrial forestry practices on local communities, examined the effects of radioactive contamination on indigenous food sources and workers' health, and evaluated pesticide exposure among farm workers; they also have been used on other environmental fronts to document concerns and needs of local communities facing environmental risks and risky technologies. Partnerships between community residents and academics within these fields, and in other fields, have started to influence university practices in general. As already mentioned, a number of universities have begun to encourage this type of outreach/inreach in the name of civic engagement and regional stewardship.[7]

For these reasons, it seems important to write about some of these emerging partnerships. In the chapters ahead, through the conversations between community and academic authors, readers will learn about collaborations that have occurred between universities and communities throughout Appalachia and the South. Readers will learn how citizens are tackling environmental challenges in partnership with faculty and students from local colleges and universities. They will hear the story of college and university faculty working with local people to develop and use new forms of civic engagement and democratic forms of discourse and science. Readers will hear, based on firsthand accounts, about conversations and meetings between academics and local residents and how these exchanges and interviews were used to recatalog and reevaluate ecological damage, environmental degradation, and potential health threats to local communities. Readers will also learn how citizens, armed with new tools and allies, have challenged official risk assessments and permit applications of agency and company bureaucrats and have begun to democratically "take back" their communities.

The stories told here are about partnerships and relationships. Like all relationships, those described in this book take work and recognition that all parties are starting from different points. Many community activists rightly view colleges and universities as strange and formidable places, while many academics may feel out of place in communities that are unlike any in which they have lived before. But whenever two people meet there is always that newness and opportunity for understanding and sharing stories and putting each other at ease. First meetings and initial encounters make for good memories later.

In those initial meetings, there is also always the question of motivations, especially among community residents who, in thinking about prospective college or university partners, ask themselves, Why is this person here and what are their intentions and motivations? To be fair, academics may be interested in a community partnership and collaboration to generate a new research project that will result in new opportunities and, potentially, publications. Academics may be motivated at least in part by generating publications to advance the state of knowledge within their academic discipline. Publications are also important for university faculty because a record of publication is often necessary to advance through the ranks of a university. This drive to publish, however, may seem extremely strange to a community resident who is primarily driven by the clear and overriding cause of combating an environmental harm or injustice and who is in immediate need of assistance and answers to confront and combat those harms. In fact, many young university academics may tend to avoid engagement with communities and community activists because long hours in a politically charged environment might take time away from the solitary time required for writing and publishing. These external pressures may have the effect of dissuading junior faculty from becoming involved precisely at that point in their career when their youth, energy, and cutting-edge knowledge could make a real difference if partnered with a community group and applied to community needs. So instead, many young faculty members keep themselves locked away in their offices writing publications based on secondary or recycled dissertation data. This represents a dilemma between traditional university practices and current university missions that encourage civic engagement. Encouraging civic engagement can have a positive impact on a young researcher's productivity by opening up layers of opportunity that previously were not available. Gaining such access involves long-term and consistent commitment on the part of university researchers to serving community interests and concerns. The investment in time by a researcher can pay off in publications later, but that cannot be the only or even the primary goal. Community partners have other, more immediate goals that must take the front seat and drive the research project and collaboration between university and community partners.

In the cases presented here, readers will meet what Scott Peters has referred to as "public scholarship." In this kind of scholarship, it is assumed and expected that university faculty members will leave their offices and work with community residents as part of their regular routine. The other assumption of such public forms of scholarship is that research will be done with university faculty and community organizers equally leading the way. Academic and community partnerships show the benefits of working together, developing levels of trust, selecting common goals to collaborate on, and ultimately effecting change. This often means educating communities with academic and scientific knowledge and, in turn, educating faculty and their students about communities and the challenges that they face. Through this process communities have the benefit of gaining knowledge and gathering resources and documentation to help support their causes, while academia can benefit from understanding how citizens organize to protect their communities.[8]

The chapters that follow were written by many experts and authors, but only some have a PhD. Readers will also learn that virtually *all* of the contributors to this volume have prepared for and spoken at public hearings; met with agency officials and legislators; filed open-records requests; checked regulatory records; reviewed statutes and regulatory guidelines; educated themselves about and deciphered the science of impact statements, risk assessments, and air, water, and soils data; and formulated lucid commentaries and critiques about the state of things at the local, state, federal, and even global levels. The book will also show how such efforts have provoked discussions among committed individuals and encouraged others, who otherwise might never have done so, to take a stand against the corporate and regulatory maneuverings that they have unearthed.

One of our intents has been to produce a highly readable book, one that is approachable and useful to a wide range of readers. Readers can be assured that we are not writing for a specialized audience of academics and graduate students, as this certainly would be out of accord with the very principles of equalizing the discourse that we are espousing here. By sharing the following cases, we want to encourage students and faculty to examine their place in their own community, their university, and how they can better position themselves between the two. We also want to help community leaders reach out to academic partners in ways that will be helpful to them and their causes. By sharing the stories and the hard work that has occurred between citizen activists and their academic partners, we hope that this book will help in further promoting a democratized civic science that bridges the divide between colleges and universities and communities within Appalachia, the South, and elsewhere. We offer no blueprint for doing so beyond the need for all parties to enter into partnerships with open minds, mutual respect, and a long-term commitment. Civic science and public scholarship should be considered more of a rubric of opportunities for engagement than a particular method or methodology. In each chapter academic and community partners use and discuss different strategies and techniques for working together. Readers might do well to take note of the different strategies and methods that are used within these pages to push the environmental concerns of local people onto the public policy–making agenda. Below, we start to summarize some of the strategies and lessons learned from each of the chapters. Throughout each chapter, different moments and memories of these partnerships and actions are shared between academic and community activists, and thus we caution readers not to just look for some "strategies" for doing action-based research, public scholarship, or civic science. Instead, we hope that readers of this volume will be inspired to engage in collaboration and public scholarship through discussions and partnerships that bridge whatever gap is found between colleges and universities and communities.[9]

Plan of the Book

Sherry Cable begins this volume with personal reflections on research with Yellow Creek Concerned Citizens (YCCC) in southeastern Kentucky. In 1987, as a brand-new assistant professor, Sherry stood in a living room and asked YCCC members to allow her to conduct a case study of the group and their efforts. When asked what the group would gain from her work, she thought and finally answered, "Nothing." After a bit of silence one of the members broke in and said heartily, "I say, let her study us! At least she didn't lie to us like the others—she didn't promise us a goddam thing!" One of the important lessons that Sherry provides is that trust is built on such forms of honesty, and developing trust and goodwill between community and academic activists is a key factor in determining the success of the partnership. Sherry reflects on her role as a "parasitic" researcher and how that experience helped her grow toward a new model of engagement.

In chapter 2 Shaunna Scott summarizes the historic work of the Appalachian Land Ownership Task Force (ALOFT), which took place between 1979 and 1980 and involved over sixty activists, citizens, and academics. Task force members were involved in collecting county data on landownership and property taxes across the states of Kentucky, West Virginia, Tennessee, Virginia, North Carolina, and Alabama. As Shaunna recounts, soon after the study's release citizens throughout the region began meeting about tax and property laws. Out of these meetings and early organizing efforts, Kentuckians for the Commonwealth (KFTC) emerged as a powerful grassroots organization working in the coalfields of rural Appalachia. When Shaunna shared her initial research, several other contributors to this volume described the formative role that the task force's study had played in their own lives and in the rise of several other grassroots organizations throughout the region.

With chapter 3, Roy Silver of Southeast Kentucky Community and Technical College provides a lesson in the types of partnerships and collaborations that can effectively link colleges and universities with the needs of communities facing an environmental crisis. This case had its origins in 1989, when the State Division of Water notified residents of the Dayhoit community in Harlan County, Kentucky, that they should immediately stop using their water for drinking and cooking. Residents and former workers at Dayhoit's National Electrical Coil plant began to raise questions about the contradictory information they were receiving. They soon realized that they needed to form a group that would represent their interests. Joan Robinett, in effect Roy's coauthor on this chapter, became the leader of Concerned Citizens Against Toxic Waste (CCATW). Roy describes the ability of CCATW members to understand the complexity of the practices and relationships that linked local, state, and federal governments and a Fortune 500 corporation, as well as their ability to describe in fine detail the harmful effects of the toxic soup of PCBs, trichloroethylene, vinyl chloride, and other chemicals that were in their drinking water. Roy may underplay his own role, and that of his students, as simply inputting data into the computer and printing a few graphs, when in fact they helped frame a survey questionnaire and interpret the results. It is also important to point out that Southeast, like other rural community colleges, draws students from the surrounding community. Some students who worked on the project were from the affected community and had family that either worked at the factory or lived near it. What comes through in this chapter is the empowerment experienced by members of a community who had help in devising a series of studies that could then be used to make their demands heard.

In chapter 4 Stephanie McSpirit and coauthors tell the story of a coal waste impoundment that, in the year 2000, released more than 300 million gallons of coal slurry and sludge materials in Martin County, Kentucky. Steph's research team from Eastern Kentucky University was made up of undergraduate students, and they became involved in door-to-door interviews that opened their eyes to both the possibilities of research and the impact of an environmental disaster on a community. Mark Grayson, editor of the *Martin County Sun,* one of the coauthors of this chapter and a member of the community advisory group with which Stephanie and her students worked, used his newspaper to document actions of the U.S. Environmental Protection Agency and other federal and state regulatory agencies in favoring the coal company over the community. Community members expected to fight those that created the spill but not the agencies they thought were there to protect the community. These are painful but important lessons for students and citizens of affected communities to learn. Out of the combined efforts of citizens, faculty, and students the research team has since been able to advocate for more citizen involvement in water testing and environmental recovery decisions, and different research teams since have been working with citizens' groups and other outside groups on water quality issues and emergency planning procedures for communities near coal waste impoundments.

Chapter 5 returns to Harlan County, Kentucky. In 1999 Robert Gipe and others looked over a mine permit map spread on a community conference table. Jericol Mining was proposing to mine above three thousand feet on Black Mountain, the state's highest peak. As a member of KFTC, Robert recounts his own experience and the experiences of several others who were involved in the movement to save Black Mountain. As he notes, one fights differently when one lives in the community. Based on his own direct involvement in the movement, Robert reflects on how local people were particularly sensible and strategic in forming and managing alliances with the media, with the Kentucky Resources Council, and with myriad other sympathetic outsiders who got involved.

One of the lessons from chapter 5 is that we should not underestimate the power of emotion to help us understand what lies at the core of the human experience. Community residents facing the potential destruction of a mountain naturally respond with a range of powerful emotions. Scientists working for corporations and governments will say that such emotional responses are detrimental to a true understanding of conditions and that what is required is a cool and dispassionate approach to the problem. But emotions are part of the human makeup—it is no more possible to imagine humans without passion than a hawk without wings. Emotions are what tie us to other people, places, and the natural world, and it is these emotions that prompt us to act when the things that we love are threatened. Robert helps us understand this point in talking about the effort to save Black Mountain from desecration. In the chapter's first pages, Robert gives homage to local community activist Hazel King, who fought the coal companies and the state government for years, and describes how, after she died, others in the community picked up the challenge to save Black Mountain, inspired by her efforts.

In chapter 6 Lynne Faltraco and Conner Bailey provide another lesson about the struggle to protect that which is loved and cherished by many people in the Appalachian region—the native hardwood forests. Lynne and Conner describe their efforts at stopping the onslaught of chip mills. Many people are unaware that chip mills are highly automated facilities that grind whole trees into woodchips for making paper, particleboard, and other wood-based materials. Between the late 1980s and the mid-1990s more than 140 large-scale chipping operations were established in the region. In the mid-1990s CCRC emerged to challenge a chip mill facility in Rutherford County. Citizens challenged the local ordinances that allowed for unconstrained clear-cutting of local woodlands to feed the mill. As a founding member of CCRC, Lynne describes the frustration she and her neighbors experienced when they realized that government agencies and even some university people were unsympathetic to their concerns. However, Lynne and CCRC also had the ability to establish working relationships with other faculty at four different universities in the region, including Conner at Auburn University.

While emotions always run high when a corporation strong-arms its way into a community, this chapter and the others remind us that facts are what make the biggest impression, whether it is at a public hearing, at a meeting with the governor, in an editorial, or in documentation of a corporation's actions and irresponsibility. Knowledge is power, and documentation of scientific and legal facts gives communities evidence to support their causes. Together Conner and Lynne reflect on the usefulness of their partnership in collecting facts to challenge the chip mill industry and on how academic research and academic publications can carry some useful weight in policy deliberations and decision making. Lynne's description of CCRC also provides a basis for understanding the sustained activity of this group. Rather than just being against something, CCRC has taken a proactive stance that includes efforts at public environmental education, the monitoring of timber harvests, and landowner education campaigns.

From the mountains and foothills of Appalachia, chapter 7 takes us to Tillery, North Carolina, and the struggle of African American residents against the environmental and public health impacts of industrial hog farming. This chapter shows how the Concerned Citizens of Tillery (CCT) promoted social change and environmental justice by forming coalitions and partnerships with local agencies and also with North Carolina's leading university—the University of North Carolina (UNC) at Chapel Hill. Steve Wing, from UNC Chapel Hill's School of Public Health, has been involved with Gary Grant of CCT in efforts to protect African American communities and local environments and watersheds from the effects of large-scale industrial hog operations.

This chapter mentions that Steve, in partnership with Gary and CCT, has received several federal grants to study the health impacts of concentrated hog farming operations on rural communities in North Carolina. In gearing up for this edited volume, we talked with Steve and Gary, and they both noted that oftentimes the leaders and organizers of movements for social and environmental justice are protected from the direct effects of injustice by their education, income, and ability to avoid poverty and discrimination. By contrast, community residents directly impacted by the injustice cannot leave their struggles at the end of the day to go home to uncontaminated neighborhoods or the privileges of their class and race. Yet ironically, environmental activists and academics have sometimes derided community residents on the grounds that they are motivated more by self-protection than by a broad critique and challenge for social and environmental change. As this book shows, however, immediate threats to health and quality of life can become powerful educational and organizational motivators for change. In chapter 7 it is the CCT that has promoted on-the-ground social change and environmental justice.

It is worth noting that the chapter is written by a former graduate student and now colleague, Mansoureh Tajik. Through her own interviews and discussions with Steve and Gary, Mansoureh provides solid insight and understanding into the partnership and alliance that developed between Steve and Gary and between CCT and the School of Public Health at UNC Chapel Hill.[10]

Chapters 8 and 9 share a common subject—demilitarization of chemical weapons by the U.S. Army—that probably is unfamiliar to many readers. In chapter 8 we read about two faculty members at Jacksonville State University in Alabama who found themselves living in a community next to the Anniston Army Depot. By international treaty the United States agreed to eliminate all chemical weapons. In Anniston the decision was made to build a large incinerator complex to destroy (burn) these weapons. Suzanne Marshall describes the historical context of industrial activities in this city, which includes being the first place where PCBs were manufactured and the contamination of African

American neighborhoods near a plant owned by Monsanto. Rufus Kinney continues by discussing his role in Families Concerned about Nerve Gas Incineration and his work with Civil Rights leaders in the Southern Christian Leadership Conference (SCLC). Antoinnette Hudson, an American history instructor, ends this chapter with reflections on her own involvement in the anti-incineration movement in Anniston. Antoinnette discusses getting involved with Serving Alabama's Future Environment, her role in organizing African American neighborhoods through churches and door-to-door canvassing, and her other organizing work through the Youth SCLC. One of the lessons from this chapter, as in the two Harlan County chapters, is that sometimes the line between academic and community activist does not hold much meaning.

Dick Futrell is a citizen-activist-scholar of the same blend as Suzanne, Rufus, Antoinnette, and others represented in this volume. Dick has been a member of the KEF and the Chemical Weapons Working Group (CWWG) since the early days when school gymnasiums in Madison County, Kentucky, were full of citizens wanting answers from the army to their most basic questions: How safe is incineration? What toxic residues would be left over? What would happen in case of an emergency? What long-term risks did incineration pose? Officials appeared unprepared for such questions and provided simple, empty assurances, asking citizens to trust them and their experts.

Dick's son Robert is lead author for chapter 9. Robert has studied and written on the chemical weapons conflict and the KEF/CWWG movement in the past, although more recently he has been involved in an extensive oral history project on the Nevada Test Site nuclear program. Robert went back over his original interviews and conducted additional interviews in preparing this chapter.

In chapter 9 Robert recounts the role KEF/CWWG played in convincing the U.S. Army to shift away from chemical weapons incineration and toward alternative disposal methods. He describes how KEF/CWWG members coordinated local activism, tied local activists into wider political networks, and built political strategies that have redirected the army's efforts away from incineration toward more environmentally sound, closed-loop disposal systems. For both Robert and Dick, the lessons are apparent. KEF/CWWG members have been successful in translating their expertise into a vernacular so that the public, the media, elected officials, and even the army have come to trust and rely on them for input and insight into the conflict and debate. They describe their approach as "holistic knowledge," in which movement members possess not only technical expertise on the specifics of the issue but also a full grasp of the entirety of the dispute, the history, the changes, the politics, and the science.

Chapter 9 provides insight into a type of civic science and public scholarship that has long characterized the environmental movement in general and that we are attempting to capture in this book. To paraphrase Craig Williams, CWWG's executive director, this approach can be likened to trying to stop a slow-moving train—you don't stand in front of it with your hand up, you get a bunch of people to stand alongside of it and begin rocking it; after a while you have enough momentum going that you can derail it or at least switch the tracks. In 2006 Craig received the North American Goldman Environmental Prize for his work with KEF/CWWG in pressing for safer alternatives for the disposal of chemical weapons. Craig's perspectives and opinions and those of other environmental activists and members of KEF/CWWG (John Capillo, Elizabeth Crowe, and Lois Kleffman) are well represented in interviews reported in this chapter.

In chapter 10 Alan Banks, Alice Jones, and Anne Blakeney talk about the Headwaters Project, based in Letcher County, Kentucky. Like the Martin County project described in chapter 4, the Headwaters Project was based at the Appalachian Studies Center at Eastern Kentucky University. Both the Headwaters and Martin County projects have served as vehicles for training university students in community-based participatory research techniques. Engaging students in community-based research provides a rich educational experience that typically cannot be matched in the classroom. This is why the move toward community engagement in colleges and universities across the United States has focused on incorporating students. We need to move well beyond internships with civic organizations to involve students in communities facing challenges and opportunities. Over the years well over a hundred students have been involved in the field in Letcher and Martin Counties, learning how to conduct surveys and interviews and do GIS mapping and water testing. University students also have gained experience presenting findings in community forums, to public officials, and to the media. These large field-training initiatives in community-based research have helped, in small part, to increase the research capacity of the region, and many students who might not otherwise have been interested in research have gone on to graduate school because of their field experiences with these community-based projects. In terms of even more tangible outcomes, the Headwaters Project has helped bring millions of dollars for much-needed water and sewer projects to Letcher County, Kentucky.[11]

One of the important lessons from this chapter is how reports generated from the Headwaters Project have since been used by local officials in lobbying state and federal agencies for water infrastructure improvement grants. The counter lesson is that for every successful community-based research project, there are probably several others that have failed outright or petered out slowly, with local residents wondering what good came of their work with university researchers. Community leaders do not want to be studied; they want partners willing to provide long-term commitments of time and energy. They want more than a report and set of recommendations. Meeting such needs is a challenge for many university researchers, but as the chapters in this volume attest, it is a challenge that can be met.

In chapter 11 Betsy Taylor discusses an innovative program that invited community organizers and academics for a semester of study and activism through the Rockefeller Humanities Fellowship Program. The goal of the program was to bring together scholars and citizen activists who are at the leading edge of innovative new models in planning for equity and sustainability. Two fellowship recipients have joined with Betsy in writing this chapter. The authors speak to their experiences with the Rockefeller program and their fellowship projects. Ana Isla talks about her fellowship work on eco-feminism and development in the context of Latin America, the United States, and Canada, while Lynne Faltraco, a member of CCRC, describes her time at the University of Kentucky and her work developing a directory of university researchers and academics who had experience working with communities or at least were sympathetic to community-based, participatory research practices. One of the important lessons from the Rockefeller program is that it brought together activists from different places and created a new institutional arrangement for dialogue on equal footing among activists, faculty, and students. The chapter ends with some final reflections and lessons on the departmentalized and isolated knowledge and practices that have too often come to characterize university life. The authors argue that we must continue to build a new type of civic engagement and civic science that transcends traditional academic boundaries and instead attempts to build new webs of civic networks that are connected by mutual knowledge and respect.

In the closing chapter we make a final effort at encouraging readers to consider the potential benefits of working closely with others toward a common end of community and environmental protection. Anyone who walks down this path needs to be aware that engagement with communities facing environmental or other crises often leads in very short order to issues of social justice, because usually the crisis is precipitated by the outside corporate, military, or governmental actors referenced throughout these pages. College- and university-based faculty and students need to know that community engagement is also engagement with power and that there can be repercussions even within the halls of academe. Faculty who have not yet earned tenure may be vulnerable to outside and administrative pressures to suspend their research. It is during these low points that the question pops into a person's mind about whether his or her time could be better spent doing something else. In this last chapter we hope to show readers that they are not alone. Their efforts are part of a long intellectual tradition of engagement and social change. In short, our general hope in putting this last chapter together is to provide some final guidance and inspiration to those who may want to work with others in protecting the environment and building more sustainable communities. We hope to persuade readers that such modes of thought, inquiry, interaction, organization, and action are highly possible, because we believe they are increasingly necessary.

Notes

1. A. Batteau, *Appalachia and America* (Lexington: University Press of Kentucky, 1983); J. Gaventa, *Power and Powerlessness: Quiescence and Rebellion in an Appalachian Valley* (Urbana: University of Illinois Press, 1980); J. Gaventa, B. Smith, and A. Willingham, *Communities in Economic Crisis: Appalachia and the South* (Philadelphia: Temple University Press, 1990); H. Lewis, L. Johnson, and D. Askins, *Colonialism in Modern America: The Appalachian Case* (Boone, NC: Appalachian Consortium Press, 1978).

2. R. Epstein, *Citizen Power: Stories of America's New Civic Spirit* (Lexington, KY: Democracy Resource Center, 1999); R. Eyerman, "Social Movements: between History and Sociology," *Theory and Society* 18 (1989): 532–45.

3. K. D. Alley, C. E. Faupel, and C. Bailey, "The Historical Transformation

of a Grassroots Environmental Group," *Human Organization* 54, no. 4 (1995): 410–16; D. Gill, L. Clarke, M. Cohen, L. Ritchie, A. Ladd, S. Meinhold, and B. Marshall, "Post-Katrina Guiding Principles of Disaster Social Science Research," *Sociological Spectrum* 27 (2007): 789–92; S. Fisher, *Fighting Back in Appalachia: Traditions of Resistance and Change* (Philadelphia: Temple University Press, 1993); R. Futrell, "Technical Adversarialism and Participatory Collaboration in the U.S. Chemical Weapon Disposal Program," *Science, Technology, and Human Values* 28 (2003): 451–82; Robert Futrell, "Framing Process, Cognitive Liberation, and NIMBY Protest in the U.S. Chemical-Weapons Disposal Conflict," *Sociological Inquiry* 73 (2003): 359–86; C. Montrie, *To Save the Land and People: A History of Opposition to Surface Coal Mining in Appalachia* (Chapel Hill: University of North Carolina Press, 2003); S. Wing, "Social Responsibility and Research Ethics in Community Driven Studies of Industrialized Hog Production in North Carolina," *Environmental Health Perspectives* 110 (2002): 437–44.

4. J. M. Glen, *Highlander: No Ordinary School* (Knoxville: University of Tennessee Press, 1996).

5. V. Friedman and T. Rogers, "There Is Nothing so Theoretical as Good Action Research," *Action Research* 7 (2009): 31–47; D. Greenwood, "Theoretical Research, Applied Research and Action Research: The Deinstitutionalization of Active Research," in *Engaging Contradictions: Theory, Politics and Methods of Activist Scholarship*, ed. C. Hale (Berkeley: University of California Press, 2008), 319–40; M. Edelstein, "Outsiders Just Don't Understand: Personalization of Risk and the Boundary between Modernity and Postmodernity," in *Risk in the Modern Age: Social Theory, Science and Environment Decision-Making,* ed. M. Cohen (New York: Palgrave, 2001), 123–42; J. Gaventa, "Appalachian Studies in Global Context: Reflections on the Beginnings—Challenges for the Future," *Journal of Appalachian Studies* 8, no. 1 (2002): 79–90; Frank Fischer, *Citizens, Experts and the Environment: The Politics of Local Knowledge* (Durham, NC: Duke University Press, 2000).

6. Suzanne Marshall, *Chemical Weapons Disposal and Environmental Justice* (Berea: Kentucky Environmental Foundation, 1996).

7. M. Cernea, *Putting People First: Sociological Variables in Rural Development* (Oxford: Oxford University Press, 1985); R. Chambers, "The Origins and Practices of Participatory Rural Appraisal," *World Development* 22, no. 7 (1994): 953–69; D. Korten, "Community Organization and Rural Development: A Learning Process Approach," *Public Administration Review* 40, no. 5 (1980): 480–511; S. Couch, J. S. Kroll-Smith, and J. Kinder, "Discovering and Inventing Hazardous Environments: Sociological Knowledge and Publics at Risk," in Cohen, *Risk in the Modern Age,* 193–95; D. Fiorino, "Environmental Policy and the Participation Gap," in *Democracy and the Environment: Problems and Prospects,* ed. W. Lafferty and J. Meadowcraft (Brookfield, VT: Edward Elgar, 1996),

194–212; R. Lidskog, "Scientific Evidence or Lay People's Experience? On Risk and Trust with Regard to Modern Environmental Decision-Making," in Cohen, *Risk in the Modern Age,* 196–219; C. O'Faircheallaigh, "Resource Development and Inequality in Indigenous Societies," *World Development* 26, no. 3 (1998): 381–94; P. Brosius and A. Tsing, "Representing Communities: Histories and Politics of Community-Based Natural Resource Management," *Society and Natural Resources* 11, no. 2 (1998): 157–69; P. Brown, "The Popular Epidemiology Approach to Toxic Waste Contamination," in *Communities at Risk: Collective Response to Technological Hazards,* ed. S. Couch and S. Kroll-Smith (New York: Peter Lang, 1991), 133–54; P. Brown, "Popular Epidemiology and Toxic Waste Contamination: Lay and Professional Ways of Knowing," in *The Environment and Society Reader,* ed. R. Frey (New York: Allyn and Bacon, 2001), 301–17; Wing, "Social Responsibility and Research Ethics"; D. Carr and K. Halvorsen, "An Evaluation of Three Democratic, Community-Based Approaches to Citizen Participation: Surveys, Conversations with Community Groups and Community Dinners," *Society and Natural Resources* 14 (2001): 107–26; L. Kruger and M. Shannon, "Getting to Know Ourselves and Our Places through Participation in Civic Social Assessment," *Society and Natural Resources* 13 (2000): 461–78; D. Quigley, D. Handy, and R. Goble, "Participatory Research Strategies in Nuclear Risk Management for Native Communities," *Journal of Health Communication* 5 (2000): 305–31; S. Cable, T. Shriver, and T. Mix, "Risk Society and Contested Illness: The Case of Nuclear Weapons Workers," *American Sociological Review* 73, no. 3 (2008): 380–401; M. Palevsky, R. Futrell, and A. Kirk, "Recollections of Nevada's Nuclear Past," *UNLV Fusion* 1, no. 1 (2010): 1–4; R. Futrell, "Technical Adversarialism and Participatory Collaboration in the U.S. Chemical Weapon Disposal Program," *Science, Technology, and Human Values* 28 (2003): 451–82; Gill et al., "Post-Katrina Guiding Principles"; S. McSpirit, S. Scott, S. Hardesty, and R. Welch, "EPA Actions in Post Disaster Martin County, Kentucky: An Analysis of Bureaucratic Slippage and Agency Recreancy," *Journal of Appalachian Studies* 11 (2005): 30–58; S. Scott, S. McSpirit, S. Hardesty, and R. Welch, "Post Disaster Interviews with Martin County Citizens: 'Gray Clouds' of Blame and Distrust," *Journal of Appalachian Studies* 11 (2005): 7–29.

8. S. Peters, *Democracy and Higher Education: Traditions and Stories of Civic Engagement* (East Lansing: University of Michigan Press, 2010).

9. Maureen Reed and Kristen McIlveen, "Toward a Pluralistic Civic Science? Assessing Community Forestry," *Society and Natural Resources* 19 (2006): 591–607.

10. Wing, "Social Responsibility and Research Ethics."

11. S. McSpirit, S. Hardesty, and R. Welch, "Researching Issues and Building Civic Capacity after an Environmental Disaster," *Journal of Appalachian Studies* 8, no. 1 (2002): 132–43.

1

Confessions of the Parasitic Researcher to the Man in the Cowboy Hat

Sherry Cable

In 1987, as a brand-new assistant professor, I stood in the center of Hotense's full-to-overflowing living room in Bell County, Kentucky, and nervously made my pitch to the assembled members of Yellow Creek Concerned Citizens (YCCC) for their permission to conduct a case study of the group. YCCC members were experienced research subjects, scrutinized several times previously by other academics. Someone asked what I would gain from the study. I answered, "If I can pull it off, I'll publish enough articles in academic journals to earn promotion and tenure, instead of losing my job." Someone else asked what the group would gain from my study. Caught by surprise, I pondered a reasonable reply. I scratched my head and cleared my throat. I squirmed and began to sweat. I finally confessed, "Nothing." The group was quiet for a moment, friendly eyes still gazing encouragingly at me. Then Gene slapped his knee, stood, and announced, "I say, let her study us. At least she didn't *lie* to us like the others—she didn't promise us a goddam thing!" With this qualified blessing, I observed and followed the group's travails until about 1990. I reported my results in several publications, then turned my full attention to a new research project. From my collaboration with YCCC members, I gained promotion with tenure, valuable research experience, increased self-confidence, solid child-rearing advice, and warm attention from kind persons. And, just as I'd promised, they got nothing.

For that, I truly apologize. I apologize to all who were YCCC members but most deeply to Larry. Larry Wilson is the Man in the Cowboy Hat, YCCC's indefatigable president for so many years. It is primarily to him that I direct these confessions, this explanation, and this testimony that I—and other academics—have learned and are changing our ways. And, in the interests of honesty in this honest book offering a warts-and-all examination of the relationships between activists and academics, I inform readers that this chapter is not cowritten with Larry because, after twenty-something years in the activist trenches, the Man in the Cowboy Hat is burned out. He is disillusioned, disappointed, hurt, tired, broke, and pissed—like many others who expend precious chunks of their lives in struggles against exploitation by power holders and, occasionally, by academics.

I welcome this opportunity to share YCCC's story, to describe my interaction with YCCC activists, and to bear witness that the times, they are a-changin' in the relationship between activists and academics.

License to Contaminate

The story of Yellow Creek Concerned Citizens is an all-too-familiar Appalachian tale of blatant and remorseless exploitation perpetrated by outsiders consorting with local politicians. It is exploitation that sucks the wealth from the resource-rich region and leaves behind the detritus of impoverishment and ecological ruin. But exploitation and contamination at Yellow Creek spurred resistance by citizens.

The headwaters of Yellow Creek lie below the historic Cumberland Gap in Bell County, Kentucky—pure Davy Crockett territory. From there, the creek winds north for about twenty miles, flowing through the county seat of Middlesboro, passing scattered dwellings and rural communities clustered on the banks, and finally tumbling into the Cumberland River at Pineville. Bell County's proud heritage—as well as its painful scourge—is coal. The valley's isolated communities are the refurbished remnants of the old coal camps that dominated the region until the mines closed in the 1950s.[1]

The legacy of the coal era is not only physical but cultural. In the 1930s the coal companies instigated intercamp competition to foster hostilities that would impede unionization. Their instigation was so successful that when the coal companies moved on to greener pastures—and mountains—valley residents retained the habit of interacting only within their own small community and kin networks. Such cultural balkanization helped block collective resistance to the pollution of Yellow Creek for many years.

A tannery built in Middlesboro by a British company in the late 1800s originally used a vegetable-based tanning process to treat cowhides and dumped the waste products directly into the creek. In the 1930s individuals' complaints about the color and smell of the water moved the municipal government to construct a sewage treatment plant that received and treated the tannery's wastes before releasing the effluent into the creek. The plant proved inadequate after 1960, when a Chicago firm bought the tannery and instituted a chromium-based tanning process that significantly worsened the pollution. The technology produced wastes far more toxic than those from the prior technology, beyond the capacity of the outdated plant equipment. Creek water often ran as thick as molasses, and the odor of the water combined with the stench of fish kills frequently drove creekside residents indoors. Individuals' complaints to city and tannery officials increased, but in 1970 the city and tannery officials signed a sixty-year contract stipulating that all tannery waste be accepted at the municipal sewage treatment plant without any pretreatment. Soon after, the city received a federal grant to renovate the sewage plant. The renovations proved inadequate for the corrosive tannery waste, and by 1976, many residents claimed, the creek was devoid of all aquatic life.

By that time changes had occurred on the national and local scenes that paved the way for collective resistance to emerge at Yellow Creek. At the national level the environmental movement significantly increased public awareness, spawning a decade of environmental protection and resource management policies under the regulatory eye of the newly created Environmental Protection Agency. Such environmental awareness was dramatically reinforced and legitimated by international media coverage of two incidents: the 1978 leaking toxic landfill at Love Canal, which stimulated the creation of the Superfund program, and the 1979 partial core meltdown of a commercial nuclear reactor at Three Mile Island, which abruptly dead-ended the nuclear power industry. These incidents profoundly shook many Americans' conviction that their neighborhoods and homes were safe places.[2]

At about the same time in the Yellow Creek Valley, the consolidation of area high schools into one large county school had the latent effect of countering the tendencies of cultural balkanization. For teenagers, attending the same high school reduced the interaction barriers previously separating communities. As teens interacted more freely, they dragged their parents along with them and the hostility gap was bridged.

Teens were crucial in the formation of YCCC in 1980. Through interaction, several high school students discovered shared parental concerns about Yellow Creek's pollution. Three couples decided to meet and talk in July 1980. With the knowledge of common concerns about the creek and the recognition that other American communities faced similar environmental threats, many residents for the first time perceived the pollution as a collective, rather than an individual, problem. The outcome was the valley-wide mobilization of a citizens' organization aimed at reversing the contamination of the creek.

YCCC members collected information about the tannery and the sewage treatment plant from public documents and former tannery workers. The nature of their grievances quickly escalated from the nuisances of odor and fish kills to concerns about the human health effects of the contamination. One of the activists referred to members' dawning recognition that "what was killing those fish could be harming us."[3]

Activists discovered that the City of Middlesboro was not in compliance with its EPA-issued National Pollutant Discharge Elimination System (NPDES) permit for operation of the sewage treatment plant. They circulated a petition requesting a public hearing on EPA's reissuance of the NPDES permit. More than a hundred residents attended the subsequent hearing, and many of them testified about the effects of the creek pollution on their family's health. But the EPA hearing officer granted the permit, insisting that any problem was due to the city's lack of enforcement of its own sewer-use ordinance. In recognition of this EPA action and similar actions, the Man in the Cowboy Hat habitually referred to the EPA as the *Industrial* Protection Agency. The EPA's reissuance of the NPDES permit was, in effect, issuance of a license to contaminate Yellow Creek.

YCCC members' research revealed that the city had no sewer-use ordinance, and the group requested that the city devise one. When city officials refused, YCCC members applied pressure by attending City Council meetings. After numerous loud confrontations, City Council meetings were quickly adjourned as soon as the Man in the Cowboy Hat showed up. An activist recalled the mayor's reaction at the sight of Wilson in the audience: "Larry would walk in, and the mayor's face would turn as red as that Coke can!"

Fearing that the creek's contamination had spread, activists asked officials of the Bell County Health Department to conduct tests on private wells along Yellow Creek. The agency refused: since agency officials considered *all* private wells to be contaminated with *something* or other, they determined that they had no basis for authorizing well testing. The health department further refused YCCC requests to post signs on the creek to warn the unwary of the potential dangers of fishing and swimming. But the agency eventually relented and authorized the placement of such signs, if citizens absorbed the costs of producing them. The health department's refusal to investigate the contamination was tantamount to a license to contaminate Yellow Creek.

The activists next requested private well testing from the Commonwealth of Kentucky's environmental agency, whose officials had previously issued citations to the city for failing to meet water quality standards but had imposed no fines and required no changes. The agency conducted tests on four wells in May 1981 and found unsafe levels of barium, chromium, and other metals. Instead of expanding the well-testing program, the agency terminated it—a termination that implicitly issued a license to contaminate Yellow Creek.

Based on the findings of the well-water tests, YCCC members conducted a health survey, aided by student volunteers from Vanderbilt University. The survey documented unusual numbers of miscarriages and high incidence of kidney disease, respiratory problems, dizziness, and nausea. Many residents subsequently stopped using their wells and for two years hauled their water at their own expense before finally securing federal funds to subsidize the installation of city water lines throughout the county.

Interspersed with these activities were pickets, peaceful marches, and an occasional protest, such as the incident in which several YCCC members drove a pickup truck loaded with wood contaminated by tannery wastes to the state capitol building and dumped the toxic wood on the steps. Activists raised funds through bake sales, yard sales, and raffles, but not all residents shared the group's grievances. Reprisals included shots fired at two activists and a dog mysteriously poisoned. As the highly visible leader, Wilson was said to be blacklisted by the mayor for any jobs in the county. I could not corroborate the allegation, but despite filing many employment applications, Wilson never worked again in Bell County.

Rebuffed by agencies at local, state, and national levels, YCCC members in 1983 requested aid from the Highlander Research and Education Center to plan a litigation strategy. Although typically wary of outsiders, YCCC members placed faith in Highlander's well-known mission of *em*powering rather than *over*powering community activists. With such aid, YCCC filed a $31 million class action suit against the city for failing to regulate tannery waste sufficiently. In this less active, litigation phase, members were limited primarily to performing legwork for the attorneys, driving sick folks to medical appointments, and presenting slide shows to educate the public and raise funds for the formidable court costs.

The class action suit was settled out of court in 1985 with a consent decree signed by YCCC representatives and officials of the U.S. Justice Department, the EPA, the Commonwealth of Kentucky, the City of Middlesboro, and the Middlesboro Tanning Company. The consent decree permitted the city to continue violating the Clean Water Act while slowly decreasing the extent of its violation. The decree specified a series of increasingly strict goals for discharges into Yellow Creek that would, over time, result in the city's full compliance with the Clean Water Act. A separate agreement between YCCC and the city established a financial settlement to be used as a medical fund for valley residents.

YCCC activists were successful, in spite of the parasite in their midst. The tannery's pretreatment of wastes, combined with the city's improved sewage treatment technology, significantly decreased the toxicity level of the effluent dumped into Yellow Creek. Legal settlements provided a cushion for residents suffering illnesses they attributed to exposure to creek water. Activists recognized the ironclad ecological principle that human-induced environmental degradation is rarely, if ever, reversible. The water of Yellow Creek runs clearer, but the sediment remains contaminated with heavy metals. That recognition drove activists to efforts to ensure that the community "wouldn't get run over like that again." Several ran for and won elective offices, substantially changing the local political structure.

And the Man in the Cowboy Hat worked for many years to aid communities in similar contaminated straits before burning out.

Apologia: My Parasitic Interaction with YCCC Activists

In ecological terms, parasitism is a form of interaction among populations coexisting in an ecosystem in which one species benefits while harming the other species. The main difference between parasitism and predation as an interaction mode—a very important difference to the prey—is that parasites act more slowly than predators and do not always kill the prey.

Between 1987 and 1990 I interacted with YCCC activists as a parasite: I diverted some of their limited resources to my own sustenance. I benefited, and they did not. I observed quietly, took notes, conducted taped interviews, and examined documents. I did not interrupt them at mealtimes; I did not call them past 8:00 p.m. We exchanged jokes, Christmas cards, tall tales, and recipes. I never sneaked with them onto tannery property at night to take water samples. I never drove anyone to a doctor's appointment. I never stuffed one envelope for them. I never gave them money. I never even *asked* if there was something I could do to help. I did not kill them as a predator would, but I harmed them: doing nothing when it would be easy to help others is a form of harm.

At the time I was unaware that I harmed YCCC activists. I simply followed the research paradigm instilled by my graduate training in sociology.

Sociology as a discipline is modeled after the biophysical sciences. The scientific study of society, particularly championed by sociology's founder, Emile Durkheim, was envisioned as the empirical observation of social life. The aim of *all* sciences is to obtain valid and reliable information on the phenomenon being studied—such as the timing of volcanic eruptions, the components of acid rain, or the reproductive habits of reptiles. But human behavior is more volatile than volcanoes, more corrosive than acid rain, and more bizarre than reptiles' reproductive habits. The complexity of human behavior poses unique problems for scientific scrutiny. How can society be studied scientifically, with the same assumptions as the biophysical sciences, that the universe is predictable and bound by causal relationships? Sociologists ultimately adopted the biophysical scientists' norm of value neutrality—the dictum that scientists not allow their personal biases and acts to influence the conduct and outcome of their research.

Max Weber supported value neutrality while acknowledging that human social life is different from the biophysical world: humans are frequently rational, deliberately organizing their efforts to reach desired goals. The sociologist must consider behavior from the viewpoint of the actor. Weber's *verstehen* method of studying society is based on using our innate understanding of human behavior to gain knowledge about others by standing in the other guy's shoes for a while. Observations are interpreted but the emphasis on value neutrality is retained.[4]

Sociologists strictly maintained scientific norms of value neutrality until quite recently, to preserve disciplinary legitimacy and to conform to rules codified in the late 1970s for the protection of human research subjects.

Disciplinary Legitimacy

Norms of value neutrality were maintained to preserve disciplinary legitimacy—to protect sociological turf. As the red-haired stepchild of the sciences, sociologists had long grappled with charges from non-sociologists that sociology was not a legitimate science. The charges were soon mirrored *within* the discipline, following the discovery of the "Hawthorne effect." Between 1927 and 1932 Elton Mayo conducted studies examining the relationship between workers' productivity levels and work conditions at the Western Electric Hawthorne Works in Cicero, Illinois. Mayo's inadvertent finding was that workers' productivity increased because they were aware that they were research subjects, indicating that researchers' actions may influence the very behavior being studied: the act of measurement itself affects the results of measurement.[5]

To counter the charges among themselves and bolster the discipline's legitimacy as a science, sociologists adopted a strong positivist emphasis, closely aping the research methods of the biophysical sciences and emphasizing value neutrality. Since value neutrality was most stringently maintained by the researcher's ability to control and manipulate variables, the most credible research strategy for sociologists was the social survey. With this strategy, researchers control variables by randomly selecting subjects from the population and using a standardized set of questions and responses to solicit information on attitudes and behaviors, allowing findings to be generalized from the sample to the larger population. This shift to a positivist emphasis embodied in survey methodology was facilitated by the increasing availability of computers and statistical software packages. By the late 1970s the survey was the model for sociological research. Mailed surveys were particularly prized—no fuss, no muss, and no interaction with subjects at all.[6]

Alternative research strategies that relied on *verstehen* methods—

observation, participant-observation, and case studies—were tolerated with the admonishment that researchers beware of influencing the behavior they intended to study, severely limit their interaction with subjects, and avoid becoming involved in subjects' activities. Even then, the methods were viewed by many practitioners as highly suspect, and such judgments heavily influenced promotion and tenure decisions at research universities. Track records in quantitative studies were more likely to be rewarded than were research careers grounded in qualitative studies.

Protection of Human Research Subjects

A second factor that reinforced quantitative surveys as the preferred research strategy was the implementation of federal policies to minimize risks to human research subjects. Worldwide horror at the revelation of Nazi scientists' biomedical experiments on war prisoners was reflected in the first principle of the Nuremberg Code, that researchers obtain prior voluntary consent from human subjects. In the United States, federal protection for human research subjects was prompted by several cases of medical research in the mid-1960s and early 1970s in which vulnerable populations were egregiously exploited. In the Tuskegee Syphilis Study, for example, treatment was withheld from black male prisoners suffering from syphilis so that researchers could track and document the disease's progress.[7]

Sociology suffered its own ethical problems. Nearly all introductory sociology textbooks criticize several studies conducted in the 1960s and early 1970s for the risks posed to research subjects. Stanley Milgram used a modified experimental design to examine Nazi-like obedience to authority by convincing subjects that they were administering electric shocks to a man against his will at the behest of a white-coated scientist. The study jolted the common belief that the Holocaust was caused by Germany's unique culture and forced many to acknowledge the more-or-less hidden authoritarian inside us all. But critics raged against the potential harm done to subjects confronted with their own cruel behavior. In a similar case, Philip Zimbardo and his associates employed a simulation design to create a mock prison in the basement of a university classroom building, where they permitted the "guards" to engage in psychological abuse of the "prisoners." The results again confounded common beliefs about social behavior by clearly demonstrating the tendencies of social control institutions to socialize individuals in the cruel and inhumane treatment of others, and the study served as the basis for numerous prison reform efforts. But detractors insisted that the tradeoff of such knowledge for the harm done to subjects was unethical.[8]

The 1974 National Research Act established institutional review boards (IRBs) to protect human subjects. A national commission established by the act produced the 1978 Belmont Report that defines principles and sets guidelines for ethical research on human subjects at institutions receiving federal funding, such as public universities. Those famous studies by Milgram and Zimbardo could not be replicated on any campus today. IRB regulation replaced self-regulation and further reinforced the emphasis on value neutrality and sociologists' trend of relying on survey research methods.

The Reformation of Parasitic Research

The preservation of disciplinary legitimacy and regulation for the protection of human research subjects imposed constraints on sociological researchers' modes of interaction with human subjects. We were trained to conduct research while we kept our views to ourselves, our hands in our pockets, and our noses out of subjects' business. In other words, we were trained to become parasites.

The product of my professional socialization, I guided my interaction with YCCC members in the late 1980s according to the disciplinary rules that defined parasitic interaction with research subjects as a necessity for career success and compliance with the ethical and professional norms of value neutrality. It may be that the activists gained some benefit simply because of my honesty or expertise or, at the very least, my genuine interest in their plight. True, I felt like suggesting that we go bomb the tannery. True, I related to them the trials and efforts of other grassroots groups, as contained in the academic literature. And true, I spoke (with passion, in the "appropriate" venues) to colleagues, students, and relatives about injustice at Yellow Creek and the courage of those who took action against it. Those efforts are just not enough. The bottom line is that, in my representation of the academy and in spite of my own predilections, I stood before YCCC activists aligned less with them than with the power structure they fought.

I never asked him, but I know that the Man in the Cowboy Hat is too kind to tell me if he agrees with my description of parasitic research. So are Gene and Hotense. But what if someone else suggested it to them?

Activists on Parasitic Researchers

Human subjects, particularly activists, are painfully aware of researchers' parasitic interaction mode. In a recent study my colleagues and I specifically asked environmental activists from across the country to describe their experiences with researchers. Tamara Mix conducted thirty-five telephone interviews with environmental activists from across the continental United States, selected from the 2000 edition of *People of Color Environmental Groups,* compiled by the Environmental Justice Resource Center.[9]

Because residents of contaminated communities frequently have health problems, activists and academic researchers have occasionally teamed up to conduct health studies or otherwise aid citizens. A small number of activists working with academics reported positive experiences. The majority of activists expressed dismay. Some activists flatly declined to be interviewed at all because of their past experiences with researchers. One response to the request was, "No! We've been screwed by researchers before!" Another explained, "Researchers have messed us over—how do I know you'll come through with your promises?"[10] A third complained, "They [researchers] want to take everything and get all the credits. Many people have sold many books off of our miseries and off of our suffering. And we don't get anything."[11]

Activists' negative characterizations of researchers indicated two major complaints. The first was that researchers exploit activists for money when it is available. Various foundations and agencies offer funding opportunities to both grassroots organizations and researchers. An activist whose group was forced to cancel a health study for lack of funding expressed deep anger over the group's interaction with researchers and research universities: "We had a grant . . . a combined grant. We got $10,000, and they got over $200,000! They got the money and we got . . . peanuts." Another activist voiced disgust at the allocation of funding: "They'll give these universities the opportunity and the big money, but they *won't* give the communities money to do the real investigation!"[12]

Activists' second major complaint was that researchers are all talk and no relevant action. One activist snorted, "I was asked to serve on a [university] panel on environmental justice. Those people have conferences, and they just sit around and talk on it! And that's it, baby—you don't get any more help!" Another echoed the complaint: "They get paid and they don't want to do nothing for us!"[13]

Activists attribute researchers' parasitic interaction to inherent power disparities in the relationship. Activists reflected that race and class divides lead to researchers' ignorance of activists' own life experiences and to condescending and patronizing attitudes. The common denominator of activists' dissatisfaction with researchers is their overwhelming sense that their voices are not truly heard and their concerns are not seriously addressed.

We can do better than that.

The Antidote to Parasitism: Participatory Action Research

Graduate studies taught me to strive for value neutrality, but long before I entered graduate study and even more persuasively, my mom taught me to be polite. In my research at Yellow Creek, maternally inspired politeness dictated that, at the very least, I listen carefully and respectfully to people and learn from them. Listening carefully and respectfully to Gene, Hotense, the Man in the Cowboy Hat, and all the others, I learned the value of what researchers call "lay knowledge."

I learned that people damn well know when they are being exploited. Viola patiently explained to me, "Appalachia has more in common with some of those countries in Africa than we do with the rest of the United States." And I learned that people who feel betrayed by the very system that they trusted and supported all their lives can exhibit a fierce energy in defense of home and family and principle. I once asked Gene why he continued to fight despite the many miles logged on his truck, the huge telephone bills, and the persistent and implacable indifference of elected officials at all levels. He gazed thoughtfully out the window a moment. Then this gentle man suddenly crashed his fist on the kitchen table with such force that the sugar bowl jumped, and he growled, "Because them big boys ought to have to obey the laws same as *I* do."

Researchers have recently developed an alternative methodology that capitalizes on the considerable knowledge of research subjects about their own situations. Advocates of participatory research methods argue that in traditional research, researchers behave as technocrats, licensed by academic and state officials as the only appropriate authorities, treating subjects simply as units of analysis.[14]

At first the call for participatory research methods was a rhetorical exhortation for the liberation and empowerment of the disenfranchised so that they could express their common grievances and fight for their common interests. Particularly in less developed countries, participatory research assigned a new advocacy role to the academic intellectual.[15]

In contrast to those early days, participatory research methods presently are discussed less as a venue for revolution than as an instrument for the enhancement and fortification of participatory democracy and transformative politics. Participatory research methods are based on a quite different epistemology from the positivist assumptions underlying social surveys. In these settings it is the subjects who actively define the research problem, and they deploy their own knowledge to comprehend and analyze the research problem in the context of their daily lives. Researchers and subjects are partners in the research effort. Participatory research transforms the exploitative and parasitic interaction between researcher and subject into an egalitarian and mutualist relationship in which each party benefits without harming the other.[16]

In ecological terms, mutualism is a form of symbiotic interaction among populations coexisting in an ecosystem in which both species benefit from the interaction. For example, algae live in the tissues of the tiny animals that build coral reefs. The algae benefit by gaining a protected living space, while the coral animals benefit from the nutrients supplied by the algae's photosynthetic processes. Everybody's a winner. The mutualist relationship developed through participatory research addresses activists' complaints registered in our study.

Researchers committed to participatory research have frequently encountered a major obstacle: the academy's disregard for such research as creditable for promotion and tenure decisions. But a movement toward an institutional change in attitude about the importance of researchers' interaction with the community has strengthened, particularly since around 2000.

In 1990 Ernest Boyer, president of the Carnegie Foundation for the Advancement of Teaching, called attention to college students' dissatisfaction with the low priority assigned to teaching and identified the crucial issue as the faculty reward system, which did not recognize teaching or service in evaluating academic success despite the great need "for connecting work of the academy to the social and environmental challenges beyond the campus." Boyer called for a renewed commitment to service. In a later article Boyer coined the term "scholarship of engagement," asserting that "the academy must become a more vigorous partner in the search for answers to our most pressing social, civic, economic and moral problems, and must reaffirm its historic commitment to what I call the scholarship of engagement."[17]

Around the same time, the National Association of State Universities and Land-Grant Colleges received a Kellogg Foundation grant to form the Kellogg Commission on the Future of State and Land-Grant Universities. Members issued six reports between 1996 and 2000. The third report urged universities to adopt reforms aimed at becoming engaged institutions. Members cited the common perception that universities are not organized to bring campus resources and expertise to bear on local problems in a coherent way. They urged that it was "time to go beyond outreach and service to what the Kellogg Commission defines as 'engagement.' . . . [Creating] institutions that have redesigned their teaching, research, and extension and service functions to become even more sympathetically and productively involved with their communities, however community may be defined."[18]

The crucial characteristic of engagement is commitment to sharing and reciprocity—interactions between researchers and their community partners must be "two-way streets defined by mutual respect among the partners for what each brings to the table." The engaged college or university is responsive, respectful of its partners' needs, accessible, and relatively neutral, while successfully integrating institutional service into research and teaching and finding sufficient resources for the effort. The report recommends that institutions make engagement a priority, a central part of the institutional mission, and that institutional leaders develop incentives to encourage faculty involvement in engagement.[19]

In 2006 the National Association of State Universities and Land-Grant Colleges and the Kellogg Foundation conducted an assessment of the Kellogg Commission's influence, based on thirty-five responses to a letter sent to presidents and chancellors asking for their views and examples of campus changes since 2001. Some universities adopted the term "engagement" without implementing the definition of engagement as mutual sharing. Several universities used the term "engagement" interchangeably with "outreach," implying one-way communication from the university out to the community. But the news is mostly good: respondents identified engagement with society as one of the primary areas of change influenced by the commission. Leading universities have reorganized their administrations to better focus on service to society, faculty involvement in engagement is recognized, and at a few institutions promotion and tenure guidelines have been reformed and incentives provided. Engagement has become part of the core mission of several universities.[20]

Reflections

I have learned a few things about research since I stood in Hotense's living room that day twenty-some years ago, sweating because I had nothing but my mom's imperative of polite attention to offer the activists in exchange for their permission to study the group. The movement toward engaged scholarship as part of institutional missions allows researchers to embrace participatory research methods as a form of interaction with subjects that is mutually beneficial.

I readily confess: if I had been studying corporate executive officers, I would not have felt at all like a parasite. As George Orwell told us in allegory, some folks are more equal than others. Parasitic research is most egregious when the folks under the microscope possess significantly less power than the university-backed researcher. Participatory research methods grant researchers the freedom to change our roles from partners in exploitation of ordinary folks to partners in the pursuit of knowledge that benefits ordinary folks. Such mutualistic research frees us to follow the imperative of sociologist and social critic C. Wright Mills: "Be a good craftsman: Avoid any rigid set of procedures. Avoid the fetishism of method and technique."[21]

We can go even further, becoming more fully engaged in the broader process of seeking social justice, of which opposition to environmental injustice is only part. As researchers, we can come out of the academic closet and practice public sociology—the current sociological term for researchers going public with their scholarship in pursuit of social justice. Michael Burawoy and colleagues offer an exhilarating description of public sociology as

> a sociology that seeks to bring sociology to publics beyond the academy, promoting dialogue on issues that affect the fate of society, placing the values to which we adhere under a microscope. What is important here is the multiplicity of public sociologies, reflecting the multiplicity of publics—visible and invisible, thick and thin, active and passive, local, national and

even global, dominant and counter publics. The variety of publics stretches from our students to the readers of our books, from newspaper columns to interviews, from audiences in local civil groups such as churches or neighborhoods, to social movements we facilitate. The possibilities are endless.[22]

"The possibilities are endless." The point of *all* disciplines should be to seek and share knowledge that benefits the whole community. Hey! Man in the Cowboy Hat! If community problems are not accepted as academic problems, then we academics really do live in ivory towers, and we should be evicted. Right?

Notes

1. Ronald D Eller, *Miners, Millhands, and Mountaineers* (Knoxville: University of Tennessee Press, 1986); John Gaventa, *Power and Powerlessness: Quiescence and Rebellion in an Appalachian Valley* (Urbana: University of Illinois Press, 1980).

2. Sherry Cable and Charles Cable, *Environmental Problems, Grassroots Solutions* (New York: St. Martin's Press, 1995); Riley E. Dunlap and Angela G. Mertig, *American Environmentalism: The U.S. Environmental Movement, 1970–1990* (Philadelphia: Taylor and Francis, 1992).

3. All quotations from activists are from interviews conducted by the author.

4. Max Weber, *Economy and Society*, vol. 1 (1909; reprint, Berkeley: University of California Press, 1978).

5. Elton Mayo, *Human Problems of an Industrial Civilization* (New York: Viking, 1966).

6. Robert K. Yin, *Case Study Research: Design and Methods*, 3rd ed. (Thousand Oaks, CA: Sage, 2003).

7. M. LeComte and J. J. Schensul, *Designing and Conducting Ethnographic Research* (Walnut Creek, CA: AltaMira Press, 1999); A. Mastroianni and J. Kahn, "Swinging on the Pendulum: Shifting Views of Justice in Human Subjects Research," *Hastings Center Report* 31, no. 3 (2001): 21–28.

8. Stanley Milgram, *Obedience to Authority* (New York: Harper and Row, 1974); Philip G. Zimbardo, "Pathology of Imprisonment," *Society* 9, no. 4 (1972): 4–8.

9. Tamara L. Mix, "Strangers in the Plight" (PhD diss., University of Tennessee, 2002); Sherry Cable, Tamara L. Mix, and Donald Hastings, "Mission Impossible? Environmental Justice Activists' Collaborations with Professional Environmentalists and with Academics," in *Power, Justice, and the Environ-*

ment: A Critical Appraisal of the Environmental Justice Movement, ed. David Naguib Pellow and Robert Brulle (Cambridge: MIT Press, 2005), 55–75.

10. Cable, Mix, and Hastings, "Mission Impossible?"

11. Environmental justice activist, interview by Tamara Mix, Donald Hastings, and Sherry Cable, 2005.

12. Cable, Mix, and Hastings, "Mission Impossible?"

13. Cable, Mix, and Hastings, "Mission Impossible?"

14. John Gaventa, "The Powerful, the Powerless, and the Experts: Knowledge Struggles in an Information Age," in *Voices of Change: Participatory Research in the United States and Canada,* ed. P. Park, M. Brydon-Miller, B. Hall, and T. Jackson (Westport, CT: Bergin and Garvey, 1993), 21–40.

15. Andrew Szasz, *Ecopopulism: Toxic Waste and the Movement for Environmental Justice* (Minneapolis: University of Minnesota Press, 1994); David N. Pellow, "Popular Epidemiology and Environmental Movements: Mapping Active Narratives for Empowerment," *Humanity and Society* 21 (1997): 307–21; Lee Williams, "Participatory Research, Knowledge, and Community Based Change: Experience, Epistemology, and Empowerment," *Research in Community Sociology* 9 (1999): 3–40; Phil Brown and Faith Ferguson, "Making a Big Stink: Women's Work, Women's Relationships, and Toxic Waste Activism," *Gender and Society* 9, no. 2 (1995): 145–72; Paulo Freire, *Pedagogy of the Oppressed* (New York: Continuum, 1970); Orlando Fals-Borda, *Knowledge and People's Power: Lessons with Peasants; Nicaragua, Mexico, and Colombia* (New York: New Horizons Press, 1988).

16. Frank Fischer, *Citizens, Experts, and the Environment: The Politics of Local Knowledge* (Durham, NC: Duke University Press, 2000); Luke W. Cole and Sheila R. Foster, *From the Ground Up: Environmental Racism and the Rise of the Environmental Justice Movement* (New York: New York University Press, 2001); Lois Marie Gibbs, *Love Canal: My Story* (Albany: State University of New York Press, 1982); Paula DiPerna, *Cluster Mystery: Epidemic and the Children of Woburn* (St. Louis, MO: Mosby, 1985); Will Collette, *How to Deal with a Proposed Facility* (Arlington, VA: Clearinghouse for Hazardous Wastes, Inc., 1987); Juliet Merrifield, *Putting Scientists in Their Place: Participatory Research in Environmental and Occupational Health* (Newmarket, TN: Highland Center, 1989); Phil Brown and Edwin J. Mikkelsen, *No Safe Place: Toxic Waste, Leukemia, and Community Action* (Berkeley: University of California Press, 1990); Randy Stoecker and Edna Bonacich, "Why Participatory Research? Guest Editors' Introduction," *American Sociologist* 23, no. 4 (1992): 5–14.

17. Ernest L. Boyer, *Scholarship Reconsidered: Priorities of the Professoriate* (San Francisco: Jossey-Bass, 1990), xii; Ernest L. Boyer, "The Scholarship of Engagement," *Journal of Public Service and Outreach* 1, no. 1 (1996): 11–20.

18. Kellogg Commission, *Returning to Our Roots: Executive Summaries of*

the Reports of the Kellogg Commission on the Future of State and Land-Grant Universities* (Washington, D.C.: Kellogg Commission on the Future of State and Land-Grant Universities and the National Association of State Universities and Land-Grant Colleges, 2001), 23.

19. Kellogg Commission, *Returning to Our Roots,* 23.

20. Kellogg Commission, *Public Higher Education Reform Five Years after the Kellogg Commission on the Future of State and Land-Grant Universities* (Washington, D.C.: National Association of State Universities and Land-Grant Colleges and the W. K. Kellogg Foundation, 2006).

21. George Orwell, *Animal Farm* (1945; reprint, New York: Signet Classics, 1996); C. Wright Mills, *The Sociological Imagination* (New York: Oxford University Press, 1959), 224.

22. Michael Burawoy, William Gamson, Charlotte Ryan, Stephen Pfohl, Diane Vaughan, Charles Derber, and Juliet Schor, "Public Sociologies: A Symposium from Boston College," *Social Problems* 51, no. 1 (2004): 104.

2

What Difference Did It Make?

The Appalachian Land Ownership Study after Twenty-Five Years

Shaunna L. Scott

In 1979–1980 the Appalachian Land Ownership Task Force (ALOFT) coordinated a team of more than sixty activists, citizens, and academics to conduct a systematic study of landownership patterns in six states: Kentucky, West Virginia, Tennessee, Virginia, North Carolina, and Alabama. The study found that land in these six states was concentrated in the hands of corporate and absentee owners who paid less than their fair share of taxes. Corporate and absentee ownership of land made it difficult for local communities to pursue alternative economic development and provide adequate housing for residents; and the low tax base resulted in poor educational systems and a lack of infrastructure development. All of this combined to make for high poverty rates, local inequality, and lower quality of life in these areas.[1]

The study concluded with a general call for land reform and a list of specific policy recommendations aimed at shifting more of the tax burden onto corporations and the wealthy, protecting surface owners' rights (e.g., elimination of the broad form deed), increasing the power of government to confiscate corporate land for alternative economic development and housing construction, protecting agricultural land, and instituting local planning and zoning to regulate land use and environmental impacts. The six-volume research report was submitted in 1981 to the Appalachian Regional Commission and published as a book by the University Press of Kentucky in 1983.[2]

This study was not meant for a dusty library shelf or agency file cabinet. Rather, it was meant as a call to action. It has been cited as a model for engaged, community-based scholarship and participatory action research. Along with Helen Matthews Lewis, Linda Johnson, and Donald Askins's *Colonialism in Modern America: The Appalachian Case* and John Gaventa's *Power and Powerlessness,* the land study helped to usher in a paradigm shift in Appalachian studies. It seems particularly fitting, then, to revisit this study in a volume documenting collaborative projects by activists and academics in and around the Appalachian region. Indeed, several projects documented in this book were inspired, either directly or indirectly, by the land study and its commitment to community-based, policy-relevant research, including the Dayhoit Listening Project (chapter 3), the resistance to mountaintop removal on Black Mountain (chapter 5), the University of Kentucky critical regionalism project (chapter 11), the Martin County coal waste disaster project (chapter 4), and the Headwaters Project (chapter 10).[3]

The Land Study: Context and History

After severe flooding destroyed homes and businesses in the coalfields of central Appalachia in 1977, citizens formed the Tug Valley Recovery Center in Williamson, West Virginia. The purpose was to respond to problems associated with the flooding, including a lack of temporary housing sites and the federal government's refusal to seize corporate land for this purpose. Frustrated by the government's response to their situation, this group invited over fifty organizations and many other individuals to a meeting in Williamson, where they formed a coalition called the Appalachian Alliance. The alliance elected a steering committee and established a landownership and taxation subcommittee at a January 1978 follow-up meeting held at the Union College Environmental Center in Barbourville, Kentucky. Of the twenty-two subcommittee members, fifteen were from citizens' groups and eight were from academic institutions. These included faculty, staff, and graduate students from Appalachian State University, the University of Alabama, the University of Kentucky, Mars Hill College, and Emory and Henry College. Of all the projects sponsored in the ten-year history of the Appalachian Alliance, the study on landownership and taxation had the most long-lasting and widespread impact.[4]

Still, it is important to note that the 1981 study was not the first project to investigate landownership in the region. As Appalachian Alliance coordinator Bill Horton observed, the study represented the culmination of decades of folk knowledge-building and activism concerning control of land, resources, and labor in Appalachia and the American South. When the War on Poverty of the 1960s defined Appalachia as a region of endemic poverty, even more attention was paid to the causes and consequences of regional poverty and inequality. A precursor from this era was Richard Kirby's report written for the Appalachian Volunteers titled "Kentucky Coal: Owners, Taxes, Profits; A Case Study in Representation without Taxation." From humble beginnings in 1963 as a student volunteer work group at neighboring institutions in Madison County, Kentucky (Berea College and Eastern Kentucky University), the Appalachian Volunteers eventually became a multimillion-dollar Office of Economic Opportunity program in the War on Poverty. The Appalachian Volunteers' brief but dramatic history of political engagement in eastern Kentucky, though interesting, is outside the scope of this chapter.[5]

While Kirby's work provided one precedent for the study, an even more direct connection can be traced to a 1971 study of landownership and taxation conducted in five eastern Tennessee counties by John Gaventa and fellow students at Vanderbilt University. This study has been cited as a primary inspiration for the start-up of the Appalachian Land Ownership Task Force member group Save Our Cumberland Mountains. In West Virginia a West Virginia University Law School survey added to the regional discussion of these issues, as did a 1978 doctoral dissertation by John C. Wells Jr. titled "Poverty amidst Riches: Why People Are Poor in Appalachia." Journalists also contributed, specifically Paul Kaufman, writing in 1972 for the *New Republic,* and Tom Miller, an investigative journalist for the *Huntington (WV) Herald Dispatch.* Citizens in southwest Virginia had brought fair taxation issues to the attention of a U.S. Senate subcommittee as early as 1973.[6]

This set the stage, then, for an October 1977 Appalachian Regional Commission (ARC) conference on balanced growth and economic development. At this meeting, chaired by former secretary of labor Willard Wirtz, participants suggested that the agency examine how corporate ownership and transfer of profits outside of the region affected the tax base of communities in Appalachia. Apparently ignoring this advice, the ARC proposed instead to conduct a study on land settlement patterns to examine population distribution among urban and rural areas within the region and how that might affect the net cost of providing public services. In August 1978 ALOFT met with the ARC research committee to criticize their refusal to address landownership questions. After meeting over a period of two days, the ARC research committee invited the task force to submit a proposal for such a study. In January 1979 the ARC awarded the Appalachian Alliance $131,100 to coordinate a citizen-led study focusing on six states: Kentucky, West Virginia, Tennessee, Virginia, North Carolina, and Alabama.[7]

Land Study Structure and Process

In May 1979 citizens, activists, and researchers met at the Highlander Center for training in how to determine ownership, location and value of property owned, and property tax amounts by examining county property tax books and deed and lease books. Representatives from each of the six target states formed working groups and elected a co-ordinator. Funds were divided evenly among the states, and each chose the counties upon which to focus, decided upon how to conduct the research, and selected which issues to emphasize. Highlander Center staff member John Gaventa and Appalachian Alliance coordinator Billy D. Horton oversaw the effort. The Appalachian Studies Center of Appalachian State University in Boone, North Carolina, under the leadership of Patricia Beaver, provided administrative support and served as the fiscal agent for the project. In addition to the ARC funding, in-kind support from colleges, universities, and community groups also underwrote the study. The Tennessee Valley Authority and Appalachian State University provided computers for data analysis.[8]

Citizen researchers collected information throughout the summer and the following fall. A follow-up workshop in September 1979 provided the venue for preliminary reports of findings. There, researchers began to identify patterns in the data and determined who would write the report and formulate its conclusions. Analysis and writing took place in 1980, and the final report, consisting of more than eighteen hundred pages of material, including a regional overview and a volume on each of the six states, was submitted to the ARC in February 1981. The ARC released the report two months later, in April 1981.[9]

Most participants reported that relationships among researchers—the activists, community organizers, citizens, and academics who collected the information and wrote the report—were collegial and cooperative. In the anonymous evaluations of the project conducted shortly after its completion, one person explained, "This whole project transcended that whole [academic-activist] tension." When interviewed, David Liden, the West Virginia team leader, agreed, stating, "The people who came to the study came with a certain open-ness about the people on the other side of the academic-activist divide—it's sort of an artificial divide. A lot of activists were open to academics and vice versa. I think they saw each other as commonly involved in this struggle for social justice in the region."[10]

Appalachian State University professor Patricia Beaver also recalled during an interview that the researchers got along well. However, she noted some initial contention between ALOFT and the ARC research team. "I think the activist/academic division wasn't really very relevant to the people who came into this project; and, after the initial confrontation, eventually the ARC research team worked through their suspicion of the process, *and* the process was honed in to suit their research standards." The Kentucky state coordinator, Joe Childers, said, "This was not a study that was done by academics, at least in Kentucky. I was a [law] student. The other folks were young, community-based people. I don't recall that we had much conflict. There were certainly frustrations, in terms of records being poor. But conflicts? I don't think so!"

To others, differences were more evident, though they were certainly resolvable. Charles "Boomer" Winfrey, Save Our Cumberland Mountains (SOCM) staffer and Tennessee state coordinator, addressed these issues during an interview:

> I know we had some lively discussions at Highlander . . . about whether we were going in the right direction or not. Some academics thought the activists had too much of a tunnel approach: that we weren't using a scientific method of "do your research *before* you come to your conclusions." And they were right.
>
> But we wanted to see some results come from this. We didn't want another study to put on a shelf that gets pulled down by some Ph.D. who wants to cite it. We wanted it to be disseminated to the region to be used as a catalyst to organize and make some changes. There was some lively debate over to what extent we should pursue that. . . . None of these discussions ended up in fisticuffs. No one ever walked out. We always resolved things.

An anonymous project evaluator similarly noted, "I think that the different elements that went into making up the study were really very valuable. . . . I look back on a couple of those early meetings where we had some real differences, where even the goals we were setting seemed very different. One was a kind of research mechanism and the other was a kind of social action group, but somehow despite those differences a lot happened with the study that wouldn't have happened otherwise."[11]

Emory and Henry professor Steve Fisher also perceived divisions among study participants, recalling in 1999, "I vividly remember being at the Highlander Center for meetings related to the land ownership study and hearing time and again that the only voices that really mattered were those of the 'real people.' It didn't take long to figure out that the real people were the community activists and organizers and the unreal people were the academics."[12] In a 2005 conversation with me, Fisher emphasized the study's success in forging connections between academics and activists. "The land study helped build some bridges and break down some distinctions, though they still exist to some extent," he stated.

Against those who would see the citizens as unqualified and inferior researchers, Gaventa argued that the local knowledge and passion of the citizens enhanced the quality of the research. "To them [citizens], the numbers and names represented power and power-holders they knew. The data quickly gave them insights into local community affairs. With such motivation, the citizen often took time to search out information that investigators who were simply in it for 'the job' would not have pursued or would have reported missing," wrote Gaventa.[13]

Any tensions between the academics and activists paled in comparison to the different orientations of ALOFT and its primary funding agency, the ARC. The land study was, in a sense, born of conflict, emerging as it did from a confrontation between ALOFT and the ARC over the inadequacies of the ARC's planned land settlement study. The ARC's agreement to fund the research came as a surprise to everyone. As Susan Williams put it during an interview, "It was sort of amazing that they [ARC] ever funded it in the first place. How did that even happen? I remember people think it was amazing that it happened."[14]

Because the ARC is a government agency that functions as a state and federal partnership, it must curry the favor of both the president and the governors of the thirteen states included in the agency's territory. The agency required detailed research methodology before it would release funds for the research. Funding was finally approved during the

May 1979 workshop, after some researchers had begun their work. The extra requirements and funding delays burdened the coordinators with additional administrative work and slowed down the momentum of the project.

The conflict between the ARC and the task force was most obvious when the final report was submitted in 1981, as Gaventa and Horton explained:

> Though the Commission had approved the methodology, it balked when it saw the findings. The 20 county case studies, where hard statistical data gave way to analysis and interpretations of what the data really meant, were particular sore spots. At the same time, the ARC itself was in trouble; threatened with abolition by the Reagan administration, it was lobbying hard in Congress to stay alive. ARC officials openly admitted that release of a controversial report wouldn't help their case.
>
> On the other hand, they did not want to be seen as suppressing the research, or to face the anger of citizens all over Appalachia who had worked so hard on it. So they finally agreed to release the report, though not without taking several steps to distance themselves from it. They refused to release the case studies, arguing they weren't objective. Despite a prior agreement, they refused to make any announcement to the press. They refused to meet the full demand for copies of the study, saying they had no money to print it. And, despite this shortage of money, they hired a blue-ribbon panel of outside academics and consultants to do an experts' study of the citizens' study. (That panel has yet to release its findings.)[15]

As of the writing of this chapter in 2008, I too have not been able to locate a copy of this alternative report in library searches, among the private papers of study participants, or in Special Collections and Archives at Appalachian State University, where many land study documents are housed.

Winfrey attributed the ARC's cool reception of the report to the change in administrations: "When this was negotiated, Jimmy Carter was in the White House. But, even though the ARC staff didn't have that much turnover, the person in the White House had an effect. By the time this was done, Ronald Reagan was in the White House. Whole different ball game! The green light had turned red!"[16]

West Virginia team leader David Liden agreed, arguing during an interview that methodological objections were motivated by political bias rather than legitimate scientific objections:

> It was a wonderful model. We had systematic approach to the issues; it was methodologically legitimate and was common to the entire study. So, we had the systematic element that we needed to be sure that we were talking about apples and apples everywhere we looked. But, then, we had the local aspect who knew the important people to talk to. If it had been an outside researcher coming in, they wouldn't have known the community dynamics well enough to know who the key people were who had the information that was important to us. It was a great combination of elements. There were people who had a college education and others who didn't. But they knew how important it was to have [the] same objective methods but also the subjective elements.
>
> We were later criticized by some for being too subjective in what we were doing. But my sense was that was coming from people who were uncomfortable with the documentation and conclusions and, by way of sounding professional, they tried to criticize the methodology which, in fact, I don't think there was any basis for. Really, they couldn't dispute the figures we were coming up with in terms of acres and dollars of taxes paid or not paid. There was nothing to dispute about that. They tried to give the impression that not all of our folks were formally trained to do this. But, in fact, our methodology was very easy to follow. And that subjective element gave a depth of understanding that would not have been possible otherwise.[17]

The task force had anticipated that the ARC would balk at the report because, as Horton wrote later, the ARC was a "federal agency not known for its propensity to share information with grass-roots groups." So the task force worked with community groups, newspapers, independent publishers, and academic presses to circulate the findings themselves. The Needmor Fund, a Toledo, Ohio, family foundation dedicated to the support of citizen and community activism, provided $6,000 to underwrite publication of the results.[18]

In addition to writing about the study for publication in academic journals and books, the task force printed pamphlets, sent out press releases, sat for media interviews, held town meetings, and wrote a book published by the University Press of Kentucky in 1983. Major regional newspapers, including the *Louisville Courier-Journal, Nashville Tennessean,* and *Charleston Gazette,* picked up on the story and published "strong editorials calling for change based on the study's findings and conclusions." Some local newspapers also called for change based on the study. The *Martin Countian,* a Kentucky paper published by Homer Marcum, ran a series on the land study that supported local efforts to implement taxation of corporate lands. (Kentucky and Alabama suffered most from undervaluation and lack of taxation of corporate land, with Martin County, Kentucky, being the most extreme example and therefore much cited.) *Mountain Life and Work,* a regional magazine published by the Council of Southern Mountains, also ran a series of articles on the study and, in addition, published a pamphlet summarizing the study for distribution to citizens, policy makers, and community organizations. *Southern Exposure,* a regional journal published by the Institute for Southern Studies, featured the land study in a 1982 issue. Church organizations also played a role in publicizing the study, including the Catholic Committee on Appalachia and the Commission on Religion in Appalachia. John Egerton published a piece on the project in the *Progressive,* and Mary Read English wrote a review of the study for *American Land Forum Magazine.* Thus its findings became a part of public discourse and an inspiration for political action in the region.[19]

What Difference Did It Make?

Most past assessments of the land study have concentrated on how it influenced politics and community organizing in Appalachia. Such influence is not surprising, given the study's stated aim: to produce information that would be useful to the citizens of Appalachia. While this retelling of the land study story includes a consideration of its political and community organizing impacts, it also considers the study's reception in academia and its impact on the lives and careers of the ten participants who were interviewed for this project.

Academic Impacts

The study had its most significant academic impact in the interdisciplinary field of Appalachian Studies, as Appalachian Studies founder Steve Fisher noted, "The whole neo-colonial model of Appalachia was a giant boost [to Appalachian Studies]. It [the land study] seemed to provide the important documentation that was needed for that new model. I think for a good number of years, it was an important reference point for academics and how they thought about the region."

In 1979 the second annual Appalachian Studies Association (ASA) Conference, held at Jackson's Mill, West Virginia, took land use as its theme and featured the study. The initiative was a formative event in the early years of the Appalachian Studies Association and helped establish a commitment to keep the Appalachian Studies conference as an inclusive forum for academics, artists, activists, and citizens to gather and learn from one another.[20] As Pat Beaver noted during an interview:

> We took the Appalachian Land Ownership Study into the ASA, and I believe impacted the evolution of that organization as not so academically driven as other professional organizations, and more attuned to issues of community participation.
>
> We had Bob Scott, former North Carolina governor who was federal co-chair of the ARC, as keynoter for that initial ASA meeting in Berea; and that, in turn, opened the door to visiting with him about the land study, which he seemed to support.

"For me, it was confirmation that academics and community people could sit together and work together and learn from one another. That helped strengthen our commitment to keep doing that through the ASA," Steve Fisher agreed. The land study functions as a touchstone for periodic reassessments of the ASA mission and performance, especially on the inclusion of community voices and academic-activist collaboration.[21]

The impact of the study was far-reaching. Bill Horton, for example, pointed out that his colleagues in the Society for Humanist Sociology were impressed with the land study and his participation in it. It served as a prototypical approach to scholarship for that group. Many have cited the project as instrumental in the creation of the field of participatory action research, a methodological approach aimed at social change and the incorporation of community participation in research problem formulation, data collection, and analysis. As former West Virginia Organizing Project activist Allen Cooper put it in an interview, "In my view, the Appalachian Land Ownership Study is like a foundational document, a foundational source in understanding the history of Appalachia. . . . [and] the history of injustice and understanding why the coal industry and its successors and helpers—why they have so much power. Any effort you make in trying to understand that, that's a basic document to frame your understanding. Almost like the air you breathe now."[22]

Personal Impacts: Reflections of Ten Land Study Participants

The political and community organizing impacts of the land study have always attracted the most attention from its evaluators, and rightly so. However, it is also worthwhile visiting the more personal impacts of the land study on its participants. Land study coordinators John Gaventa and Bill Horton and four of the six state coordinators agreed to share with me their thoughts on how the experience fitted into the trajectory of their lives. The four state coordinators I interviewed were Joe Childers (Kentucky), David Liden (West Virginia), Tracey Weis (Virginia), and Charles "Boomer" Winfrey (Tennessee). Patricia Beaver, the administrative coordinator; Steve Fisher, a report writer; and researchers Joe Szakos and Susan Williams also shared their thoughts. The interviewees fall into three basic categories: those who identified the study as a positively transformative experience; those who viewed the study as a nontransformative event—just another step on a personal journey that preceded the land study; and those who were ambivalent about their experience with the project.

The Land Study as Transformational Event

Five of the ten individuals I interviewed identified the study as a positive, transformational event in their lives—one that had long-lasting effects on their career choices, personal identities, and political engagement. "It was probably the most influential thing that I did in the course of directing what my career was going to look like," said Joe Childers, Kentucky state coordinator. "I was really interested in working through the legal system to address some of the issues that we pointed out [in the study], particularly in Kentucky." Childers followed through with that commitment. In 1981 he took a position at the Appalachian Research and Defense Fund of Kentucky (AppalReD), where he was the recipient of a Reginald Smith Fellowship. The fellowship required him to devote half his time to community service, and, with the support of AppalReD director Joe Rosenberg, Childers devoted his community service time to Kentuckians for the Commonwealth (KFTC). He represented KFTC in its legal challenges to the broad form deed, which advantaged mineral owners' rights of recovery over the rights of the surface (land) owners, as well as in its quest for a state tax on unmined minerals. Childers currently has a law firm specializing in environmental law in Lexington, Kentucky.[23]

Tennessee community activist and land study researcher Susan Williams also saw her work on the project as a key experience influencing her future career path and general outlook. Williams had just taken a staff position at SOCM when she was assigned to work on the land study. In addition to providing her with an opportunity to meet people and visit places in the area where she was to work, this work helped Williams attain valuable knowledge about landownership, corporate power, and political dynamics in Tennessee. Equally important, the project introduced her to participatory action research and changed her perspective on the definitions of research, knowledge, and expertise. Williams credited the project with empowering her to engage in research and in community organizing. In her words, "It was all new to me. It made me feel like I could do stuff I didn't [previously] know anything about. That was really helpful. I grew up thinking that you had to be a scientist in order to do research." Williams worked at SOCM from 1979 to 1989 and then went on to become coordinator for the Highlander Library/ Resource Center.

Tracey Weis was a young college graduate working on a government flood recovery program when she was invited to serve as the Virginia state coordinator for the landownership research. "I learned so much from the Appalachian Land Ownership project that I scarcely know where to begin," she said. "It was life-changing; it has served as a compass for my personal and political life. In particular, the land study demonstrated the power of participatory research; this served as the template for what I've tried to do in subsequent efforts." Her desire to learn more about the historical dynamics behind the concentrated patterns of landownership that characterized Appalachia in the late twentieth century was what "catapulted" her into graduate school to study history. As a member of the history faculty at Millersville University, she has applied the land study's "participatory research model in just about every arena of my academic career: graduate school courses and research, teaching at Millersville University, participation in the American Social History Project's New Media Classroom, and the formulation of grant applications for the National Endowment for the Humanities."[24]

While the study led Weis into an academic career, it took David Liden in the opposite direction. Liden had earned a PhD in political science from the University of Michigan before he joined the faculty of Bethany College in West Virginia. While there, he became increasingly interested in the politics of the region and found himself getting "a little bit restless in the college environment." So when friend and colleague Joe Hacala (Wheeling Jesuit College) invited him to join the Appalachian Land Ownership Study, he "signed on" as West Virginia coordinator. "At that point, I moved from academia to this participatory community research way of doing things," he observed. After the study Liden moved to North Carolina, where he helped start the Western North Carolina Alliance, and then "I went on to a career basically in development work, fund-raising, for non-profits here in our community, our medical center and others. And it influenced the way I worked."

When asked how the project affected his subsequent career and life, John Gaventa replied, "You couldn't be involved in something that exciting and intense for three or four years and not have an impact. I did devote a fair amount of energy trying to build on participatory action research. I didn't work on land per se as much. But I was then linking to an international group of people thinking about this new research approach. It certainly influenced me to pursue that." Gaventa had completed his doctoral work in politics at Oxford University before he became the coordinator of the land study and the codirector of research at the Highlander Center. By 1989 he had become the director of research at the Highlander Center, a position he held until 1994. In 1986 he joined the sociology faculty at the University of Tennessee (UT) and helped found and codirect UT's Community Partnership Center from 1994 to 1996. From there he took a fellowship and then a professorship at the Institute of Development Studies at the University of Sussex. The study continues to be relevant to his work today: "Now, of course, I'm working in a research center that does a lot of community research all over the world in developing countries. I talk about it in classes, [especially] in research methodology classes. It links me to issues of land all over the place. I was raised in the Niger delta where now the troubles around oil are like the troubles around coal. So, those insights I bring there. I also work in Angola where companies are taking over the resources there. My experiences on land help me think about these issues in other parts of the world."

The Land Study as Stepping Stone

Joe Szakos, who after the study became a KFTC organizer and then a staff member of Virginia Organizing Project, did not regard the experience in this transformative light. As he put it, "For me, the Appalachian Land Ownership Study was just an excuse to get things started. It wasn't a life-changing project." Having already left Chicago for a career in community organizing in eastern Kentucky, Szakos found the project to be a good opportunity with fortuitous timing. It merely provided a conduit for the work that he had already committed himself to doing.

Steve Fisher likewise had already embarked on his life's work, studying political science at Emory and Henry College. For him the project represented a step in a journey that he had already begun rather than a life-changing event. He explained,

> For me, it was confirmation that academics and community people could sit together and work together and learn from one another. . . .
>
> I did a lot of land reform research after that. . . . It gave me contacts with activists and academics that have been important to me throughout my career. It reinforced my educational philosophy. In some ways, my work at Emory and Henry [College] and Just Connections [a service learning program] grew out of that philosophy [of the land study]. . . .
>
> [At the time,] I was still struggling with all of that; but the land study was my confirmation to me that this was what I needed to be doing.

Study coordinator Bill Horton had also embarked on an academic career when the project began, and his decision to leave academia temporarily to work on the project "was part of a career stream" that grew out of his "frustration in academe." He explained further,

> Part of the reason I left the academic context to get involved in the land study was that I was looking for ways to connect the scholarly and activist sides of myself. The land study, it seemed to be what it was about, on one level, it was trying to make scholarly work practically useful in terms of bringing about social change. . . . I'm not sure that the land study had a dramatic impact on my subsequent career and life as much as it was part of the ongoing interest that I had felt about connecting those two parts of my life.

After the land study Horton briefly worked for the Highlander Center but then moved to New Hampshire, where he taught sociology and pursued a career in college administration until 2001. He is a founding member of an organization to prevent farmland loss in New England and currently works on a federal project aimed at integrating persons with developmental disabilities into the community.

Burnout and Unfulfilled Potential

Patricia Beaver credited the land study with "launching" her into Appalachian Studies but also noted that the study in combination with her instructional and administrative duties at Appalachian State University and her first foray into motherhood contributed to her desire to leave Appalachia and Appalachian Studies, at least temporarily. After the study's publication in 1983 she found herself "eager to go far away [to visit] exotic places and understand other revolutions." So she spent a year in China, conducting research that occupied her attention for the subsequent decade. By 1993, however, Beaver turned her attention again to Appalachian topics and has since played an important role in research, teaching, community activism, and mentoring the Appalachian Studies Association at Appalachian State University. She retains a "deep respect" for her colleagues and for the project but articulates some lingering regret that the project did not have the major impact that it should have.

The land study put a strain on everyone, Charles "Boomer" Winfrey said, especially the state coordinators. "If anything, it contributed to my burnout. It was such an intense and more time-consumptive project than we expected. By the time that was over, I was ready to move on. As far as working with SOCM, it was a negative effect. That land study burned us all out." Like Szakos, Fisher, and Horton, he did not identify the study as a transformative event in his life: "Personally, it didn't have a big impact. . . . For me it was another piece of the continuing work that we had done for 10 years." Winfrey departed SOCM within six months of completing the study. While the taxing duties of coordinating the Tennessee segment of the land study played a role in his "burnout," Winfrey also acknowledged that "ten years at a non-profit organization is a long time. . . . It was probably time [for me to leave] anyway." Even though the study did not change his perspective or life's work, as it did for others, Winfrey nevertheless recognized the continued legacy of the project in his later life as a "ball-busting" newspaper editor and in his quest to "afflict the comfortable and comfort the afflicted." Though he retired as editor of the *LaFollette Press* in 2001, Winfrey continues to work as a consultant and trainer for nonprofits, including KFTC, Appalshop, and the Community Farm Alliance (all in Kentucky) and writes a weekly newspaper column for the *LaFollette Press*.

Critiques of the Land Study: Insider Perspectives

Though they generally thought that the positive aspects of the study far outweighed its problems, landownership researchers were keenly aware that the study had shortcomings. Many of the problems with the study resulted from difficulty in collecting data, a problem that was out of the control of the researchers. Counties recorded landownership and valuation information in different ways, sometimes kept inadequate records, and did not always cooperate with the researchers, which made access to the data difficult. The variation in data access combined with the different backgrounds and skills of the researchers meant that the quality of data varied from county to county. In spite of this, the study participants all felt satisfied that their findings were valid and their research was, if not perfect, at least competently done.

At the state level, "Boomer" Winfrey regretted the narrow focus taken by SOCM, the organization that coordinated the study in Tennessee:

> One of the drawbacks was [that] we [SOCM] were an existing organization with an agenda. . . . We were working on strip min-

ing, coal issues, and tax issues. And we really needed information from the counties outside of those five counties [where the original study was done]. So, we picked the Cumberland Plateau (the coal counties) for our studies.

We didn't look at counties with national forests. We didn't look at counties where timber was the main resource, rather than coal. Some of the other states did look at those things. They had a more broad-based research focus.

We were restricted because of our agenda at looking at coal.

. . .

I wish we had done more. SOCM now is working on a lot of issues. Some of the data from the other states, like Alabama and North Carolina, would be valuable now to us. But you can't have everything.

David Liden traced the study's limitations to its "federated" structure, a feature that was also regularly regarded as a strength of the study:

It was a federated structure and each state faced different tax law and realities and different ownership issues and different environmental and socioeconomic consequences. So, maybe because of the federated nature of what we were doing, there couldn't have been any larger strategic initiatives, region-wide. Maybe they had to be state-wide or even at the community level.

That's an interesting thought: how strategically can you think on a regional level when you're dealing with this sort of federated mechanics and information that relates more to the state level and county level and even the community level? I don't know, that's just an observation.

Steve Fisher noted that the report-writing group had trouble "thinking outside the box" in terms of policy recommendations but, more importantly, not enough planning had been devoted to using the results as a region-wide organizing strategy:

We needed more focus on strategy for organizing around the results.

There were frustrations that grew out of the workshop in the effort to write up the recommendations. We did pretty well on how to protect the land but, in terms of land reform, we were stymied. We had a three- or four-day workshop in which we tried to do exercises on that. . . . But we couldn't break out of the box on that. . . .

It didn't offer us a vision of what Appalachia should be in terms of land ownership. It wasn't for lack of trying. We could've started earlier and we needed more follow-up.

Finally, the ARC's failure to make better use of the research in policy formation was a disappointment to Liden. "If there were any disappointments," he said, "a big one was the ARC didn't follow through with what we presented to them. We knew that it would be a sensitive thing for them. But some of us hoped they would use it." Horton concurred, saying, "I sometimes have mixed feelings about how much change has actually resulted. On the one hand, you see some laws changed, some practices changed, and some funding mechanisms changed. On the other hand, you see some of the same battles going on in Central Appalachia that were going on a long time ago, preceding the land study."

The Appalachian Land Ownership Study has been cited in Appalachian Studies and in the field of participatory action research as a foundational study that instituted a paradigm shift in how some scholars viewed the world, how to study it, and how to change it. In Kentucky the project leveraged resources and created networks that laid the foundation for the creation of Kentuckians for the Commonwealth in 1991. That group has since played an important role in state politics, legislation, and policy formation. The study also can be linked (indirectly, at least) to a variety of other organizations in the six study states, organizations that have become players in community development, environmental activism, and democratization in their states. In addition, some of the researchers and coordinators of the project identify the study as a transformative event that inspired them and trained them for a career in community organizing or academia—or both. The study also influenced some of the authors of chapters in this volume, including Robert Gipe, Roy Silver, Betsy Taylor, Stephanie McSpirit, and Alan Banks. As Silver explained,

Just after I moved to Eastern Kentucky in 1980 to teach sociology at a small liberal arts college they published the *Land Ownership Study.* This publication and the subsequent interactions
I had with participatory action researchers like John Gaventa,
Helen Lewis, Juliet Merrifield, et al. exposed me to the value
of serving communities through participatory action research.

To this day the *Land Ownership Study* serves as foundational
work for academics who strive to serve communities.

Like Silver, I credit the land study as a personal inspiration, even though
I did not participate in it directly. As an undergraduate student and Appalachian Studies minor at the University of Kentucky at the time of
this research, I read the study in draft form before it was published as a
book. It had a profound impact on how I understood the development
of underdevelopment and poverty in Appalachia and my ideas about the
research-activism relationship. It is fair to say that this study paved the
way for my participation in research on the community impacts of the
Martin County coal waste disaster of October 2000 (see chapter 5). Even
though that project has not had a similarly transformative impact on
ARC policy, federal and state taxation structures, landownership, poverty, and private property in the region, it remains a significant force in
Appalachian Studies, community-based research, and activism in our
region. The land study inspired many of us to question the boundaries
between expert and citizen knowledge and actively engage our theories
in action. Most important of all, it encouraged us to believe that change
is possible.

Notes

A version of this chapter first appeared first in *Appalachian Journal* 35, no. 3
(Spring 2008).

1. Appalachian Land Ownership Task Force, *Who Owns Appalachia?
Landownership and Its Impact* (Lexington: University Press of Kentucky, 1983).

2. Appalachian Land Ownership Task Force, *Who Owns Appalachia?*

3. P. D. Beaver, "Participatory Research on Land Ownership in Appalachia," in *Appalachia and America: Autonomy and Regional Dependence,* ed. A.
Batteau (Lexington: University Press of Kentucky, 1983), 252–66; P. Park, M.
Brydon-Miller, B. Hall, and T. Jackson, *Voices of Change: Participatory Research
in the United States and Canada* (Toronto: Ontario Institute for Studies in Education, 1993); H. M. Lewis, L. Johnson, and D. Askins, *Colonialism in Modern*

America: The Appalachian Case (Boone, NC: Appalachian Consortium Press, 1978); J. Gaventa, *Power and Powerlessness: Quiescence and Rebellion in an Appalachian Valley* (Urbana: University of Illinois Press, 1980).

4. Beaver, "Participatory Research," 255, 257; C. Montrie, *To Save the Land and People: A History of Opposition to Surface Coal Mining in Appalachia* (Chapel Hill: University of North Carolina Press, 2003), 193; R. Couto, *Making Democracy Work Better: Dedicating Structures, Social Capital, and the Democratic Prospect* (Chapel Hill: University of North Carolina Press, 1999), 137–42.

5. B. D. Horton, "The Appalachian Land Ownership Study: Research and Citizen Action in Appalachia," in Park et al., *Voices of Change,* 85–102; R. M. Kirby, "Kentucky Coal: Owners, Taxes, Profits; A Case Study in Representation without Taxation," *Appalachian Lookout* 1, no. 6 (1969): 19–27.

6. J. Gaventa, E. Ormond, and B. Thompson, *Coal Taxation and Tennessee Royalists* (Nashville, TN: Vanderbilt University Student Health Coalition, 1971); D. McAteer, *Coal Mine Health and Safety: The Case of West Virginia* (New York: Praeger, 1973); T. D. Miller, *Who Owns West Virginia* (Huntington, WV: Huntington Publishing, 1975); B. Privratsky and J. Randalf, "Coal Taxes in Southwest Virginia" (unpublished report for the U.S. Senate Subcommittee on Intergovernmental Relations by Citizens for Fair Taxes, 1973).

7. Beaver, "Participatory Research," 255–56; Appalachian Land Ownership Task Force, *Who Owns Appalachia?;* J. Gaventa and B. D. Horton, "Who Owns Appalachia?" *Southern Exposure* 10, no. 1 (1982): 35; J. Gaventa and B. D. Horton, "Land Ownership and Land Reform in Appalachia," in *Land Reform, American Style,* ed. C. G. Giesler and F. J. Popper (Totowa, NJ: Rowman and Allanheld, 1984), 233–44.

8. B. D. Horton, "How to Find the Facts," *Southern Exposure* 10, no. 1 (1982): 42; Gaventa and Horton, "Who Owns Appalachia?" 35; Beaver, "Participatory Research."

9. Beaver, "Participatory Research," 258–59; Appalachian Land Ownership Task Force, *Who Owns Appalachia?* xviii; Gaventa and Horton, "Land Ownership," 235.

10. Gaventa and Horton, "Who Owns Appalachia?" 37.

11. Gaventa and Horton, "Who Owns Appalachia?" 37.

12. J. Williamson, "Anger and Hope, in Nearly Equal Measure: An Interview with Steve Fisher," *Appalachian Journal* 26, no. 2 (1999): 170–87.

13. J. Gaventa, "Land Ownership in Appalachia, U.S.A.: A Citizens' Research Project," in *Research for the People/Research by the People,* ed. T. Erasmie (Linkoping, Sweden: Linkoping University, 1980), 118–30; Beaver, "Participatory Research," 260.

14. Beaver, "Participatory Research"; Gaventa and Horton, "Land Ownership and Land Reform."

15. B. D. Horton and J. Gaventa, "A Citizen's Research Project in Appalachia, USA," *Convergence* 14 (1981): 37.

16. Unless otherwise indicated, all quotes are taken from the author's interviews conducted in 2005 and 2006.

17. D. Liden, "Pulling the Pillars: Energy Development and Land Reform in Appalachia," in Giesler and Popper, *Land Reform, American Style,* 101–16.

18. Horton, "Appalachian Land Ownership Study," 89; Needmor Fund, "Mission, Vision and Values Statement," at http://www.needmorfund.org/mission.htm.

19. Horton, "Appalachian Land Ownership Study," 89–101; Catholic Committee on Appalachia, "This Land Is Home to Me: A Pastoral Letter on Powerlessness in Appalachia, by the Bishops of the Region" (Prestonsburg, KY, 1975); J. Egerton, "Appalachia's Absentee Landlords: A Ground-Breaking Study Shows the Causes of Poverty in the Mountains," *Progressive* 45 (1981): 42–45; M. R. English, "The Uses of Participation," *American Land Forum Magazine* 5, no. 2 (1985): 63–65.

20. The Appalachian Land Ownership Study is cited as a key event in the Appalachian Studies Association's "Appalachian Studies Time Line," at http://appalachianstudies.org/archives/timeline.php.

21. K. Tice, D. B. Billings, and A. Banks, "Sustaining Our Region-Wide Conversation: Founding Hopes and Future Possibilities of the Appalachian Studies Association," *Journal of the Appalachian Studies Association* 5 (1993): 3–19.

22. Beaver, "Participatory Research," 252; Park et al., *Voices of Change.*

23. Kentuckians for the Commonwealth, "State Finally Gets It Right! 1980's Unmined Mineral Case Settled," *Balancing the Scales* 24 (2005): 1–2.

24. K. M. Brown and T. M. Weis, "Producing for Use and Teaching the Whole Student: Can Pedagogy Be a Form of Activism?" in *Taking Back the Academy! History of Activism, History as Activism,* ed. J. D. J. Manion (New York: Routledge, 2004), 161–76.

3

Participatory Action Research

Combating the Poisoning of Dayhoit, Harlan County

Roy Silver

In February 1989 residents of the community of Dayhoit in Harlan County, Kentucky, received the following notice: "Due to organic chemicals found in the well water supply at the Holiday Mobile Home Park, the Division of Water has placed a ban on consuming water from this supply. Residents of the Holiday Mobile Home Park must immediately stop using this water for drinking and cooking. The division recommends residents not use the water for bathing or showering."[1]

The Kentucky Division of Water informed residents of the mobile home park that owners of the facility would furnish water for drinking and cooking until they established a permanent alternative. Initially, households were given two gallons of bottled water per day, as if this would satisfy their daily cooking, bathing, drinking, and cleaning needs. The Division of Water also instructed domestic well users who resided near the mobile home park to contact the division so they could find out if their wells required testing.

Within two weeks of the initial notification "ten additional wells within a one-mile radius of the trailer park" were found to have levels of vinyl chloride, a carcinogen, well above the U.S. Environmental Protection Agency's (EPA) maximum contaminant levels (MCLs). On March 9, 1989, more than two hundred residents of Dayhoit attended a meeting where state officials advised them once again "to discontinue use of the water. They were further advised boiling the water does not alleviate the problem but in fact worsens the situation." Some residents were concerned about possible damage to water lines. They were told "vinyl chloride does permeate through plastic piping, but not copper or lead. They were told their private wells could not be flushed free of the contaminant."[2]

The primary concern of most of the residents of Dayhoit, expressed at the March meeting, was the health of their children and family. What the state officials told them did not alleviate their fears. While they were told that they should not drink, cook, or bathe with the contaminated water, they were also informed that their health was not likely to be adversely affected. This did not make much sense to many in attendance. The state had not identified the source of pollution. They told the people "there was no way to arrive at a definite answer" about how long they had been using contaminated water.[3]

Unearthing Seeds of Fire

After their initial encounters with state and local officials, citizens of Dayhoit began to understand that the answers to their most compelling questions would not be forthcoming. They discovered that they needed to form a group that would represent their interests. They incorporated under the name Concerned Citizens Against Toxic Waste (CCATW). Joan Robinett, chairperson of CCATW, outlined the purpose of the organization to a reporter for the *Harlan Daily Enterprise:* "All we want is to see that this situation is rectified. Everyone deserves clean water, healthy air to breathe and safe soil to live on. . . . The people of Dayhoit are no exceptions." Reflecting frustration with elected officials, Robinett told the *Lexington Herald-Leader,* "We'd vote for a person and thought he would take care of our needs. And that's wrong."[4]

CCATW began to prod county, state, and federal officials. They educated themselves about the nature of the toxic soup of chemicals they were exposed to and their harmful effects. As more test results became public, CCATW discovered that the extent of the poisoning was more dangerous than they had envisioned. Water and soil samples taken in Dayhoit established that arsenic, barium, cadmium, chromium, lead, mercury, selenium, silver, cis-1,2-dichlorethene, 1,2-dichlorethane, naphthalene, PCBs, trichloroethylene (TCE), and vinyl chloride were above MCLs. Residents also discovered that they had some common health problems. Typically, they complained that their hands and feet would peel and blister. Former workers at the National Electric Coil (NEC) plant, next to the Holiday Mobile Home Park, exhibited the most severe symptoms.

CCATW was formed because county, state, and federal governments and Cooper Industries, owner of the NEC plant, would not answer basic questions. What was the effect of this poisoning on the health of their children? What chemical poisons had they been exposed to? For how long? What was the extent of the poisoning? What could the combination of these chemicals do to them? What agency would help? Their minimum demands were long-term health monitoring for all present and former NEC workers and residents and medical treatment for those whose health had been affected.

Letters written by CCATW to the governor of Kentucky went unanswered. An aide to the attorney general of Kentucky responded to requests for assistance with declarations of limited resources. On one of their frequent visits to a state office to review the Dayhoit file, CCATW members were pushed into a corner of a room and told that they were becoming a nuisance. At one of the early public meetings with the CCATW, state representatives claimed they were not aware of the existence of NEC until 1987. CCATW uncovered records that suggested the state knew NEC was polluting as far back as 1985. According to Bill Bishop, former editorial columnist with the *Lexington Herald-Leader,* the state's Cabinet for Natural Resources and Environmental Protection was "grossly understaffed."[5]

CCATW Reactive and Proactive: Participatory Action Research

The poisoning of Dayhoit exposed the complicity of county, state, and federal governments with a Fortune 500 company against the stated objectives and concerns of citizens. What unfolded was a remarkable testimonial to the capacity of people to educate themselves on complex scientific information and the intricacies of public policy in order to establish control over their lives.

CCATW learned that if they were going to get answers to their questions and solve their problems they needed to take a more proactive approach. In 1990 Joan Robinett explained to a reporter, "A year ago, I would have assumed that someone, somewhere in government would have done something. Now, I don't assume anything." CCATW initiated four projects to answer questions that Cooper Industries and county, state, and federal governments appeared reluctant to pose.[6]

The first of these projects was begun in the midsummer of 1990 when CCATW initiated, at its own expense, blood lead testing. Residents and former NEC workers went to a local clinic to draw blood samples and sent these specimens to a lab for testing. Of the sixty people tested, thirteen, or 21 percent, displayed perceptible amounts of this hazardous heavy metal.

Community Survey

In January 1991 CCATW initiated a second project, a community survey to collect information on the extent of the adverse effects of the poisoning in the Dayhoit community and among former NEC workers. The survey not only collected information but was designed to correct misinformation. Through a grant from the Highlander Research and Education Center, CCATW worked with Rural Southern Voices for Peace (RSVP) and Southeast Kentucky Community and Technical College (SKCTC) in Harlan County. These outside groups worked with CCATW to construct a survey and train members of the citizens' group.

CCATW felt the need to conduct a door-to-door survey in Dayhoit because "the state, EPA and Cooper Industry [owner of NEC] were spending a lot of time in the community, talking to community people and telling them one thing while the reports showed something else. There was a lot of conflict and misinformation about what was actually going on."[7]

The citizen's group compiled a list of approximately seventy-five questions before they began working with the participatory action researchers. CCATW wanted help in "figuring out a way to shorten the questionnaire and make sure that they worded it properly so people could understand it." Health was one major area of concern. Based on more than a year and a half of experience, CCATW learned that residents and former NEC workers had similar illnesses. Both independently and with the assistance of the staff of Highlander and Roy Silver they were also able to research some of the common health problems associated with exposure to the toxins found in their water and soil. They needed to determine how many residents had their wells tested. "We knew there were a lot of people still on well water," Robinett explained. "We just didn't know exactly who they were. We knew that there had only been two initial rounds of well sampling, in March of 1989 and July of 1989."[8]

Since the area around the NEC facility was in a floodplain, CCATW was concerned about the absorption of the poisons through the root systems of garden vegetables. They also wanted to know how many people had eaten fish from the Cumberland River, which runs behind the plant. Former NEC workers who were members of CCATW talked about dumping toxins behind the plant and into the drains that emptied into the river.

CCATW wanted to find out how the residents felt about Cooper Industries, the state, the U.S. EPA, and CCATW itself. Since the company and the state were giving the public conflicting information, CCATW also wanted to know how the community perceived their efforts. There were reports that some homeowners had been denied loans on their property because local banks assigned their homes a value of zero. Were residents blaming CCATW, the messenger, for their predicament?

CCATW established a working relationship with RSVP through networking with the Highlander Center and the center's Environmental Economic Program. This program involved five citizen groups working on environmental problems. For one year, the groups participated in a series of five workshops, either at the Highlander Center or in a participating community. The program provided training in which groups learned from one another and learned about the relationship between environmental and economic issues.

RSVP works with community groups by providing them training for listening projects. Listening projects are designed to find and involve new people in social change work; teach groups to communicate and work with others, even those opposing them; identify information needs in a community; clear up misinformation; begin educating people on the issues; better understand community hopes, values, and concerns; and empower people to think of and act on creative solutions to problems. A listening project has one primary goal: communication that increases understanding and the potential for positive social change.[9]

Although RSVP had not worked with groups on environmental issues before the Dayhoit community survey, their program matched CCATW's needs. Listening projects do not just attempt to solicit information. The survey is designed to simultaneously ask questions and share information about the issues. For example, survey questions included the following: "Former workers at National Electric Coil have reported that poisonous chemicals from the plant were dumped into the Cumberland River for over thirty years. Some of those same chemicals have been found in Dayhoit drinking water. Within the past thirty years, have you eaten fish from the Cumberland River below National Electric Coil?"

RSVP trainers visited the community and met with residents and former NEC workers. CCATW shared with RSVP the questions they had written and educated them about the problems that they were experiencing. A four-page questionnaire was developed. One Saturday morning in January 1991 CCATW gathered ten two-person teams for a training session. The underlying philosophy of the listening project is that those conducting the survey function as active listeners. While many of the questions can be answered with a yes or no, most require some elaboration. By conducting the survey in people's homes, in face-to-face encounters, CCATW was better able to get to know people in their community.

RSVP staff spent the morning going over their philosophy and had each person rehearse a question-and-answer session. Participants were instructed to keep their opinions out of the discussions. The goal was to remain nonconfrontational and not to try to convert the people to CCATW's point of view. In the afternoon, the teams went out into the community and interviewed for two hours. When they returned, each team discussed its experiences and evaluated the questionnaire and the process. All of the teams were welcomed into residents' homes and spent from twenty to forty minutes with each family.

During the next two months CCATW conducted interviews in 120 homes. The next stage of the project put the survey material in a form that CCATW could use. Robinett explained that they worked with SKCTC "to get the information put into the computer. This was done so that we could get statistics and graphs."[10] The working relationship between CCATW and outside institutions illustrates a fundamental element of participatory action research: "Participatory research attempts to break down the distinction between the researchers and the researched, the subjects and objects of knowledge production by the participation of the people-for-themselves in the process of gaining and creating knowledge. In the process, research is seen not only as a process of creating knowledge, but simultaneously, as education and development of consciousness, and of mobilization for action."[11]

Robinett described how working with Highlander, RSVP, and SKCTC was different from working with other institutions: "It was a lot easier working with these groups because they do community work. They regularly work with community groups. They followed our lead. The questionnaire, for example, did not go to print until it had our final approval. It was the same thing with you [Silver] and the college, we worked together. One or two members of the citizens' group helped put some of the data into the computer. Some of the other people, from the college, who worked with you, were familiar with the community."[12]

The interaction between the participatory action researchers and the community was in stark contrast with interactions between Cooper Industries and the community. At a company press conference that CCATW turned into a public meeting, company representatives discovered that Roy Silver was a professor with a PhD. During a break company representatives cornered him and gave him a book that they believed would explain how the threats to community health were overblown. Simultaneously other company representatives gave Joan Robinett a videotape. This incident became the source of laughter within CCATW. The company clearly believed that the professor was a skilled reader and the community leader was skilled at watching television.

The alliance between SKCTC and CCATW was facilitated by three factors. First, as a community college, SKCTC drew students from the county where Dayhoit is located. Many students or their relatives either lived in Dayhoit or worked at NEC. The student who helped put information in the database, for example, lived in a community adjacent to the plant. Another student who helped with the survey was from the community. The second factor was that as part of the mission of SKCTC, faculty are required to perform community service. All the work that Roy Silver did with CCATW earned him community service credit.

Finally, the successful partnership between SKCTC and CCATW was based on a shared philosophy that guided the work. The central principles of this philosophy included avoiding the tendency to impose an external definition of need, understanding that the community must maintain control over the process, and recognizing that professionals have to work in solidarity with community groups, sustain a respect for the knowledge of community, and learn from them the different dimensions of the problem. At the same time that professionals are being educated by the community, they have an obligation to transfer their skills to the community.

CCATW, through the survey and other participatory research projects, systematically identified what they needed to know. They organized to gain and create knowledge. What they discovered was extremely valuable because they employed this knowledge for further citizen action. The survey showed that there were thirty-five homes less than two miles downstream of NEC that were still using well water. Of these, twenty-eight had never had their wells tested, and the remaining seven wells had been tested only once. CCATW learned that the nature of groundwater poisoning was such that a well that was found uncontaminated one day could be found contaminated the next. The findings from the survey were significant and frightening: 53 percent of the households had eaten fish from the Cumberland River; 73 percent had eaten vegetables grown near the plant; 23 percent reported that someone in the household had kidney problems; 54 percent, an itching rash; 59 percent, dry, scaly, or cracked skin; and 61 percent, experiences of dizziness. Among survey respondents, 76 percent had strong concerns about the health and well-being of the children in their community, and 82 percent were highly concerned about the effect of toxic waste.

Any apprehensions that CCATW may have had about their support in the community were put to rest. Ninety-seven percent of the households surveyed recognized, along with CCATW, that there was a need to test and monitor the wells for at least ten years. Ninety-eight percent of the 120 families surveyed agreed that citizens should have a chance to be involved in developing a cleanup plan and should be able to influence and monitor the implementation of the cleanup plan.

All of the survey respondents wanted free comprehensive medical evaluations to be offered to those who had lived near NEC or had worked there. Every one of the respondents also said that residents and workers should be offered ongoing medical testing and help for any health problems related to NEC's dumping of toxic wastes. Respondents were also unanimous in their opinion that soil around NEC should be thoroughly tested for toxic waste and that thorough testing of the floodplain for at least two miles downriver was necessary.

The citizens used the survey for a variety of actions on behalf of the community and former NEC workers. According to Robinett,

We have used it to get the federal EPA to do more well testing. In the printouts, there was a list of names and addresses of people who had not had their wells tested. We have used it in reference to health problems and statistics.

We used it during the hazardous ranking system scoring for Superfund. One of the major factors for getting a site ranked for Superfund is surface water contamination, particularly if the river is used for fishing. Our local fish and game commissioner stated that the river was not used for fishing. So we pulled the graphs from the door-to-door survey, verified the number of people who have eaten fish from the Cumberland River and lived downstream from NEC.

We have used it a couple of times in a press release, in trying to get more testing done. We are going to be using it again under a public comment period that we have on the permitting process for the air-stripping unit. There is information we are going to use, because we are against it, because the extent of the contamination hasn't been determined.[13]

CCATW was skeptical about the ability of the air-stripping unit to remove contaminants. Air stripping was the method proposed by the U.S. EPA and Cooper Industries to treat the poisoned groundwater. It pumps water out at a rate of six hundred gallons per minute and runs it through a number of filtering devices. CCATW was opposed to its use because the extent of the contamination had not been determined. It could remove any trace of toxics from wells that had not been tested. They were also opposed to the use of the air-stripping unit because it could convert the water pollution into air pollution. There are families who live within one hundred yards of the unit.

Robinett continued to comment on the impact of the survey:

A substantial quantity of unanticipated knowledge was gained.

We had a lot more community support than I thought we had. Because people were not physically active in the group, I thought that maybe they weren't supportive. I was wrong in thinking that. We found out that they were indeed supportive, and in fact had very good reasons for not being active. Some offered to be active with the group.

We also found out that there was a problem with illiteracy. People could not read, some [had] very low education levels.

We found some learning disorders, which could very well be linked to lead.[14]

Learning these things helped provide a new direction for CCATW. They realized that the problems they encountered were not solely related to their poisoned water and soil. One of the causes of their problems was their relative degree of powerlessness. This was grounded in the considerable number of residents and former NEC workers who cannot read or were low-level readers.

Through the survey the CCATW learned that people wanted more information. This information had to be presented in a manner appropriate for the reading level of most residents and former NEC workers. An impediment to making the material comprehensible is that much of it is highly technical material replete with scientific jargon. As other researchers have recognized, "The arcane and highly specialized language used in communication of scientific research makes it hard for anyone untrained to get information they may need about particular problems. The availability of scientific journals is also restricted to university and other specialized or large libraries. For rural communities in Appalachia and the South, where the nearest public library may be in a small county town a 30 mile drive away, such information is almost unobtainable."[15]

CCATW decided to publish a one-page newsletter that covered topics relevant to the needs of the community. As the writer and editor, Roy Silver made every effort to write the material on a third- to fifth-grade reading level without diluting the content.

CCATW also learned a lot from the process of executing its participatory research survey. Robinett noted,

It was something that we felt that we needed to do. When we realized the seriousness of the groundwater contamination, that it wasn't something that you could clean up like a house, we knew that we needed to build our organization for a long-term basis. One way to do that was to see if the majority of the community had the same view as us. We realized that our organization wasn't just about groundwater contamination. There were other social issues, economic issues, educational issues. . . . I mean there were just a lot of other things that were major problems in the community. The community already knew this, and the survey helped bring this out. We probably learned more from the community than they learned from us.[16]

The success of the community survey and the partnership between CCATW and RSVP led to RSVP working with another local group, Partners Affirming Community Transformation, to address prescription drug problems.

Kidney Study

The third project CCATW completed was a kidney study, funded with a $10,000 grant. Dr. J. D. Miller of the Clover Fork Clinic in nearby Evarts, who aided the study, called it the Pee for Justice Campaign.[17]

A research scientist worked with CCATW on this project and visited the community twice. The first time, he toured the community around the site and met with residents and former NEC workers. On the second visit he was asked to explain the nature of the testing to a CCATW citizens' meeting. He was apprehensive about addressing the citizens' meeting. He had thought he was going to address a small group that would coordinate collection of the urine samples and was not prepared to explain the nature of the study to this group. CCATW, however, wanted the residents and former NEC workers to understand the rationale for the Pee for Justice Campaign.

The researcher's reluctance to explain the study at the citizens' meeting was illustrative of the scientific establishment's distance from the lived community reality. This can also be true for members of the politically progressive sector of the community. CCATW's experiences in the past led the group to conclude that it was kept in the dark about scientific and technical issues. In an effort to democratize the process and shatter the cycle of imposed ignorance, the group believed it was necessary to have citizens participate in the production of knowledge and decision making.

CCATW collected more than 240 urine samples. It recorded names of each participant and kept extensive records on whether the participants were workers, children of workers, or residents who lived near the NEC plant. Urine samples also were collected from a control group. The samples were packed in dry ice and shipped to Cincinnati for testing. Using state-of-the-art equipment, which until this time had been used only on diabetics, the research scientist Roy Silver and CCATW found that everyone in the control group had protein levels well within the normal range. (The healthier a person is, the lower the level of protein found in his or her urine.) Results for thirteen of those in the exposed group indicated kidney problems. The median protein level recorded in the exposed group was higher than that of the control group.

Accounting for the Cost of Water

In its fourth project, CCATW worked with the Kentucky Open Government Project to bring affordable water to residents whose wells were contaminated. Staff members from the project trained members of CCATW to research county government and the Black Mountain Utility District. After the initial discovery that the water was poisoned, Cooper Industries gave the county government $500,000 for construction of a water line to connect those affected to city water. This seemingly became pork-barrel funding, used to distribute rewards.[18]

Many homes did not get connected to the city line. Those living next to NEC, in the Holiday Mobile Home Park, were given only one water meter for all the trailers. The county sent the bill to the owner of the park, who then divided it equally among households. This meant that a single person paid as much as a family. The new lines were hooked up to the old, contaminated lines, which could not take the pressure of the municipal water system.

People began to receive bills as high as ninety dollars for a single month's water. Residents of the community received their water bill every third month, so they did not see a bill until higher rates had been in place for some time. Black Mountain Utility District would not accept partial payment. This left many, particularly those on fixed incomes, with the choice of no water or contaminated water. Since the pipeline was paid for by Cooper Industries, the water bills these customers received should have been lower, rather than higher. CCATW found out that the utility district had treated the $500,000 as a loan. The Kentucky Open Government Project, through its training and assistance, provided CCATW with the tools it needed to correct this injustice.

CCATW used participatory action research in its struggle to combat the poisoning of its community and former NEC workers. Participatory action research strives to fracture the differentiation between the investigator and the investigated. It achieves this through the participation of those who lack information in the process of gaining and creating knowledge. Research is then conceived not solely for developing knowledge but also for education, extending awareness, and mobilization for action.

Joan Robinett, while concerned about the health and well-being of the people of Dayhoit and the former NEC workers, understands the need for broader, democratic changes in society. "We are going to have to fight for local changes," she told a reporter, "because if we don't, our children won't have anything."[19]

CCATW responded to a myriad of challenges during the first four years of its existence, from the pressing everyday problems associated with the contamination of the community to the psychological trauma associated with the poisoning. Many citizens of Harlan County contacted CCATW when they became aware of their own victimization at the hands of the polluters. Participatory action research provides a model for those in the academy who are interested in bridging the gap between the needs of community groups and the best means of meeting them.

Notes

1. "Notice to the Customers of the Holiday Mobile Home Park, Dayhoit, Kentucky," Division of Water, Cabinet of Natural Resources, Commonwealth of Kentucky, 1989.

2. Lisa Fee, "Residents Present Questions on Health, Other Concerns," *Harlan Daily Enterprise,* March 10, 1989; Daniel G. Todd, Michael A. Brown, Julie Stickney, and Mario J. Citra, *Draft Toxicological Profile for Vinyl Chloride* (Atlanta, GA: U.S. Department of Health and Human Services, Public Health Service, Agency for Toxic Substances and Disease Registry, 2004).

3. Fee, "Residents Present Questions."

4. Bill Bishop, "Governor's Silence Doesn't Deter People of Dayhoit," *Lexington Herald-Leader,* December 13, 1990; Lisa Fee, "Woman Helping Citizens Find Answers on Dayhoit Contamination," *Harlan Daily Enterprise,* July 25, 1989. The title for this section is borrowed from Frank Adams with Myles Horton, *Unearthing the Seeds of Fire: The Idea of Highlander* (Winston-Salem, NC: John F. Blair, 1975).

5. Bishop, "Governor's Silence."

6. Bishop, "Governor's Silence."

7. Joan Robinett, interview by Roy Silver in her home, October 30, 1991.

8. Robinett interview.

9. Rural Southern Voices for Peace, Listening Project, www.listeningproject .info.

10. Robinett interview.

11. John Gaventa, "Participatory Research in North America," in *Action and Knowledge: Breaking the Monopoly with Participatory Action Research,* ed. Orlando Fals-Borda and M. A. Rahman (New York: Apex, 1991).

12. Robinett interview.

13. Robinett interview.

14. Robinett interview.

15. Juliet Merrifield, *Putting the Scientists in Their Place: Participatory Research in Environmental and Occupational Health* (New Market, TN: Highlander Center, 1989).

16. Robinett interview.

17. Bishop, "Governor's Silence."

18. Robin Epstein, *Citizen Power: Stories of America's New Civic Spirit* (Lexington, KY: Democracy Resource Center, 1999). In the late 1990s the Kentucky Open Government Project became the Democracy Resources Center. The center was dissolved in 2005.

19. Bishop, "Governor's Silence."

4

The Martin County Project

Students, Faculty, and Citizens Research the Effects of a Technological Disaster

Stephanie McSpirit, Sharon Hardesty, Patrick Carter-North, Mark Grayson, and Nina McCoy

The Big Branch Coal Waste Impoundment, owned and operated by the Martin County Coal Company, a subsidiary of Massey Energy (MCCC-Massey), occupied approximately seventy-two acres in Martin County, Kentucky. It rested at the top of the stream head to two of the county's primary creeks: Coldwater and Wolf Creeks. Most of Martin County's eleven thousand inhabitants live between these two creeks, and therefore most of the county's inhabitants were affected in some way by the events of October 2000.

At midnight on Thursday, October 12, an employee of MCCC-Massey was working near the west mine portal when he noticed that the belt line had stopped. Based on documented events in one investigative report, the employee then radioed the dispatcher, and other coal company employees were directed to travel to north-end mine operations. There they observed coal slurry flowing out of a mine portal at a mounting velocity. By the night's end the Big Branch Impoundment had emptied its seventy-two-acre contents of black water, coal slurry, and sludge into underground mine works below the impoundment. The Mine Safety and Health Administration (MSHA) estimated that 300 million gallons of the slurry and sludge materials escaped into the county's two principal creeks. One Martin County citizen who had long been involved in the coal mining industry commented on what came down Coldwater and Wolf Creeks that Tuesday, "The coal company and the EPA like to call it slurry. Slurry is a fast moving substance. What came down Coldwater . . . was very, very slow moving. Its magnetite, very thick, thicker than any mud you'll ever see. Magnetite is used in the processing of the coal. . . . That magnetite settles to the bottom of the impoundment. There is so much weight to that magnetite that you can take a five-gallon bucket of it and you can hardly carry it. It's that thick."[1]

In the following days coal sludge from the devastated creeks slowly traveled toward the Tug Fork of the Big Sandy River and then snaked its way through to the Ohio River. Through it all, town water systems along the affected rivers were forced to close their water intakes while the massive sludge plume moved past. According to official state estimates, nearly twenty-eight thousand people were without public water while emergency water lines were established by contingency teams of state, federal, and coal company personnel.[2]

Meanwhile, people in Martin County were describing the coal waste disaster as one that paralleled the *Exxon Valdez* oil spill. The mayor of the City of Inez, Martin County, made such a comparison in an open letter to the governor of Kentucky. Calling for disaster relief, the mayor went on to say, "Not only am I concerned about our water supply, residents and wildlife, I am also concerned with the environmental impact and economic damage that this disaster will cause to Inez and Martin County. This could possibly set Martin County back for many years to come. The economy in Martin County is already bleak but this could be the straw that broke the camel's back."[3]

During the weeks, months, and years to follow, no federal disaster funds or federal emergency relief monies were forthcoming, and many Martin County citizens asked why. In later field interviews, citizens continued to comment on the lack of federal relief for the disaster. Reflecting frustration that nobody seemed to care, one interview respondent commented, "I know there were no lives that were lost, but this was a big, a huge environmental disaster. . . . But it happened in Martin County, maybe ten, eleven thousand people living here. The coal communities, you know, we're kind of forgotten anyway." Another local resident said, "The coal company had it in the newspaper, saying this was 'an act of God' and that they were doing everything that they could to clean up the mess. But everybody knows it's not an act of God, it's a disaster."[4]

A Technological Disaster

Less than a week after the disaster, before full chemical testing on the sludge was even complete, state and federal officials attempted to allay public concerns. Agency press statements reported detectable levels of heavy metals and other compounds in the sludge but "not in harmful amounts." A spokesperson for the state of Division of Water was reported as saying, "We're saying right now the water is safe. If we determine there is a long-term problem we will let people know." On October 18 the U.S. Environmental Protection Agency (EPA) released a press statement claiming that they found "no acute toxicity levels in aquatic organisms used in tests." A consultant for MCCC-Massey was reported as stating, "There were some metals in the sludge, but the amounts were below drinking water standards." By the next week a Coast Guard official stated that "the metals pose no hazard to public water supplies with full treatment."[5]

Competing definitions of risk tend to contribute to heightened levels of anxiety and stress among residents living in potentially contaminated communities. In his classic work, Allen Barton describes individuals and communities struck by natural disaster following a clear course of events: the predisaster period, the period of detection and warning, the period of immediate and relatively unorganized response, the period of organized social response, post-disaster equilibrium, and the subsequent move back to the status quo. William Freudenburg describes differences in the stages of technological disaster. He points out that residents and communities confronting an impending, sometimes slow, long-term threat of toxic contamination are typically left in a suspended state of uncertainty. Stephen Kroll-Smith likens this suspended state to living in a "*what if*" environment, as in, What if the environment is not safe? What if the cause of my neighbor's cancer is the drinking water?[6]

In one letter to the editor, a mother in Martin County expressed such fears of "ontological uncertainty." She wrote,

> We are faced with a situation that warrants major and immediate attention and begs a multitude of questions. Number one, we are being told that our water contains a list of chemicals that it would take a team of scientists to hold a class about for understanding to seem possible, so is our water safe to drink? We are also being told that the chemicals contained in our water are

at acceptable levels for "non hazardous" ingestion. What is an acceptable level of arsenic, barium, beryllium, etc.? After years of consuming these "acceptable" levels of chemicals, will there be any long lasting, extremely painful, physically noticeable or perhaps fatal effects? If the answer to this question is no, then comes How do they know? Have they exposed other people to this exact mixture of chemicals for extended periods of time and had no ill effects? . . . I don't know about you, but it scares the hell out of me. It is not my life I am concerned about. I have a thirteen-year-old son who has his whole life ahead of him. At least, he's supposed to, bar[r]ing some "Act of God." . . . He is a wonderful boy who makes straight *As* and has a very kind heart. I have done the best I could. He is doing his best as well. I would find it unforgivable to learn that all of his efforts are in vain because someone decided to cut corners and some money by not disposing of dangerous contaminants properly.[7]

"Knowledge gaps" about the safety of the local biosphere tend to breed not only fear and uncertainty but also heightened levels of suspicion about state and federal agencies that are supposedly mandated by law to protect the public and keep people safe. Freudenburg has described this loss of legitimacy by regulatory institutions after a technological break-down as "recreancy," which he describes as "the failure of an expert, or for that matter a specialized organization, to do the job that is required." Rebecca Richards and Michael Womersley describe the same pattern of recreancy after a toxic spill in California.[8] Expressing a common view, one Martin County resident blamed both company and government officials for not preventing a disaster that, according to him, could have been prevented: "Everyone that is involved in this, I'm talking your state inspectors, your federal inspectors and the people over this mine, that had anything to do with this, should be fired."

In the aftermath of technological disaster, Kroll-Smith identifies fear, uncertainty, distrust, and suspicion as leading to retreat and in-ward withdrawal among some residents. This psychic retreat, according to Kroll-Smith, contributes to the further decline of community and a community's civic capacity. Others have also written on social corro-sion after a technological or human-made disaster. Kai Erikson wrote of the 1972 coal waste flood that annihilated communities along Buffalo Creek in West Virginia and the social psychological stressors that ensued among survivors due to the loss of community. The 1972 Buffalo Creek coal waste flood released more than 120 million gallons of slurry and killed 125 persons. The Martin County coal waste spill, in comparison, released more than 300 million gallons of slurry and sludge materials, luckily with no loss to human life.[9]

The rest of this chapter describes the partnership between a research team of faculty and undergraduate students from Eastern Kentucky University and residents in Martin County, Kentucky. We also present findings from interviews and a formal survey to describe the impact of the coal waste spill on residents of Martin County.

The Martin County Project

Soon after the coal waste disaster in Martin County a team of sociology students and faculty at Eastern Kentucky University started to talk about the disaster and the prospects of starting a research project. If we initiated such a project, we would have to rely on undergraduate students for field assistance and research support, since the sociology department had no graduate program. We asked ourselves if this was possible. Was it possible to involve a large team of undergraduates in a sensitive and potentially litigious research project? Was this a good plan?

We decided to call Duane Gill at the Social Science Research Center, Mississippi State University, and ask his opinion. He listened intently and by the end of our conversation had agreed to visit our campus. In less than a week's time he was at Eastern Kentucky University, talking with students and faculty in both lectures and in seminars about researching communities hit by technological disasters. Beyond theory and case descriptions, he also spoke about methods and research design. He advised our team to replicate and fine-tune methods that he had used in the past in his work on the *Exxon Valdez* disaster: personal interviews, survey research techniques, random-sampling strategies, and the use of control communities. On the last day of his visit Gill traveled with our team to Martin County. During the three-hour drive up the Mountain Parkway, he provided more field advice and, more important to the team, enthusiastically advised us to go ahead with our original plan of involving a large team of undergraduate students in our research and field efforts. After spending several days with undergraduate students in lectures, seminars, and on the road, Gill concluded that such a research project on a relatively isolated community "could only be done well with the help of university students"—many of whom, as he observed, were themselves from the region.[10]

In the weeks that followed our research team made more visits to Martin County. We scheduled meetings with state emergency management personnel and coal company officials. We also attended public meetings. At these public meetings we started to establish more and more contacts with area citizens. Some of these initial citizen contacts proved crucial in getting our research project fully off the ground in Martin County. One of our field contacts was Mark Grayson, an alumnus of our university who proved to be an ideal key informant and gatekeeper and became so fully involved in our project that he is a coauthor of this chapter. Early on Grayson devoted much of his outside time to helping our research team get started. In informal conversations and in some formal lectures to students, he patiently explained the history of the county and its history with the coal mining industry. By January we had set up a formal special topics course, Field Practicum in Community-Based Research, and had twenty-five students from sociology, anthropology, social work, and geography enrolled.

It's hard to forget the time one Saturday when we first brought our research team to Grayson's small editor's office at the *Martin County Sun.* As students filed in and squeezed along the walls of his small office, Grayson turned to a friend and said, "It looks like we need to find a different place to hold this meeting." We subsequently went across the street to the county courthouse, and it was there that Grayson and another community leader and organizer explained the history of the county. While students sat on the floor and took notes, the two described the impact of a railroad spur opening up Martin County to coal production. At that time, they explained,

> Any man who wanted a job was quickly hired. . . . By the late 1960s as many as five thousand coal miners were eventually employed by five major coal companies. A county with just two doctors and one dentist and no drugstore and two lawyers soon had ten doctors, three dentists, five drugstores, and at least ten lawyers. When the 1974 OPEC oil embargo took place, causing the price of coal to go from $10 per ton to more than $100, Martin County really exploded. More and more mines were opened,

many of them [by] wildcat strip miners who literally stole coal from unsuspecting landowners. The local bank suddenly had assets totaling nearly $100 million. Even though people had jobs and plenty of money, there were no sewer systems and the tiny Inez water system was stretched for miles in all directions so that Big Coal could keep from paying damages to landowners who either lost well water completely or had it sullied by waste. The Martin County government was controlled by Big Coal and the few, now wealthy, landowners [were] using vote-buying methods that would put Knott County to shame. In the 1985 primary election, for example, voters were being paid as much as $200 each for voting for a slate of candidates hand-picked by Big Coal.

And that is where our own story picks up again. Other citizens provided similar stories to attentive students. Several residents and local professionals explained the nuances of federal, state, and local politics as well as the politics of regulating the coal industry. Later, when it was time to conduct field interviews with affected citizens, Grayson and several other contacts helped us compile lists of people in the county that we "should probably talk to." The method that was emerging in Martin County was expanding beyond traditional field and survey practices and was becoming increasingly more democratic and participatory, with Martin County residents taking an active hand in providing direction to our research team of twenty-five students and three faculty.

Field Interviews

After that initial site visit with our undergraduate research team, we began to gear up for the field interview phase of our project. In preparation, we called Shaunna Scott at the Sociology Program/Center for Appalachian Studies, University of Kentucky. Scott had done extensive fieldwork and case study work on Appalachian coal mining communities. When we called Scott, she, too, listened thoughtfully and agreed to meet with our research team at a weekend workshop to talk about field interview methods and case study research in Appalachia. Grayson also joined us for that weekend of intensive discussion and field preparation. By the end of the weekend Grayson and Scott had helped our research team draft our field interview questions.[11]

By mid-February our research protocols, in which we gave assurances that we would protect resident confidentiality and anonymity, had been approved by our university's institutional review board, and it was time for us to make plans to conduct our first field sweep. During the last two weekends of February twenty or so university students, now trained in field interview methods, conducted tape-recorded interviews with area residents. Interviews typically lasted thirty to forty minutes, and each student usually conducted two. Upon leaving the field, as part of their course requirements, students were expected to transcribe their taped sessions with residents. In the end, this resulted in a qualitative database of approximately thirty-five transcripts. These interviews and transcripts would be used later in several reports and publications to document regulatory and coal company responses to the disaster as seen through the eyes of local residents.[12]

During these home interviews, following the set of field interview questions, students recorded residents' recollections of the first days of the disaster as well as residents' comments about the spill's impact on the local environment and watershed. Residents also commented on cleanup efforts and how the coal company and state and federal agencies were handling the disaster. With respect to the first stages of disaster response, several citizens expressed anger that, at the time of the impoundment break, there was no warning or contingency plan in place to warn residents living downstream of the impending disaster. One local resident complained, "No warning! Absolutely no warning! At any time! And during one of the community meetings I asked [the coal company president] as to why and who made that decision and he said that he made that decision. I don't want [the coal company president] making that decision with my life and my family's life . . . but that was their answer to it, they just made that decision."

Shattered confidence in state and federal regulatory agencies was a constant theme in our field interviews with Martin County residents. Many residents expressed complaints with how state and federal agencies, especially EPA Region 4, conducted their mitigation and assessment strategies. To many of those we interviewed, it seemed that Region 4 was deferring to MCCC-Massey and allowing the coal company to take the lead in environmental cleanup and environmental assessment. Several citizens we interviewed were outraged over this. One said,

I guess one of the main things that people were more troubled about more than anything else was that they thought that, because of taxpayers' money, that MSHA, the EPA, that those agencies were in here to protect the citizens. But really the EPA set their command station up behind coal company guards, who guarded the EPA to keep the people away from them. It is my understanding that the EPA either did not or could not release a press statement or any information without the permission of Martin County Coal. Now, that's, that's very disturbing. That they would try to hide behind Martin County Coal and that they would let the coal company approve any release that they would want to make. It's very disturbing. The only people satisfied with the cleanup are the EPA!

This respondent went on to say where the real blame resided: "In my opinion, the coal company is not the problem. The coal company has done what it has been told to do. The problem is EPA and MSHA. The people who are supposed to be working for us and protecting us are acting like they work for the coal company, protecting the coal company. They think that because we are mountain people that we are ignorant. They are the ignorant ones—to think that we are going to believe that."

Nina McCoy, a high school biology teacher at Sheldon Clark High School and like Mark Grayson a long-time community partner and co-author of this chapter, wrote the following about the EPA:

Our community has always felt a general mistrust in our regional representatives of this agency, which was proven at the first large county wide public meeting in the week immediately following the spill. One lady got up to the public microphone during the question period and told the EPA representative (who, we had been told, had flown in from Washington, probably to make us feel a little safer) that we did not trust our "local" EPA and that she wanted the water tested by the "federal" EPA.

At a conference call . . . during June 2004 designed to update the public about the status of the cleanup, I was finally able to ascertain that the coal company or its representatives had conducted most tests that EPA had used to assure our community that the air, water and soil were safe. Previously the EPA had forced companies to provide communities new drinking water sources affected by much less contamination than in our community. One such case involved the Eastern Coal Company in Pike County, Kentucky. According to 1985 EPA documents, "the slurry contains a number of chemical contaminants in excess of Primary Drinking Water Standards. These standards were established to prevent adverse health effects from chemical contaminants in drinking water. Excessive amounts of these chemical elements are capable of causing acute toxic effects." However, in our case, we had 306 million gallons of the stuff released into two streams that both end up at about the spot where we get our drinking water, but apparently this was not enough to constitute a public health hazard.[13]

In March 2001 MCCC-Massey, along with the regulatory agencies, held their last county-wide public meeting. This is when we got to meet our representative from the Kentucky Division of Water face to face. By this time the community was absolutely irate, and tempers flared. One woman got up and, with tears of anger, told the agency and company representatives that if they really believed that she should give her baby this water and bathe her baby in this water, then they should drink it. Someone went to the water fountain to fill Styrofoam cups with the water. Coal company representatives stayed out of it. As usual, they were absolutely silent during this part of the debate. The EPA lawyer laughed out loud, and the on-site coordinator from Region 4 of the EPA announced, "Look, you live in coal mining country, and coal mining is dirty business!" The representative from the Kentucky Division of Water acted like he was ready for a fistfight. He slammed down a stack of papers and shouted, "Here, if you want to see what is in your water, here it is. Look at these." After the meeting one of us walked up to the panel and asked for the papers he had offered, and we still have them. While they are difficult to read and impossible to interpret, it is very easy to see that all the information was collected before October 11, 2000.

Surveys

Based on what we heard in our interviews with residents and through our long conversations with key informants, our research team started to build a survey. Given what we heard, we included survey questions on water quality and water treatment and other standard inventory questions that measured levels of government trust, perceptions of risk, and views on regulatory policy, environmental recovery, and community quality of life. While we wanted our survey to be relevant to the people who received it and developed our questions accordingly, in building our survey instrument we also modified social impact surveys previously developed by Gill and Steven Picou (see also chapter 3) and drew from other social impact and risk assessment surveys.[14]

Our student-faculty research team held several weekend seminar sessions to discuss and devise a sampling and distribution method for our survey. In the end we devised a residential sampling strategy and "drop-off/pick-up" method similar to the sampling method described by Jennifer Steele and colleagues. The method they describe has been used in communities in Pennsylvania and in other western states. Before our survey was conducted, no comparable hand delivery method had been used in surveying communities in Appalachia.[15]

In March 2001, less than a month after conducting preliminary field interviews with area residents, our research team used the formal questionnaires to survey the affected area of Martin County during a weeklong survey sweep (spring break week). During the survey sweep, students and faculty had more opportunities to talk on porch steps with a wider range of area residents; they heard their points of view and their perspectives and comments on things, but this time students had to politely excuse themselves and move on to the next house. It was clear, however, that many residents in the affected communities wanted to talk. By the week's end our research team had collected 290 surveys (response rate = 62 percent).

With survey work in Martin County completed, our research team made plans to survey a control community in accord with the research plan. We selected Perry County, Kentucky, as our control site because of several broad similarities with Martin County. Both Martin and Perry Counties, for example, are defined by the Appalachian Regional Commission as "distressed counties" and "core coal producing counties." Using a similar drop-off/pick-up residential sampling design as before, our research team was able to collect 250 surveys from the Perry County area by the start of the next academic year, September 2001 (response rate = 50 percent).[16]

Patrick Carter-North was an undergraduate student who joined our research team during this second survey phase, and as coauthor of this chapter shares his experiences in surveying Perry County:

When I reflect on experiences that have shaped me as a person I inevitably think about the Martin County Project. I joined the project in fall of 2001. My specific role was to aid in the administration and analysis of the second phase of written surveys that were distributed to citizens in the control community of Perry County, Kentucky.

Our research team divided into groups and set out systematically traversing the community, knocking on doors, hoping to find the residents home and willing to participate in the survey. We often parked the car in a certain area and set out on foot. It was a lot of fun, as most citizens seemed eager to talk to us—to know more about who we were and what we were doing. On numerous occasions they invited us into their homes not only to hear more about our work but also to voice their opinions and concerns regarding coal mining and other community issues. One older couple even invited us to stay for dinner. With other cases, I remember sensing a bit of surprise and even shock among several of the citizens I encountered, as if they couldn't believe that there was a team of academics interested in listening to their stories. A few citizens were a little hesitant to participate in the survey and seemed a little distrustful of us. Those personal interactions on the front porches and inside homes were just as valuable as the data gathered through the surveys—the emotion, compassion, and nonverbal expressions captured in those moments is something that couldn't be captured through a paper questionnaire.

Survey Findings

A comparison of household demographic data for Martin and Perry Counties indicated some striking parallels between samples on dimensions of gender, length of residence, public water use, voter turnout, and income.

Though there were broad parallels between households at both sites, based on our analyses it appeared that citizens in Martin and Perry

Counties were thinking differently on issues related to their community, their economy, and their environment. Martin and Perry County citizens were asked to rate the quality of life in their community on the following scale: very good, good, fair, poor, and very poor. Sixty-two percent of Martin County citizens rated the quality of the natural environment in their community as "poor or very poor," compared to only 23 percent in Perry County. On outdoor recreational opportunities, 79 percent of Martin County citizens rated them "poor or very poor," in comparison to only 35 percent in Perry County. Ninety percent of Martin County residents and 57 percent of Perry County residents rated job opportunities in their community "poor or very poor."

On another set of community livability questions, Martin and Perry County citizens were asked to rate community concerns on the following scale: not a problem, a slight problem, a moderate problem, a serious problem. Crime and drugs were the highest rated problems among Perry County citizens, but Martin County citizens reported drinking water as their number one concern. Eighty percent of Martin County citizens compared to only 24 percent of Perry County citizens rated drinking water "a serious problem." Coal waste also rated high as "a serious problem" in Martin County. Nearly seven out of ten of Martin County citizens (69 percent) rated coal waste a serious issue facing their community, compared to 12 percent of Perry County citizens.

Based on survey comparisons, it appears that on standard community, quality of life, and livability scales Martin County citizens tended to think differently about their environment, the economy, their community, the local watershed, and the public water system than other citizens from the region. Strong differences were also noted on reported levels of trust in the U.S. Environmental Protection Agency and in state regulatory agencies. Survey findings showed that Martin County citizens were three times more likely than Perry County citizens (35 percent to 12 percent) to "strongly disagree" with the statement that they "have trust in the Environmental Protection Agency." Similarly, Martin County citizens (31 percent) were more likely to "strongly disagree" that they "have trust in state agencies" than were citizens in Perry County (11 percent).

Formation of Our First Citizen Advisory Committee

Using these survey numbers we wrote a grant proposal to the Appalachian Regional Commission (ARC) requesting some funds to continue our research and to help build civic capacity so that the county could begin to address some of the long-term issues of community recovery. In September 2001 our research team received ARC funding ($9,800) through the Flex-E-Grant initiative. This funding not only allowed us to complete survey data collection efforts in the control community of Perry County with a new undergraduate research team, as described above, but it also allowed us to start to assemble a citizen advisory committee (CAC). Through grant-writing efforts and dialogue sessions, citizens developed an eight-year strategic and civic action plan to move their community toward economic and environmental recovery. This particular case study, rather than the wealth of literature on community trauma and victimization in the face of disaster, provided us with a more positive, policy-oriented model in moving forward with our work and research in Martin County.

When we received ARC funding in late 2001, nearly a year after the spill, our research team began working closely with our CAC to identify the issues facing Martin County and build a set of recommendations to assist the community in tackling some of these issues. With CAC input and sharing, our research team initiated a content-review of regulatory documents and other regulatory agency records on file at the state Division of Water and available through the administrative record from EPA Region 4. We started a content-review of agency reports and water test data with initial guidance and instruction from biology and earth science faculty at our university. Along with our review of the regulatory record, we began a separate content-review of local newspaper accounts based on a year's collection of the *Martin County Sun.* We started a catalogue of events (spreadsheets) based on the regular on-the-ground reporting that Lilly Adkins and other reporters on Grayson's staff had done over the year since the spill.[17]

Our systematic review of regulatory and newspaper records confirmed citizen suspicions regarding the on-site response structure established by EPA to guide cleanup operations and conduct environmental impact assessments after the coal waste spill. It appeared, for example, based on our review of enforcement documents, that in March 2001 EPA Region 4 had indeed ceded substantial authority to the responsible party—MCCC-Massey—to handle site cleanup, site monitoring, and development of site mitigation strategies. As one citizen stated, "It is like a fox guarding the chicken coop." Early on in their field interviews and subsequently through participation in our CAC, local residents had expressed grave concerns over this response structure and questioned water quality and environmental monitoring data collected and analyzed by the coal company. Citizen distrust was more than a lack of confidence in the scientific and technocratic discourse of regulatory experts and agencies and cut to the core of the legitimacy of process and structure. In short, many citizens simply distrusted the environmental impact statements and mitigation plans that were being conducted and filed by MCCC-Massey, and for good reason.[18]

This response structure, along with a number of other documented events, many of which were conveyed to us by our CAC through their own document requests, seemed at odds with several environmental statutes designed to promote citizen involvement in environmental recovery decisions at contaminated sites. It appeared, based on testimony from our CAC and our own content review of site-relevant documents, that citizens were being routinely excluded from environmental recovery decisions in Martin County.[19]

Instances of citizen involvement effectively being bypassed by EPA Region 4 were documented in our final report on civic capacity to the ARC. We argued in our final report that active citizen participation in community and environmental recovery would have to be a central component both for civic capacity building and environmental recovery initiatives in Martin County. We recommended that the channels for citizen input in environmental recovery be expanded, specifically for citizen involvement in stream reclamation and recovery strategies and, more importantly, water quality testing and monitoring. These recommendations were developed in close consultation with our CAC and were consistent with information gained and views heard from both field interviews and our more formal survey.[20]

Notes

A version of this chapter first appeared in *Southern Rural Sociology* 18, no. 2 (2002): 162–84.

1. U.S. Department of Labor, Mine Safety and Health Administration, "Report of Investigation, Surface Impoundment Facility Underground Coal Mine, Non-Injury Impoundment Failure/Mine Inundation Accident, October 11, 2000," 2001, accessed January 10, 2003, http://www.msha.gov/impoundments/martincounty/martincounty.htm.

2. L. Mueller, "Spill Looks Like One of the Worst in Nation," *Lexington Herald Leader,* October 19, 2000, 1.

3. R. Penix, "Inez Mayor Asks Governor for Help in Sludge Crisis," *Martin County Sun,* October 18, 2000, 7.

4. M. Grayson, "Martin Countians Blindsided by Spill," *Martin County Sun,* October 25, 2000, 13.

5. R. Alford, "Industries to Bill Coal Firm for Losses in Sludge Spill," *Lexington Herald Leader,* October 18, 2000, 1; L. Mueller, "Coal Firm Says It's Working on Spill: Residents Worry about Harm from Sludge," *Lexington Herald Leader,* October 18, 2000, 1; Associated Press, "Groundwater Feared Threatened by Sludge," *Lexington Herald Leader,* October 21, 2000, 1.

6. M. R. Edelstein, *Contaminated Communities: The Social and Psychological Impacts of Residential Toxic Exposure* (Boulder, CO: Westview Press, 1988); S. J. Picou and D. A. Gill, "Commercial Fishers and Stress: Psychological Impacts of the Exxon Valdez Oil Spill," in *The Exxon Valdez Disaster: Readings on a Modern Social Problem,* ed. Steve Picou, Duane Gill, and Maury Cohen (Dubuque, IA: Kendal/Hunt, 1999), 211–32; A. H. Barton, *Communities in Disaster: A Sociological Analysis of Collective Stress Situations* (New York: Anchor, 1970); W. R. Freudenburg, "Contamination, Corrosion and Social Order: An Overview," *Current Sociology* 45, no. 3 (1997): 19–39; J. S. Kroll-Smith, "1994 MSSA Plenary Address: Toxic Contamination and the Loss of Civility," *Sociological Spectrum* 15 (1995): 377–96; D. A. Gill and S. J. Picou, "Technological Disaster and Chronic Community Stress," *Society and Natural Resources* 11 (1998): 795–815.

7. P. Hall-Smith, "Smith Has Questions about Chemicals in County Water," *Martin County Sun,* October 24, 2001, 4.

8. W. R. Freudenburg, "Risk and Recreancy: Weber, the Division of Labor, and the Rationality of Risk Perceptions," *Social Forces* 71, no. 4 (1993): 909–32; Freudenburg, "Contamination, Corrosion and Social Order," 33; R. T. Richards and M. W. Womersley, "Toxic Contamination, Community Health, and the Attribution of Blame: The Dunsmuir Metam Sodium Spill," *Society and Natural Resources* 11, no. 8 (1998): 817–29.

9. Kroll-Smith, "1994 MSSA Plenary Address"; Gill and Picou, "Technological Disaster"; R. Gramling and N. Krogman, "Communities, Policy and Chronic Technological Disasters," *Current Sociology* 45, no. 3 (1997): 41–57; Edelstein, *Contaminated Communities;* A. M. Shkilnik, *A Poison Stronger than Love: The Destruction of the Ojibwe Community* (New Haven, CT: Yale University Press, 1985); K. T. Erikson, *Everything in Its Path: Destruction of Community in the Buffalo Creek Flood* (New York: Simon and Schuster, 1976); G. Ball, "Coal Sludge Release Doubles That of 1972 Buffalo Creek Disaster," *Mountain Citizen,* October 18, 2000, 1.

10. Gill and Picou, "Technological Disaster," 802.

11. S. Scott, *Two Sides to Everything: The Cultural Construction of Class in Harlan County, Kentucky* (Albany: State University of New York Press, 1995); S. Scott, "Dead Work: The Construction and Restoration of the Harlan Miners Memorial," *Qualitative Sociology* 19, no. 3 (1996): 365–94; S. Scott, "Drudges, Helpers and Team Players: Oral Historical Accounts of Farm Work in Appalachian Kentucky," *Rural Sociology* 61, no. 2 (1996): 209–26.

12. S. Scott, S. McSpirit, S. Hardesty, and R. Welch, "Post Disaster Interviews with Martin County Citizens: 'Grey Clouds' of Blame and Distrust," *Journal of Appalachian Studies* 11 (2005): 7–29; S. McSpirit, S. Hardesty, and R. Welch, "The Martin County Project: Researching Issues and Building Civic Capacity after an Environmental Disaster," 2002, accessed January 25, 2012, https://martincounty.eku.edu:4530/sites/martincounty.eku.edu/files/Martin_County_Project_Final_Report.pdf

13. U.S. Environmental Protection Agency, Eastern Coal Corporation, Docket No. IV-85-UIC-101, 1985 (Proceeding under Section 7003 of the Solid Waste Disposal Act, 42 USC 6973).

14. Freudenburg, "Risk and Recreancy"; W. R. Freudenburg and T. Jones, "Does an Unpopular Facility Cause Stress? A Test of the Supreme Court Hypothesis," *Social Forces* 69 (1991): 1143–68.

15. J. Steele, L. Burke, A. E. Luloff, P. S. Liao, G. L. Theodori, and R. S. Krannich, "The Drop-Off/Pick-Up Method for Household Survey Research," *Journal of the Community Development Society* 32, no. 2 (2001): 238–50.

16. Kentucky Appalachian Commission, *Pursuing the Potential of Appalachian Kentucky: Kentucky's Appalachian Development Plan* (Frankfort: Kentucky Appalachian Commission, 2000).

17. U.S. Environmental Protection Agency, Administrative Record, Martin County: KYN000407233, 2001, EPA Region 4, 61 Forsyth Street SW, Atlanta.

18. U.S. Environmental Protection Agency, Administrative Order on Consent, In the matter of Martin County Coal Slurry Spill Site, Martin County, Kentucky, Martin County Coal Corporation, Respondent, EPA Docket No. 01-19-C, DOW File: 0054810-680-8002, 2001, EPA Region 4, 61 Forsyth Street SW, Atlanta.

19. A. Szasz, *Ecopopulism: Toxic Waste and the Movement for Environmental Justice* (Minneapolis: University of Minnesota Press, 1994), 133.

20. McSpirit, Hardesty, and R. Welch, "Martin County Project."

5

Unsuitable

The Fight to Save Black Mountain, 1998–1999

Robert Gipe

A hawk flying over the southern edge of the Kentucky coalfields sees Black Mountain sprawled like a bear across Harlan County's border with Virginia. Kentucky's highest point is the arch of the bear's shoulders. To the northeast Big Black drains into Looney Creek through the mining towns of Benham and Lynch and into Poor Fork at Cumberland. To the southwest Big Black drains into Clover Fork through Holmes Mill, Louellen, and Evarts and joins with Poor and Martin Forks behind the Dairy Queen in the city of Harlan to form the Cumberland River. It is on the Clover Fork that the story begins of how Black Mountain became ground zero in one of the first mountaintop removal strip mining disputes.

Clover Fork has seen its share of coal mining. The bloodshed at the Battle of Evarts, a 1931 shootout between union miners and company-hired gunmen, was carried away by the Clover Fork. The Brookside strike of the 1970s, chronicled in the documentary film *Harlan County, USA*, took place on the Clover Fork. After Congress passed the Surface Mining Control and Reclamation Act (SMCRA) in 1977—the intent of which was to grant citizens protection against water destruction, blasting, and unreclaimed land that results from strip mining—the first strip job shut down for abusing the law was on the Clover Fork.

In the case of that early SMCRA enforcement, newly hired federal regulators were alerted to the violation by a retired army sergeant, Clover Fork native Hazel King. Hazel lived in a green-and-white block house, a swinging bridge's walk across the Clover Fork from Highway 38, just above the Louellen coal camp. Hazel marched dozens, maybe hundreds, of journalists and other visitors through the hills so they could experience both their beauty and their destruction. When the mining operation of a local coal operator crossed onto Hazel's property, destroying her land and taking her coal, she won a judgment against him and used much of the money she recovered to finance helicopter rides to show visitors the destruction visited on the mountains by strip mining.

Hazel showed anybody willing to come look at the cost of coal mining. She put her hand in the silt that filled the creeks where she once fished. She stuck the ski poles she used for walking sticks in the orange, acidic water released by mining that often rendered the fork unfit for swimming, for drinking, and on some days for washing one's face or clothes. She would walk people along the twisting roads of Clover Fork, laying her foot on the broken edge of the pavement, hanging her toe over the ten- and twenty-foot-deep voids that yawned below. And when she stood with visitors on those roads as the coal trucks rumbled by, she did not need to explain how the roads were not wide enough. People could feel it as the breeze created by the trucks rustled the hairs in their noses.

About eight miles downstream from Hazel King's house is Evarts, home to the Clover Fork Clinic. In July 1998 the chief of the medical staff at the clinic was J. D. Miller. J. D. came to Harlan County in the 1970s. Along with Hazel, J. D. had been one of the early members of Kentuckians for the Commonwealth (KFTC), an environmental and social justice citizens' group with chapters across Kentucky. That July Roy Silver, my colleague at Southeast Kentucky Community and Technical College, and I met with J. D. and health educator Elaine Stoltzfus at the clinic. J. D. spread a mining permit map on a table in a conference room. The map was for state permit application 848–0140, amendment 2. Jericol, a coal company owned by the Sigmon brothers, was applying to extend an existing permit on Black Mountain. In their initial application they mentioned that they might want a permit for a mountaintop removal (MTR) strip mine. It seemed to us that that MTR request, if approved, might take the mining operation right across the highest point in Kentucky.

Roy and I took the information that J. D. shared with us to a meeting of the reconstituted Harlan County chapter of KFTC, a chapter that had lapsed after being one of KFTC's first. One of the attendees at KFTC chapter meetings in Harlan in the summer of 1998 was Gary Short. Gary and his family lived in Holmes Mill, at the head of Clover Fork. Gary started his family in Michigan, but he came home to Harlan County because he wanted his kids to grow up in the same mountains he had, to run through the same woods and splash in the same creeks. Gary was upset by the way the mountains were being mined. He was angry not just because of the disruption of habitat that strip mining on Black Mountain was causing but also because he had cracks in the foundation of his house as a result of excessive blasting on the strip jobs around his home.

At the end of July, at the chapter's request, representatives of the state Division of Mine Reclamation and Enforcement and the federal Office of Surface Mining (OSM), agencies charged with the permitting and regulation of strip mines, came to a local meeting and answered our questions about Jericol's permit application. No, they said, this wasn't a mountaintop removal permit, and no, it wouldn't take out the state's highest point. But yes, it was in the highest reaches of Black Mountain, above three thousand feet, in the habitat of the Indiana bat, a federally endangered species. That was important to know, because proving threat to the habitat of a federally endangered species is one of the best ways to draw the federal government into closer scrutiny of a mine permit application. Under SMCRA, states have primacy in the permitting of surface mines. At that time, citizens seeking stricter enforcement of SMCRA often looked for ways to draw OSM, the federal agency, into discussion around the permitting of particular mining operations. Whether it was true or not, OSM was perceived by citizens' groups at that time as more likely to attend to environmental protection and the rights of citizens outside the mining industry than were the state agencies. During the summer of 1998 Jericol withdrew its initial permit application and put in another one without mention of the MTR method.

Amendment 2 to Kentucky state mining permit application 848-0140 turned out to be the permit application that led to a statewide battle to have the highest reaches of Kentucky's tallest mountain declared unsuitable for mining. Before the conflict was over, Trout Unlimited; the Sierra Club; schoolkids across the state; veteran activists from outside the county, like Linda Brock, Kenny Rosenbalm, and Larry and Sheila Wilson; expatriate Kentuckians who hadn't seen the state in years; bird-watching clubs; wildflower clubs; an association dedicated to the protection and enjoyment of the highest point in each of the fifty states; and various individuals, including the governor, would be involved. But the effort to protect Black Mountain began with people on the Clover Fork—J. D. and Elaine, Hazel and Gary—who lived beneath a Black Mountain that was already ringed round with strip mines and whose homes sat beside a Clover Fork already clogged with silt. It began with Hazel, Gary, Roy, Earl Ball, Joan Robinett, Terry Blanton, Monetta Gross, Linda Brock, Roger Noe, Elaine Stoltzfus, Robin Lambert, Darlene Wilson, David Rouse, me, and others beginning to meet to discuss strategies to get some relief for our friends on the Clover Fork.

During July 1998 attorney Tom FitzGerald, director of the Kentucky Resources Council (KRC), began advising the Harlan chapter about how to respond in the Black Mountain case. KRC advocates in courts and in front of the legislature for responsible environmental laws and enforcement of those laws. FitzGerald is based in Frankfort but has long been among the best friends coalfield communities have had in their struggles for justice and community health against corporations and governments with other priorities to consider.

A man like Fitz is critical to the work of community change. FitzGerald argued Hazel King's case in the suit she won against the coal company that trespassed on her land. FitzGerald was there for the citizens of Dayhoit and the employees of Cooper Industries struggling against PCB contamination in the Cumberland River. FitzGerald was there when the water supply of Middlesboro was threatened by mining around Cannon Creek in Bell County. Activists from all these efforts converged in the Black Mountain campaign. All were enthusiastic about engaging Tom FitzGerald in our efforts. A gifted lawyer and skilled negotiator and writer, Fitz never charged the community group for his service. And through it all—even when our difficulty in reaching consensus made his negotiations more difficult—he always made us feel like he was working for us.

In July, on the eve of our first informational conference with state and federal officials about Black Mountain permits, Fitz prepared a memo that put our concerns into the language of the law and the bureaucrats. Morgan Worldwide Engineering also helped us understand the technical aspects of the permit. In the memo we expressed concern about groundwater monitoring, that the impact of the mining be adequately measured, that the federal Clean Water Act not be violated by hollow and valley fills, that the impact on federally endangered species such as the Indiana bat be adequately assessed, that the slopes of the hillside were too steep for reclamation, and that permit language was inconsistent. We also asserted that the permit application needed to be withdrawn until a full environmental impact assessment could be completed.

Another of the attendees of those early meetings was Judy Hensley, a schoolteacher at Wallins Elementary School in Harlan County. I have known Judy since 1989, when I was working at Appalshop. She was teaching at Wallins, and we met because of her participation in the Eastern Kentucky Teachers Network, a part of Foxfire Teacher Outreach. Judy is a proponent of the Foxfire teaching approach, which is grounded in principles that student work should be community-based, that students should have a voice in the means by which material is learned, and that schoolwork should have real-world ramifications.

Over the course of her career at Wallins, Judy's students had written their own reading texts, created local history books, and in 1995, taken on the protection and purchase by the state of one of the last patches of old-growth forest in Kentucky, a two-thousand-acre tract known as Blanton Forest.

The Blanton Forest project was a collaboration among Judy's fourth graders, the education reform group Forward in the Fifth, the Mountain Association for Community Economic Development (MACED), and the Kentucky Natural Lands Trust. In 1995 Blanton Forest was privately owned. Judy's students, as well as those of Wallins teachers John Slusher and Ingrid Partin, studied the forest's ecosystems, endangered species, and watersheds. They hiked into the forest, which was near their school, to do field studies. The students also got involved in a letter-writing campaign to appeal to the landowners and potential contributors to help preserve the forest. They exhibited their photos of the forest at the capitol in Frankfort. They appeared in magazines and newspapers and on television. In the end, more than two thousand acres were set aside and taken over by the Kentucky Natural Lands Trust. Judy said in an interview that "after that, the students had a taste for studying something, trying to help preserve it, publicity and public support, and sticking with a project until it reaches a successful end."

Judy's teaching assignment changed in fall 1998, and she had as seventh graders the students she had taught in fourth grade three years earlier and who had worked on the Blanton Forest project. They were, as Judy says, "itching to do something good." When they asked what project they could tackle that year, Judy left it to them to come up with an idea relevant to science, the subject she was assigned to teach. The local newspaper had recently carried stories about the mining proposed near Black Mountain's peak. When one of the students, Elizabeth Saylor, brought in a letter expressing her concerns about the possibility of destroying the state's highest peak, other students became interested and began to study the uniqueness of the mountain's flora and fauna and the methods used to mine coal. In an almost unanimous decision, the students agreed that the proposed mining was not a good idea and wanted to express their opinions to the appropriate officials. The students began a letter-writing and public information campaign. The students who wanted to see the mining take place were also given appropriate opportunities to express their convictions.

As the Wallins students began their work, the Harlan County chapter of KFTC began holding meetings nearly once a week through the fall of 1998. These meetings saw a steady stream of visitors from the media as well as activists from other parts of the state. In October and November the group discussed various strategies to protect Black Mountain and the surrounding mountains and communities.

By late October the struggle to protect Black Mountain was becoming a statewide one. Eighty-five hundred brochures about Black Mountain were distributed at a University of Kentucky (UK) basketball game by students from UK, Berea College, and Eastern Kentucky University. Southeast Kentucky Community and Technical College students distributed an informational brochure, created as part of their classwork, at local shopping areas. Spokespeople for the project appeared on *Issues and Answers,* a public affairs program on WYMT, a television station in Hazard, Kentucky, and on WMMT, a community radio station in Whitesburg.

As the effort drew more participants, the state office of KFTC held fast to its guiding principle that most of the strategy decisions on the issue be made at the local level, by the Harlan chapter of KFTC. At that time it was a core operating principle of KFTC to give primacy to the local chapter on a local issue. Understanding that fact is central to understanding how the Black Mountain protection campaign felt from within Harlan. The protection of Black Mountain became a statewide issue, fraught with symbolic significance for a great many people. Local KFTC organizer Kevin Pentz did a great job of mediating between the local chapter and the statewide organization.

In October Fitz presented a set of options to us: (1) challenge every permit to mine on Black Mountain as it was filed; (2) file a lands unsuitable for mining petition, which would define a specific boundary of land that could never be mined; or (3) seek a conservation easement and a way to buy the land outright. The right of citizens to petition the state government to have certain lands declared unsuitable for surface mining is a provision of SMCRA. According to federal legislation, lands can be declared unsuitable if mining would be incompatible with existing state and local land use plans; significantly damage lands having important historic, cultural, scientific, and aesthetic value and natural systems; create a substantial loss or reduction of long-range productivity of the water supply or food or fiber products; or substantially endanger life and property by mining on areas subject to frequent flooding and areas of unstable geology. Fitz advised us that the highest elevations of Black Mountain stood a good chance to qualify as unsuitable for mining because they included not only habitat for the federally endangered Indiana bat but also a number of other plant and animal species that occur only in Kentucky at the highest elevations of Black Mountain. In October we directed Fitz to prepare a lands unsuitable petition, in case we needed it.

In October students from Wallins Elementary went to the Middlesboro office of the Division of Mine Reclamation and Enforcement to present their concerns. Judy Hensley described the scene in a 2008 e-mail message:

> We took three busloads of students and teachers to the Middlesboro office of Surface Mining. When we pulled into the parking lot, there were at least a dozen eyeballs peering at us through the Venetian blinds of the office. The students disembarked with their posters and stacks of letters. They knew they were exercising their constitutional rights for peaceful protest and freedom of speech and took it very seriously. They were extremely well-behaved. Their letters were accepted and they were allowed to hold their posters and stand in front of the building while those inside sorted things out. We were chastised by the office for not

letting them know ahead of time we were coming, but those in charge recovered from their surprise and were gracious to the students. The officials talked to them about surface mining in a favorable light. Jennifer McDaniels from the *Harlan Daily Enterprise* was there to cover the story. It made the front page and was then picked up by the Associated Press. That was the beginning of the snowball of attention and publicity.

Later in the fall the Wallins students were joined by students from Rosenwald-Dunbar Elementary School in Nicholasville. Some of Sandra Adams's Nicholasville students made an overnight visit to Harlan County and met with the Wallins students. In December state representative Herbie Deskins invited the Wallins and Rosenwald students to share what they'd learned and their opinions about it before the Agriculture and Natural Resources Committee of the Kentucky House. Judy Hensley also described that experience:

When we went to Frankfort, private donations paid for the cost of bus and driver for this trip. On the bus, students rehearsed among themselves what they wanted to say and answers to potential questions they might be asked. They knew what was in their hearts and what they wanted to say. When they got there, however, it was all a bit overwhelming. One student said he had never seen so many suits in one place besides in J.C. Penneys. They were intimidated and although they made their point, they did not say all of what they had planned to say. The one student who had so adamantly opposed saving the mountain declined to make the trip with the rest, but his statements were tape recorded and presented by the other students.

In December KFTC filed a petition with the state to have approximately ten thousand acres on Black Mountain declared unsuitable for mining. The specifics of the lands unsuitable for mining petition included declaring all land above three thousand feet in elevation unsuitable for any kind of mining, the contention being that it is fragile, historic land and mining it would create a natural hazard. Once the petition was filed, the state had to rule whether or not the petition was complete. In the meantime, mining stopped on the land included in the petition boundary.

On December 9 we found out the permit conference we had requested was scheduled for December 29, in the middle of the Christmas holidays, a prospect that would force many to choose between family observance of the holiday and testifying at a mining permit hearing. We suggested to the state that this was not in the holiday spirit and asked that the conference be moved to a later date. Eventually that hearing was changed to January 14.

During the Black Mountain campaign Harlan KFTC held several meetings in the Evarts Multipurpose Center, a now-demolished remnant of the War on Poverty, built in the 1960s of stone from local mountains and creeks. On January 14 at least 150 people attended the permit hearing at the center. Forty people spoke, most questioning the merits of Jericol's permit application. A delegation of Evarts High School students unfurled a roll of butcher paper with two hundred handwritten letters attached. It was at this hearing that Darlene Wilson first decried what she saw as industry collusion with the regulatory agencies to issue permits for mining on relatively small acreages that adjoined existing strip mines. This practice, while technically legal, turned small mines into massive ones without attracting the attention that a proposal for a massive mine would draw. "Creeping permititis," Wilson called it. Through several hours of testimony state officials sat in stone-faced silence.

Soon thereafter the lands unsuitable for mining petition was deemed complete by the state, and we were granted an April 6 hearing on it. That is when a campaign to get letters in support of Black Mountain protection went into full swing. In February we picketed a campaign appearance by Governor Paul Patton, who was running for reelection. We questioned him on what he thought ought to be done about Black Mountain. At that time Patton said that resolving the matter was the job of Natural Resources and Environmental Protection Cabinet Secretary James E. Bickford.

Also around that time some KFTC members began seeking support for the petition from local city councils and the county government in Harlan. We sought support from the Harlan County Fiscal Court for our petition. Local coal companies, miners, and their families turned up to oppose. Benham and Lynch passed motions in support of the petitions. When representatives from Arch Mineral, one of the big landowners and mining concerns in the area, showed up at the next town meetings to say that the petition would put an end to underground mining on the mountain (which led to an exchange of letters between Fitz and the officials defining more accurately what the petition meant for underground mining), the Benham and Lynch councils rescinded their earlier support.

John O'Hara of Arch Mineral came to the Cumberland Council, where Gary Short and others confronted him. Cumberland did not pass a resolution. O'Hara also went to Judy Hensley's class to talk with the Wallins students about the petition. *Ace Magazine,* a weekly newspaper based in Lexington, chronicled O'Hara's exchange with the students. Arch Mineral's contention, which O'Hara made in Wallins, was that if people knew this wasn't mountaintop removal they wouldn't be so vehement in their opposition to the mining. "How many of you think this is about mountaintop removal?" O'Hara asked Hensley's students. None raised their hands.[1]

Early in 1999 the commissioner of the Kentucky Division of Mine Reclamation and Enforcement was quoted as saying that emotion and not practical concerns were driving KFTC's efforts and, in particular, the efforts of the Harlan County chapter of KFTC. After our local meeting on February 11 we responded to the commissioner's remarks by issuing a statement suggesting that he should recuse himself from participation in the decision about the lands unsuitable for mining petition and the protection of Black Mountain, claiming he was showing bias before all the evidence was in.

By this time, however, most of our local meetings were focused on Fitz's negotiations with the state and the coal companies. It was suggested that the companies might want to reach a settlement rather than let the petition process play out. We were asked if we would be interested in delaying the permit hearing. Our response was that until we had a written promise that there would be no mining and that they would allow biologists to survey the petition boundary for bats and other potentially endangered federal species, we were not inclined to postpone the meeting.

By March draft agreements were starting to circulate. On March 25 the Kentucky Environmental Quality Commission recommended a compromise, suggesting that the state find money in the budget for purchase of the concerned lands. On April 4 the *Lexington Herald-Leader,* the state newspaper most widely read in the coalfields, carried a series of full-color photos of Black Mountain and a banner headline reading

"Black Mountain Majesty" on top of a large-print editorial stating that Governor Patton should take a hand in deciding the landmark's fate. Beneath that ten citizen letters suggested that the mountain be spared.[2]

On April 10 there was a three-hour negotiating session in the basement of the governor's mansion. At that meeting the governor committed to securing state funding to compensate landowners within the petition boundary. On Wednesday, April 21, a tentative settlement was announced at Wallins Elementary School, with an April 30 deadline for working out the details. The agreement committed the companies to binding negotiations with the state, KFTC, and KRC that would result in protection of the highest reaches of the mountain. Under terms of the agreement, the summit of the mountain would be open to "researchers" but not the general public. The mountain would be off-limits to logging and mining above elevations of thirty-eight hundred feet. Sustainable forestry practices would be required between three thousand and thirty-six hundred feet in elevation. Companies were to make "best efforts" to sell all coal above three thousand feet to the state. Existing mines would be permitted to continue operation. Underground mining would continue to be permitted. In large part the deal was settled because Governor Patton guaranteed that the state would find the money to compensate the companies for the value of their holdings on Black Mountain.[3]

After the agreement was signed at the end of April, the lands unsuitable for mining petition was withdrawn. On May 4 there was a celebration of the settlement at the Evarts Fish and Game Club at Louellen. The students from Harlan and Jessamine Counties who had spent a whole school year working toward the protection of Black Mountain joined hands in celebration with many others from the community and elsewhere. "I think this is just a great big dream," Rosenwald-Dunbar student Andrew Conn was quoted as saying. On May 8 KFTC and those seeking better enforcement of mining law everywhere in the mountains held a rally in Frankfort. On Friday, May 21, author Wendell Berry spoke at a picnic in the park in Benham in between performances by local bluegrass and country bands.[4]

On June 30, 1999, the *Louisville Courier-Journal* reported that the companies involved were willing to sell their coal and timber interests on Black Mountain for approximately $10 million. Three of the interests—Arch Coal, Incorporated, Richard Gilliam, and Nally and Hamilton

Enterprises—donated their interests on the mountain. Jericol Mining, Penn Virginia, and Pocahontas Land Corporation agreed at that time to sell their interests. In August 1999 *Balancing the Scales,* the KFTC newspaper, reported that the companies' offer had been reduced to $7.7 million. The state hired appraisers to establish market value for the coal and timber in the affected area. Governor Patton requested $4.1 million to compensate property owners in his budget request in early 2000.[5]

In the end the state paid about $4.2 million to various companies for the mining and timber rights above the thirty-eight-hundred-foot level and the surface mining rights from thirty-two hundred to thirty-eight hundred feet. The 2000 Kentucky General Assembly approved a bond issue to provide funding for the payout. Most of the money was distributed in August 2000. The *Lexington Herald Leader* reported that Jericol received more than $1.2 million for its mineral rights. Penn Virginia Corporation received more than $674,000 for its mineral rights and $100,000 for its timber rights. Blackwood Coal Company received more than $104,000 for its mineral rights and $70,000 for timber rights. Pocahontas Development Corporation received more than $1.8 million for timber rights. At the time, coal company lawyer Joseph Zaluski was quoted as saying, "The general management of this thing was quite a challenge at times," adding that "it felt good to do this one."[6]

And that was it. Four million dollars of taxpayer money went to compensate the industry in exchange for protecting the highest reaches of Black Mountain. Within months of the payout, the Harlan County KFTC chapter and KRC would be involved in another lands unsuitable for mining petition around the Pine Mountain Settlement School. What difference did it make? In a 2008 telephone interview Tom FitzGerald said,

The Black Mountain case was a textbook example of how KRC ought to work with a community group. KRC laid out options, and the community group made decisions about which option they wanted to pursue. There were compromises. We did not have the legal tools to prevent all logging and mining on Black Mountain. We traded continued mining at the lower elevations on the mountain for protection we could not otherwise have gotten at the higher levels. We leveraged the lands unsuitable for mining petition process to limit both mining and logging.

Under the interpretation of SMCRA that prevailed at that time, the law covered surface mining and the surface effects of underground mining. The provision including surface effects of underground mining is what caused so many other coal companies with interests further down the mountain to come to the table, companies that might not otherwise have been interested in Jericol's dispute with KRC and KFTC. And it is what brought the timber interests to the table, because there is not an effective program or set of laws for limiting clear-cutting on biologically sensitive land. We leveraged the petition process to protect the habitat from logging. We could have protected the habitat from strip mining and then seen it destroyed legally through logging.

During the George W. Bush administration, OSM reinterpreted SMCRA to say that it no longer included surface effects of underground mining. We challenged that interpretation in court, saying that it strained the language of the law. The courts ruled that in the absence of explicit language in the legislation that defined the exact intention of Congress, that the court would defer to the regulatory agency. It would have been much more difficult to negotiate the protection of the highest reaches of Black Mountain without the inclusion of protection against the surface effects of underground mining in SMCRA.

Judy Hensley had this to say:

The thing that sticks with me most is the number of students I still run into out in public who will come up, hug me, chat a bit and remind me of the work they did on the Save Black Mountain project. "We made a difference, didn't we, Ms. Hensley?" they often say. I had one student who had dropped out of high school say regarding the project, "At least I did one good thing in my life." I wish the Black Mountain Project would have influenced lawmakers to abolish mountaintop removal forever. But as a teacher, my primary responsibility was to create a learning environment for the students that provided them with the opportunities to learn at their highest and best potential.

In the end, I felt the money the coal and timber companies got was too much but was still money well spent. It was a landmark decision that proved some really important things: Public outcry can make a difference. People working together can accomplish far more than they think they can. If all parties in a problem can sit down at the table together and listen to each other, there are solutions to even the biggest problems. Not being able to go visit the top of the mountain is peculiar to me. It makes you wonder what there is about Black Mountain that someone in high places wants to keep secret.

Hazel King, the mountains' fiercest defender, died in 2007 at age eighty-seven. Often during those weekly chapter meetings through the gray winter of 1998–1999 our will to continue would ebb. Hazel would inspire us to stay at it. When she was unable to inspire us, she would scold us. When that didn't work, she would shame us. We all loved and admired Hazel, and if it were not for her, I do not know that we would have stuck it out. We would often cheer ourselves by imagining that one day there would be a Hazel King State Park on Black Mountain. So now, when most of the higher elevations of Black Mountain are closed to the public and strip mines cut into her beloved Slope Holler on Black Mountain's lower elevations, I cannot help but think that we let Hazel down.

I asked Judy about this and she said, "I still think about Hazel a lot. Every time I see strip mining or mountaintop removal, it tugs at my heart and I think about the sadness in her eyes when she talked about it. She would be heartbroken to see how much more has gone under since she was out and about. But I don't think we let her down. I think in the time she knew us, she knew we were with her. And it's not all over yet. Who knows what will happen in the future or what fights there are left to fight?"

Our chapter meetings during 1998 and 1999 were often very divided. Many people within our group felt that we were not going far enough in challenging the mining industry. That we were not radical enough. I remember that by the spring of 1999 I was very tired. We had been meeting at least once a week since July. I remember thinking that if we came all that way and did not get something, some protection, some progress in the effort to find balance between the needs of industry, the community, and the environment, I wasn't sure I could stand it.

As of the fall of 2008 my wife and I still live here in Harlan. I teach Appalachian studies at the community college, and in those classes I ponder our shared past, present, and future with coal miners and their families. I laugh with former students as they lean out drive-thru windows. I share the stage with friends and neighbors in our community dramas made from stories and music that grew out of this place. I go to weddings and funerals and visit people in the hospital and rehab. I wave at the coal-truck drivers as we share roads too small for their trucks. I cannot help but feel that we are all in it together. That we all wish for some way to work and live in peace in this beautiful place and that in our heart of hearts we all want the place to remain beautiful. I look back on our struggle over Black Mountain, remember the angry faces of friends who thought we were taking food off their plates, remember the arguments within our group that we were not going far enough to fight strip mining, and I wonder what has happened to our ability to operate from a sense of what we have in common, instead of what divides us. Why have we allowed others to promote selfishness as our national ethic, to define the pursuit of happiness as a private affair? That is not what we see when we look one another in the eye. We see something far better there. We see ourselves.

Notes

1. M. Downs, "How to Save a Mountain: And a Little Child Shall Lead Them," *Ace Magazine*, May 12, 1999, 12–17.

2. "Black Mountain Majesty," *Lexington Herald-Leader*, March 25, 1999, 1B.

3. A. Mead, "Tentative Accord Reached on Black Mountain's Fate," *Lexington Herald-Leader*, April 21, 1999, 12A.

4. "Upper Elevations of Black Mountain to Be Protected," *Balancing the Scales*, May 5, 1999, 1.

5. "Offers Made to Sell Black Mountain Mining, Timber Rights for $7.7 Million," *Balancing the Scales*, August 12, 1999, 1.

6. "Black Mountain Deal Done: State's $4.2 Million Ends Threats from Logging, Mining," *Lexington Herald-Leader*, August 2, 2000, 3B.

6

Building Partnerships to Challenge Chip Mills

Citizen Activists Find Academic Allies

Lynne Faltraco and Conner Bailey

Community activists must quickly come to grips with the nature of power. Distilled to its essence, power is the ability to make things happen (or keep things from happening) despite opposition from others. In modern industrialized societies, power is found largely within large institutional settings, such as government or corporate bureaucracies or even universities. Such organizations control financial and human resources, often work together, and can make things happen even when people in a community oppose their plans. People have power only when they become organized and focus on common goals.

The challenges are daunting when people wake up to find that a threat to their community has emerged, not on the distant horizon but on their front steps, and that local, state, and even federal governments appear more interested in the prospects of economic growth than environmental quality or public health and safety. Fear easily can turn to despair as people realize that their governments are aligned with corporate interests and that political elites gain economic wealth and influence through such alignments. And yet we live in a democracy, and many books (including this one) are full of stories of citizens who rose up in righteous indignation to defend their homes and communities.

In this chapter we describe how residents of one community responded to a threat to hardwood forests that protected watersheds, provided shelter and forage for abundant wildlife, and provided employment and recreation opportunities for local residents and visitors.

Rutherford County, the setting for this chapter, is a predominantly rural community in the eastern foothills of the Appalachian mountain chain in North Carolina. In the late 1980s and early 1990s the pulp and paper industry established nearly 150 chip mills throughout Appalachia and the South. Chip mills cost relatively little to build ($8–10 million) and employ relatively few people (five to eight per mill, not counting loggers and truck drivers). Chip mills take whole logs and grind them into chips, load them onto railroad boxcars, and ship them considerable distances to pulp and paper mills. Chip mills encourage clear-cutting and in particular target the hardwood resources of the region, creating problems of erosion and loss in soil fertility as well as disrupting wildlife habitat and adversely affecting water quality. As a result of the spread of chip mills, local sawmills and furniture makers that depend on local resources for their livelihoods find themselves in competition with some of the nation's largest corporations. The impacts of chip mills were potentially devastating to resources and communities throughout the region. The Concerned Citizens of Rutherford County (CCRC) emerged in response to the threat chip mills posed to local forest resources and the local environment, organizing resistance first in Rutherford County and then throughout Appalachia and the South.

CCRC was successful in finding a common set of goals that everyone could support and then developing a set of programs that promoted positive values through environmental education and monitoring activities. Along the way, community activists met and found support from individual faculty at three different universities but also encountered other faculty who were less sympathetic. This interaction with academics provided the first author of this chapter, Lynne, with a broader understanding of commonalities between her community's struggles and those occurring elsewhere. The second author of this chapter, Conner, is an academic interested in how communities organize in response to environmental crises, and working with Lynne provided a learning opportunity to be shared with students.

The Resource and the Threat

The forest products industry has long played a dominant role in rural economies across the South and Appalachian regions. Several factors made this region attractive to the industry, including abundant rainfall, long growing seasons, and the facts that most forestland in the region is privately owned and that environmental and natural resource management standards are relatively weak. In the Pacific Northwest, by contrast, shorter growing seasons, the prevalence of public ownership of forest resources, and relatively strict standards for logging operations represent a challenge to industry. This challenge became increasingly severe in the early 1990s, when the federal government restricted timber harvests from public lands.

In Appalachia and the South the pulp and paper industry is the dominant actor in the forest products industry, accounting for roughly half of all timber harvests. This region produces approximately three-quarters of total paper products in the United States, from disposable diapers to newsprint, fine writing paper, and cardboard.

During the 1980s and 1990s hardwood forests of the South attracted the attention of pulp and paper companies looking for new sources of fiber. Their approach was to establish satellite chip mills. The logic behind this strategy was simple enough. Due to the high cost of trucking logs, pulp and paper mills generally drew on timber resources within a fifty-mile radius of the mill. Contemporary integrated pulp and paper mills are enormous facilities, with capital investments commonly more than $1 billion. These mills operate twenty-four hours a day, seven days a week, and require enormous supplies of timber. Chip mills connected by rail or barge to pulp and paper mills effectively extend the "woodshed" of a pulp and paper mill into multiple fifty-mile radii. Big trees, small trees—any trees!—are chewed up in the voracious maw of chip mills, which grind up whole logs.

The rapid expansion of chip mills raised both ecological and social issues that are related to broader impacts of the forest products industry. Research on resource dependency in the South has documented a negative correlation between economic dependence on forestry and a range of quality of life measures, including infant mortality, poverty, unemployment, and out-migration. Further, counties that hosted large pulp and paper mills gained little benefit because generous tax abatements undermined the tax base. Moreover, our research showed that technological changes in harvesting and processing followed the familiar pattern of displacing labor with capital so that relatively few jobs were created in the forest products industry. Finally, given the nature of the labor market, the best jobs went to white males while African American men and women of both races were effectively excluded. Even those employed in the mills did not necessarily live in the host county, and many preferred to live where better schools and health care facilities were to be found.[1]

The Concerned Citizens of Rutherford County

In June 1995 one of Lynne's neighbors read a short public notice in the local newspaper, the *Daily Courier,* stating that a chip mill was going to be built in their rural community of Union Mills. No one in the community knew what a chip mill was. All they knew was that the ex-lieutenant governor of North Carolina, Robert Jordan, was promoting the project with the promise of jobs and tax revenue for the community. As people began to ask questions, the community learned that Jordan was working closely with the local economic development director. Further research made it obvious that employment and tax revenue gains would be minimal compared to the potential threats of the proposed chip mill.

Concerned Citizens of Rutherford County became the first non-profit, community-based grassroots group focusing on timber resources to form in North Carolina. CCRC included a diverse group of people, including farmers, housewives, teachers, salespeople, children, coaches, nurses, doctors, veterinarians, and others. Some were "locals"—people whose families had lived in Rutherford County for more than 150 years. Others were "outsiders" who had moved in from elsewhere, attracted by the beauty and serenity of the area. This mismatched group came together to oppose the construction and operation of a high-capacity satellite chip mill in the community of Union Mills. First Jordan and then Willamette Industries tried to divide the community and thereby defuse opposition, but this strategy did not work because the people of Union Mills now had a common cause.

As CCRC was getting established, Saturday morning meetings were held at the Union Mills Community House, drawing fifty to seventy-five people. In 1996 CCRC hosted a rally attended by nearly eight hundred people. A local veterinarian said, "I can't believe that an event like this could draw so many people—locally, regionally, and nationally." The 1996 rally was a key event in the early history of CCRC, demonstrating the importance of networking and building support both within Rutherford County and beyond. The community truly began to understand that there were others interested in their issues and concerns, and more importantly, that they were willing to help. Among those willing to help were several university professors and both undergraduate and graduate students from Appalachian State University, who worked on projects that centered around CCRC, chip mills, and forestry. The students helped organize meetings, stuffed envelopes for mailings, made flyers, posted notices, and taught community members how to appreciate the energy of youth and understand that they would soon be taking older people's place in the world of activism.

During the early years CCRC filed an injunction against Jordan based on inaccuracies on his local industrial bond application; filed a sixty-day notice of intent to sue the Army Corps of Engineers; participated in numerous public hearings addressing water quality and the mill's stormwater general permit; addressed logging truck traffic safety issues and legislation and community chip mill concerns; participated on the North Carolina Advisory Board for a state study of the impact of chip mills; met and talked with local, state, and federal agency officials; gave presentations in North and South Carolina, Virginia, West Virginia, Georgia, and Kentucky; incorporated and acquired nonprofit status; and conducted outreach and provided support in communities where chip mills are located (in North and South Carolina, Virginia, and Pennsylvania). Whew!

At first CCRC was primarily concerned with local impacts, and because members of the group were novices at community organizing most of this time was used to get up to speed. They needed to learn more about the impacts of logging, logging truck safety, devaluation of private property, degradation of water quality, the loss of jobs for local sawmill owners and loggers, the aesthetics of local tourism, and how our community's quality of life would be affected by the chip mill in Union Mills. Chip mills in our area, as with most chip mills in the region, were focusing on converting hardwood forests into chips for making pulp and paper. CCRC members had to learn what effects clear-cutting would have on the health of forestlands and how this would affect people and communities in Rutherford County. The more the group learned, the more they realized that this was not just a local issue; it had state, regional, national, and even global implications.

The efforts and attention that CCRC raised concerning chip mills compelled Governor James B. Hunt in October 1996 to commission a statewide study on the economic and ecological impacts of chip mills. This study, titled "Economic and Ecologic Impacts Associated with

Wood Chip Production in North Carolina," was conducted through the North Carolina Department of Natural Resources (NCDENR), North Carolina State University, and Duke University and was funded in part by the U.S. Environmental Protection Agency.[2]

The timber industry did not want the community component included in the study, but fortunately some key people from NCDENR and academia were convinced that this section deserved attention. As a member of the advisory committee, Lynne had limited expectations regarding CCRC's ability to influence the study as a whole, but along with Mary Kerley from the Hickory Alliance, the group was able to gain the attention of other study members within the academic arena. In the following sections Lynne tells the story in her words.

CCRC Meets Academia

In February 1997 I attended a public hearing addressing the North Carolina stormwater general permit. Chip mills are required to have such permits, which come up for review every five years. The purpose of this hearing was to hear public comments and address water quality issues regarding on-site and off-site cumulative impacts. The public hearing was held at Piedmont Community College in Morganton, North Carolina. The timber industry (Willamette Industries and Godfrey Brothers with the support of the North Carolina Forestry Association) had wined and dined loggers and sawmillers, loaded them on two Greyhound buses, and transported them to the hearing. The auditorium was overflowing with intoxicated loggers and sawmillers, leaving very little space for citizens and others. The hearing was facilitated by a Duke University professor and NCDENR. Shortly after the hearing began, the facilitators lost control of the hearing. By the time I was called upon to present my comments, the drunken audience was cussing, jeering, and shouting at me! I informed the audience that they were behaving in an irrational and rude manner and proceeded to conclude my remarks. After I sat down, someone passed me a note. The note was from Dr. Fred Cubbage, apologizing for the rudeness of the timber industry, asking me for a copy of my comments, and requesting a meeting with me. That was my first introduction to Dr. Cubbage, who was from the Department of Forestry, North Carolina State University, and the start of a second partnership with university professors.

Although nearly all of my dealings with academia were positive, educational, and helpful, some were not, and clearly the forestry industry took great offense to our being involved in the chip mill study. To most in the industry, we were just people living in communities where chip mills were located or slated to be built, and were simply whiners without credibility or credentials. However, over the two years in which the chip mill study was completed, I met and developed remarkable and incredibly supportive relationships with many professors and graduate students. There was one notable exception, however. For reasons unknown, one of the key researchers was opposed to using CCRC and the Union Mills community and the Hickory Alliance and Pine Hall community in her socioeconomic research. This was a slap in the face to our organizations and communities. It is still unclear why, but she seemed to have concerns that our involvement would compromise the objectivity of the study. We had to push for our voices to be heard and to ensure that the chip mill study would reflect community concerns in a fair and equitable manner. Dr. Cubbage was instrumental in making sure that this happened.

For some of the people in the academic community, the chip mill study was the first opportunity they had ever had to talk with community members living near a chip mill. I met and talked regularly with the researchers, graduate students, and professors, and the process became an excellent educational experience for me. I also began to understand the kind of curricula being taught through state forestry schools at land-grant universities. Citizens typically have difficulty accessing and processing research data. It became clear to me that universities were an important resource to be cultivated and understood. And just as there were people at some universities who might not be sympathetic to the views of community activists, there were others who were willing to work together with communities on the basis of mutual respect.

As the chip mill study was progressing I learned of the work being done on the pulp and paper industry by a rural sociologist at Auburn University, Dr. Conner Bailey. One morning in January 1999 I called Conner to talk with him about CCRC and how difficult it is for communities to access and understand scientific data. Conner understood what I was saying, as he had spent years studying grassroots environmental groups fighting hazardous and solid waste landfills. He described the research being done on social aspects of forestry at Auburn and sent me a set of publications that had come from this work. One article in particular caught my eye, "Pulp Mills and Public Schools: The Tax Abatement Connection." Even though it was based on a lengthy doctoral dissertation, the article was simple, concise, and easily accessible for a lay reader. Moreover, it was exactly what we were looking for to support our case that the forest products industry should be understood as an extractive industry that often generates little employment or other benefits for rural counties in the South.[3]

Published studies carry weight in settings such as the committee that produced the North Carolina chip mill study. Simply stated, publications that have been through a rigorous peer-review process are hard to ignore or dismiss. When you as a community activist find an academic doing work that addresses concerns at a community level, such work can be a very powerful resource to counter claims by industry or government agencies (in this case, the USDA Forest Service) that community concerns do not reflect sound science, are narrowly focused, and are based purely on emotion. Frequent phone calls and subsequent face-to-face conversations with Conner helped me and others within CCRC understand that the issues over which we were fighting were in fact matters of global concern. Clearly, the problems resulting from corporate dominance were much bigger than the one chip mill in one community.

Conner also was very much interested in bringing community insights into academia and organized a panel of community forestry activists, including me, at the 2000 meeting of the Southern Rural Sociological Association in Lexington, Kentucky. Panel discussions and additional conversations at the conference opened our eyes further to the possibilities of forging working relationships with sympathetic academics. Continued exchanges between CCRC and our academic partners have become a vital part of developing joint knowledge and sharing educational experiences. These relationships helped CCRC become more familiar with socioeconomic and quality of life issues, the concept of sustainable community development, and the importance of ensuring that local governments are responsive to citizen needs. Personally, I have built on this experience. Having grown comfortable with the strange world of academia, I was honored to receive a fellowship funded by the Rockefeller Foundation at the University of Kentucky that allowed me to work with faculty and graduate students there and elsewhere around the Southeast. Not only did I gain from this exposure, but my academic colleagues came to understand something of what motivates a woman from Appalachia to defend her community.

Over the years CCRC has grown from a small, rural organization to become a primary voice for all communities in Appalachia and beyond dealing with the impacts of satellite wood chip mills and unsustainable forestry practices. The main reason we were successful is that we not only opposed chip mills but also developed a set of programs to educate ourselves as well as others.

CCRC Programs

With over ten years of grassroots experience, CCRC has used key leverage points, strategies, and tactics to provide organizational support for other communities where the threat of wood chip mills is occurring and for leaders in those communities; to encourage private woodland owners, foresters, and loggers to adopt sustainable forestry methods; and to educate the public about the broader threats that lie behind the immediate battles. Three CCRC programs have been the focus of our efforts over the past decade: Landowner Outreach and the Hemphill and Robbins Demonstration Forest, Forest Watch, and the North Carolina Democracy Schools.

Landowner Outreach and the Hemphill and Robbins Demonstration Forest

Despite creative efforts to block construction, the chip mill in Union Mills finally opened its gates in March 1998. This was a pivotal point in the formation of CCRC. We could have decided we were going to give up but instead decided that we needed to address issues of the nonindustrial private landowners. CCRC has never taken a position against logging, and many forestland owners were anxious to have their timber cut. We have always felt that it is a landowner's right to sell his or her timber. We established the Landowner Outreach Program in April 1998 to encourage private landowners to develop a relationship with an ethical forester, have a comprehensive forest management plan, and seek out responsible loggers to harvest their timber. The first program meeting was held at the Rutherford County Agricultural Extension office and was attended by nearly seventy private landowners, timber industry representatives, public officials, concerned citizens, and members of the media. This program developed into a series of well-organized educational meetings and field-based demonstrations on sustainable forestry.

In 1999 CCRC sponsored its first annual Horse Logging and Saw Milling Fun and Field Day. More than two thousand people have attended these events to learn more about sustainable forestry. With help from CCRC, the Hemphill and Robbins families developed a demonstration forest to show how selective cutting, preservation of diversity, management of individual "crop" trees, and careful harvesting practices will provide steady long-term income, preserve wildlife habitat, and protect water quality. CCRC awarded a Good Logger Award in 2003, which spotlighted the efforts of a young local logger harvesting timber in an ecological and ethical manner. This award helped convince loggers and others that CCRC was not against logging or the timber industry as a whole. Rather, our primary concerns are the use of chip mills to extend the reach of paper mills into the hardwood forests of North Carolina and the impact of clear-cutting on ecosystems and social systems.

Forest Watch

In response to calls from local residents distressed by the impact of logging on water quality, during May 2000 CCRC began a Forest Watch Program to promote best management practices (BMPs). We soon received calls from Henderson, McDowell, Buncombe, Burke, Haywood, Union, Chatham, Polk, Brunswick, and Wilkes Counties.

Forest Watch was the first forest monitoring program in North Carolina. We documented logging activities in Rutherford County and surrounding counties by taking pictures and video and filing site evaluation forms. In so doing we helped build the case for protective forestry legislation in North Carolina. These efforts encouraged inspections of active logging sites. We promoted local, state, and federal incentives that could provide landowners with the ability to practice sustainable forestry, and we promoted regulations that would require prior notification of timber harvesting. We also pushed for mandatory BMPs (e.g., streamside buffers) and logger registration and certification. To assist landowners in finding ethically responsible loggers, CCRC compiled a resource list by talking with local loggers and landowners. This list includes loggers who harvest timber following BMPs, are sensitive to the landowners' objectives, and follow sound aesthetic and ecological principles.

To date, CCRC has evaluated more than 256 logging sites and sent written reports to the North Carolina Division of Forest Resources (NCDFR) and the North Carolina Division of Land Resources. Of the sites visited and documented, 75 percent were active logging sites. CCRC set up a filing system that included written evaluations of each site. CCRC designed its own evaluation form, and evaluations included topographical and road maps and panoramic photographs. When CCRC receives a phone call or notification of an active logging operation, the person's contact information is taken along with the site location. The site is visited and evaluated to scope, inspect, photograph, and document the harvesting activity. Information is recorded about the logger, type of forestland and timber (hardwood, mixed species, or pine), kind of operation (clear-cut, selective cut, thinning, or other cutting process), diameter of the trees cut or left on site, amount of acreage, potential violations or problems, and people talked to. The evaluation also includes a narrative description. Evaluations are then sent to the NCDFR. This provides the division with the data it needs to conduct on-site inspections, monitoring, enforcement for compliance, education, and restoration options. CCRC reports have led to notices of noncompliance and violation being issued on sites evaluated by the NCDFR. Since the inception of CCRC's Forest Watch Program, the NCDFR has been very supportive of our reporting efforts, and we feel that we have a good working relationship with them.

In 2002 CCRC received the Governor's Award as Conservationist of the Year from the North Carolina and National Wildlife Federations for our Forest Watch Program. Eileen Conti, Caroline Edwards, and Lynne Faltraco traveled to Raleigh to receive this award and attend a banquet. Everyone who was anyone was there. Imagine—a community-based organization receiving an award of this caliber—what an honor! Such recognition increases the legitimacy of our work with Forest Watch and the belief that it is everyone's responsibility to protect the integrity of our human and natural communities, to have the forethought to think about long-term sustainability, and to preserve the legacy of our forests and communities for many generations to come.

North Carolina Democracy Schools

CCRC has faced many adversities and has also partnered with communities that have faced similar situations. Time and time again, communities find themselves in situations where they are essentially powerless. How do communities oppose corporations and the power, influence, and money that they wield?

In November 2004 CCRC hosted the first Democracy School in North Carolina at the YMCA Blue Ridge Assembly in Black Mountain. The Daniel Pennock Democracy School was named after a young man who died in Berks County, Pennsylvania, after being exposed to sewage sludge. The school was established as a training school for activists and community leaders. Its focus is simple—exploring how to build a new model of organizing that is not anchored in the regulatory arena but empowers communities to confront corporations. The central question we asked was, By what authority are corporations making decisions that govern our communities?

Democracy School sessions begin with an analysis of current environmental organizing and then examine how peoples' movements in this country have successfully organized. A written curriculum for communities and citizens focuses on the period from the early 1900s to the present; it covers the history of corporate expansion and power and the limited nature of regulatory protection from government agencies. Participants then examine organizing in specific situations and how that organizing has sought to stop imminent harm in ways that reveal the larger issue of community dominance by corporations. Democracy School then concludes with a session in which a selected single issue is reframed using that organizing model.

These approaches focus directly on re-democratizing our communities and taking power away from corporations. The Democracy School approach does not depend on lectures and speeches but rather encourages dialogue, conversation, debate, candor, listening, and earnest rethinking of strategies and tactics. Little attention is paid to specific issue strategies except for historical examples and analyses of their strengths and shortcomings. The purpose of the school is to empower participants to apply the collective wisdom in their respective communities. To strengthen and build the overall democratic movement, the Democracy School facilitates a strong network of individuals who stay in touch and, when appropriate, engage in common, connected strategies.

Partners

During CCRC's early years several organizations played a vital role in spotlighting our issues and concerns. The Western North Carolina Alliance was the first organization CCRC joined, in 1996. The alliance provided personnel as well as organizational and financial support. Although the alliance was focused on several broader issues, they were pivotal in supporting the early stages of our Landowner Outreach and Forest Watch Programs. CCRC also joined the Dogwood Alliance, which was the first regional coalition formed to address the acceleration of clear-cutting and construction of chip mills throughout the Southeast. In conjunction with the Dogwood Alliance, CCRC became the poster child for other communities addressing chip mills and unsustainable forestry practices.

As CCRC's strength and credibility grew, our efforts expanded to address regional impacts. Our concerns included clear-cutting and the loss of eight thousand to twelve thousand acres of hardwood and softwood forests per year, conversion of native forestlands to pine plantations, watershed degradation, elimination of wildlife habitat, stresses on the fine furniture industry, the loss of opportunities for nature-based recreation and tourism, and compromised nonmarket values related to natural aesthetics and scenic vistas associated with community landscapes. We studied property and landownership profiles and inadequately protective forest legislation. Many community-based organizations enjoy a brief period of growth followed by rapid decline as people tire or issues become settled. This has not been the case with our group. As individuals and as an organization, we grew to understand the connection between our local concerns and the larger world of politics and corporate greed that threaten our quality of life.

Our mission focused on developing partnerships and promoting education and support for communities and organizations from Alabama, Kentucky, Missouri, North Carolina, Pennsylvania, and Virginia. Each of the groups we worked with has its own story to tell and has overcome huge obstacles while reaching out to others in need, providing an example of what courage, tenaciousness, and hard work can do. In working with these groups CCRC has cultivated a broad base of support throughout the region.

Most groups are not able to draw on the support of others or do not have the expertise to oppose large corporations. The community development model on which CCRC is based is specific to our own community but also one that can be replicated in other communities throughout Appalachia. This model builds partnerships from the bottom up and inside out, involving citizens, local and state officials, agency and industrial representatives, traditional environmental groups, faith-based communities, academics, the medical profession, and the media. Over the years the strength and value of CCRC's networks has grown, allowing us to address local, state, and federal problems while setting an example of how to protect our local community.

What started out as a mission to keep one chip mill from being constructed in our community turned into a lifetime journey to help others, based primarily on faith. We are often approached by other communities for our expertise when they are addressing environmental, social injustice, and quality of life issues. We know something about the encroachment of extractive industries and businesses that violate and jeopardize our health, safety, and prosperity. We have come to recognize the limited ability that communities have to protect themselves in the absence of local zoning laws or in the presence of greedy local elites. Thus CCRC feels a great sense of responsibility in partnering with and mentoring other groups in communities struggling against corporate power and the timber industry.

CCRC has published several documents to help communities learn from our experiences. Grassroots leaders and their groups use our "Guide to Environmental Action Resources (GEAR)" to quickly and effectively find contact information on grassroots organizations and activists, environmental attorneys, media resources, environmental contractual services, scientists, academics, foresters, foundations and institutes that provide grants, and local, state, and federal agencies.[4]

CCRC, along with the Hickory Alliance (located in Pine Hall, North Carolina), Dogwood Alliance, and Appalachian Voices, compiled a "Landowner's Help Guide to Low-Impact Forestry in Western North Carolina." The guide provides educational information to nonindustrial private landowners. Chapter topics include sustainable forestry options for landowners, good forest management, resources, North Carolina's Forestry Present-Use Value property tax program, priorities for a forest plan, the appeals process for property tax evaluations in North Carolina, low-impact forestry in hardwood stands, Pioneer Forest (a sustainably managed forest in Missouri), and land conservancies.[5]

CCRC also received a grant from the Mary Reynolds Babcock Foundation and published a leadership manual with the help of other community-based grassroots groups. This manual provides tools to help leaders organize effectively in their communities and impact state policy. The manual includes chapters on running productive meetings, cultivating nontraditional communities, fund-raising, grant writing, lobbying, office tips, outreach tactics, editorial writing, building coalitions, working with the media, incorporation and establishment of nonprofit status, a glossary of legal terms, and other helpful information.[6]

Taking Things Personally

Not many people are comfortable being criticized on a regular basis. In this section I want to explain the personal and emotional side of a decade-long struggle in the hope that this will help citizens elsewhere understand what it's like to be personally attacked and have their loved ones threatened, then decide if the fight is worth the effort.

At some point, we all take things personally. For example, logging trucks on small county roads was one of the scariest concerns for our community. I will never forget receiving a call from our son telling me that he had almost been run off the road by a logging truck. It was in the late afternoon, and he was on his way back to the high school to help with an evening program. He was upset, and I was terrified. My husband was at work, and I called my neighbor, Mike Conti. I needed to talk with Shannon Buckley, the procurement forester and manager of the chip mill. I didn't trust myself to be calm—after all, this was my child—our only child. Mike agreed to pick me up and drive me to the chip mill. We walked into Mr. Buckley's office, and I proceeded to tell him that a logger had nearly run my child off the road. I was furious, scared, and really, really mad. I leaned over his desk and told him that if one hair on my child's head was ever harmed there would be ramifications for Willamette Industries and him. Later, Mr. Buckley attended our landowner outreach meeting, as we always made a point of inviting landowners, local and agency officials, foresters, loggers, and representatives from the industry. He came up and spoke to me after the meeting and, like me, was clearly upset about what had happened to our son. One thing we both definitely agreed on—truck traffic safety was paramount in our minds. Fast-moving logging trucks loaded with tens of tons of logs on narrow, winding roads are a threat to the lives of everyone who lives and works in the area. Truckers are paid by the number of loads they carry, so speed equals money. This creates unsafe conditions on local roads, a problem that continues to be one of our primary concerns.

What to Do If the FBI Comes Knocking

Over Labor Day weekend in September 2002 the Willamette Industries chip mill was sabotaged, and the Federal Bureau of Investigation (FBI) and the State Bureau of Investigation (SBI) came knocking on my door. I knew that they would come because I was a leader of CCRC, and we were the ones who had challenged construction and operation of this facility and had monitored its activities for the past seven years.

I had just returned from giving a presentation to Fred Cubbage's class at North Carolina State University in Raleigh. The telephone rang, and it was a reporter from our local paper, the *Daily Courier,* asking me for a statement. "A statement about what?" I asked. He explained what had happened and asked me if I or CCRC had anything to do with the incident. This was the first time I heard about the incident. Since CCRC has always taken a nonviolent approach, it was not a difficult task but was nevertheless disconcerting. All kinds of questions were flying around in my head. Was it someone we knew or could it have been an inside job? Or were they trying to blame us for something that we hadn't done?

The local newspaper ran articles, and we knew that the FBI was investigating the crime. We also wanted to be prepared if the FBI came for a visit. We contacted our environmental attorney, Thomas Linzey of the Community Environmental Legal Defense Fund. He advised us of our legal rights and helped us understand just how much information we were required to provide before requesting that legal counsel be present to continue an interview. The chip mill was shut down for two weeks in order to make repairs, and the perpetrators were never arrested. Since this incident took place during the acquisition of Willamette Industries by Weyerhaeuser, we have often wondered if it was an internal job, allowing the company to upgrade equipment that could later be written off on its taxes.

We are the only organization working on environmental issues in Rutherford County, and the finger was frequently pointed at us. The procurement forester had initially suggested that the FBI question our organization. It was just like in the movies: two agents drove up our driveway in a dark SUV with tinted windows. They came up to the door and asked to speak to me. My husband requested identification and asked that they remain on our deck until I was dressed.

The visit lasted about forty-five minutes, and although the FBI and SBI were very thorough, it was clear that they didn't have any suspects and were simply gathering information. I didn't offer any additional information except what was asked of me, and my husband was present during the entire interview. The FBI agents asked questions about our board of directors and our activities and associations with acquaintances we had worked with since 1995. After the interview was completed, I learned that the agents had also visited my neighbor and his wife, Mike and Eileen Conti. They had been active in CCRC since its inception and continue to be well-respected members of the community. A small, feisty Italian lady, Eileen was always working behind the scenes to encourage everyone, keeping track of our activities and contacting and following up with local public officials. She is one of the reasons why this journey has had such a huge impact on my life. Although she battled cancer seven times, she always attended meetings, was on the board of directors, and continued to be the inspiration that we all looked to when things weren't going our way. This part of my chapter is dedicated to Eileen and her tenacity, love, the lessons she taught me, and her gentle spirit. Those who were fortunate enough to meet her were truly blessed.

The long-term effects of this visit are a constant reminder of how vulnerable citizens can be when they do not understand their constitutional rights and how to behave in these kinds of situations. It is critical for citizens to understand that honesty and truth must always be uppermost in their approach to organizing and working on these types of campaigns. It is also imperative that citizens have accurate information, which helps any organization take the moral high ground when faced with potentially stressful and intimidating situations. Never, ever lie!

To Thine Own Self Be True

Fighting for your community takes extraordinary amounts of time. The fight intrudes on dinner hours, conversations between husbands and wives, vacations, work, relationships, and other activities and is always on your mind. At some point the fight takes on a life of its own, dominating your own life. Rather than remembering to eat, you are typing or talking on the phone, and forgetting to make dinner, sleep, or even take a walk. All too easily you forget to take a moment to appreciate the very nature of the community you are trying to protect, because the fight becomes more important than anything else. You get tired physically, mentally, emotionally, and spiritually. You may become cranky, making life difficult for those you love.

You have to consider very carefully whether you are cut out for this type of activism. Your husbands and wives, children, and friends also pay a price for this commitment. I was fortunate to have the unwavering support of my husband, Mike, and our son, Joey, but other community activists paid a heavy price for engaging in community activism. Family and friends may think that you are spending too much time on the issue and not enough time with them or that you may just be crazy. Personal relationships are either strengthened or broken when one family member becomes involved in a local struggle. I saw families become fragmented, jealousies surface, and some marriages end in divorce.

At first, the fight is fun—it creates a sense of empowerment—but when others are criticizing you or you read the morning paper and find that you have been slammed in an editorial, sometimes the fun is replaced by self-doubt. Do you take public criticism personally, or do you see it as an opportunity to educate and set the record straight? When you receive a letter from the president of the corporation that you are at odds with, does it scare you or compel you to respond in a professional and firm manner? Would the president of a corporation write a letter to a citizen unless the citizens in her community were making a difference? Absolutely not!

The danger of burnout is ever present. You will wonder if you can stay in the fight for the long haul or if you will just give up if you are not quickly successful. You need to realize that the other side of the fight knows that they have the resources for a long fight and is counting on community activists to burn out, give up, and go home. If you decide to get into the fight, prepare for the long haul, and this includes pacing yourself and having fun along the way. One way to avoid burnout is to be sure you are not in the struggle alone. Community struggles are collective efforts. You need to work with others and not try to do everything yourself.

You have to ask, continually, if the cause is worth the price you are paying. I can't answer that question for others—I can only talk about my own situation. And believe me, at times I wondered. But when I look back at all of the wonderful people that I have met and the positive achievements that would not have happened had we not been willing to stand up for our communities, the answer in my case is clear. Yes, it really was worth it!

What Have We Learned from Each Other?

Through our collaboration, we have learned and confirmed what we knew. Lynne found in Conner an academic who understood the struggles that people go through when confronted with threats to their communities. Conner found in Lynne an activist leader who understood that her struggle was part of a larger tapestry, who knew she was in for a long journey and was eager to learn from any source.

Lynne knew intuitively that the battle she found herself in was connected to phenomena well beyond Rutherford County, a reality confirmed through public hearings and the chip mill study. Coming into contact with Conner helped Lynne understand some of these larger connections, which in turn informed many of Lynne's and CCRC's actions in the years that followed. A central realization was that rural communities often find themselves at the mercy of corporations or industries that are making decisions without consulting the citizens who live in the affected areas. Often a community becomes aware of a new industry only after all the decisions have been made. Communities often find themselves reacting to problems rather than developing proactive visions and programs around which the public can be mobilized. In Union Mills the realization came too late to stop the chip mill, but the organizational efforts of CCRC were effective in drawing public attention, university support, and a major state award. More importantly, once CCRC was established, no additional chip mills were established in North Carolina. CCRC has been in operation for more than a decade and has adopted proactive programs of community and landowner outreach and public and environmental education to make sure its message is understood and widely disseminated.

One factor that distinguished CCRC from other community-based citizen groups was that CCRC reached out to and became actively involved with different universities in the region, finding sympathetic professors who provided data and helped the leaders of CCRC understand the broader context of their own unique struggle. This understanding in turn led CCRC to move beyond simple opposition to a specific facility to a more holistic understanding of what was needed to protect local forest ecosystems and the communities that live in and depend on such ecosystems. As a result, CCRC became actively involved in developing environmental education programs, monitored logging sites, and organized a democracy school to educate citizens about the nature of power in an era of corporate ascendency. The central understanding was that citizens must educate themselves and become involved in local government. They must understand that they have a fundamental right to protect their children, families, and neighbors from harmful industrial impacts. And they must understand that being proactive is more effective than being reactive.

As CCRC developed, members realized that their challenges were part of a much wider struggle and that other communities were facing the same challenges. In part, this realization came about through interactions with academics who have been studying such phenomena for a long time. Many economically distressed communities are desperate for jobs, any jobs, and therefore are vulnerable to purveyors of snake oil treatments in the form of environmentally destructive enterprises masquerading as economic development.

Ironically, in a democracy such as ours, politics and power at the local level are a point of significant vulnerability. Corporate investors are quick to form alliances with local elites who see personal and political benefit in aligning themselves with corporate power and wealth. Through such alignments, the power of local elites is enhanced at the same time that distant corporations gain access to the local levers of power. This coalition of internal and external actors often is able to establish substantial domination, to the point where local residents cannot even imagine challenging their power. But sometimes, as detailed in this book, local residents reach a point where they rise up, fight back, and effectively challenge corporate power. Lynne lives in such a place, and Conner has studied communities that struggled successfully as well as those that failed.[7]

The mantra of new investment and jobs is seductive in many parts of Appalachia and the South. Academic partners can help community activists effectively challenge corporate promises of economic development by documenting experiences in other communities where promises were made but not realized. Armed with data and supported by professional expertise, community activists are better able to challenge corporate or governmental actors who might otherwise claim that objective scientific and technical reasoning supports their position. Those who promote chip mills base their arguments on technical efficiency and economic benefit as measured by profit and economic growth. Community activists and their academic partners are no less objective in focusing their attention on ecological impacts of chip mill technology or how the benefits of economic growth are distributed. These, too, are valid values, and this line of reasoning is best made through the combined voices of academics and activists.[8]

Academics who are interested in working with community activists face significant challenges within the academic culture where they are employed. Sometimes university administrators are influenced by corporate sponsors and will discourage critical work. This happened to Conner and his colleagues at Auburn University, when an administrator stopped publication of a report that might have been seen as critical of the forest products industry in Alabama. Here, too, good research can trump administrative obstructionism, and publishable results can not only attain credibility but protect an academic from unwarranted challenges.

There are real challenges for a researcher wanting to ensure quality of data and analysis who also wants to work with community activists. What might be a poorly drafted research document to a researcher might be perfectly adequate for a community group trying to get a handle on public concerns and interests in taking action to address a particular problem. Understandably, community partners faced with real-world challenges might be impatient with the pace of academic research, particularly when the researcher also has classes to teach, papers to grade, and myriad other professional responsibilities. Community interests have little to do with publishing, and the drive to publish has to be understood as a point where interests diverge.

That said, the publication record of an academic is an important component of professional credibility, which in turn is an important resource for community activists. Jokes about absentminded professors notwithstanding, academics make good expert witnesses at public hearings, in courtroom proceedings, and elsewhere. This is because professors are not on the payroll of community groups (or industries) and generally are seen as independent and credible. And published work, particularly work published in peer-reviewed journals, can be a powerful tool to counter arguments made by corporate and governmental actors.

What academics can bring to the struggle is understanding based on research about what has worked in other communities. But academics generally must approach community struggles with a profound sense of humility, understanding the limits of their knowledge under local conditions and most importantly that the struggles they document are real in their consequences for the people who live in those communities. These are among the lessons we must share with our students, our children, and our neighbors.

Notes

1. John C. Bliss, Conner Bailey, Glenn R. Howze, and Lawrence Teeter, "Timber Dependency in the American South" (SCFER Working Paper no. 74, Southeastern Center for Forest Economics Research, Research Triangle Park, NC, 1993); Mahendra Joshi, "Industrial Recruitment Policy and Rural Development: A Case Study of the Pulp and Paper Industry in Alabama" (PhD diss., Auburn University, 1997); Mahendra Joshi, John Bliss, and Conner Bailey, "Pulp Mills and Public Schools: The Tax Abatement Connection," *Highlights of Agricultural Research* 45 (1998): 23–24; Mahendra L. Joshi, John C. Bliss, Conner Bailey, Larry J. Teeter, and Keith J. Ward, "Investing in Industry, Underinvesting in Human Capital: Forest-Based Rural Development in Alabama," *Society and Natural Resources* 13 (2000): 291–319; Conner Bailey, Peter Sinclair, John Bliss, and Karni Perez, "Segmented Labor Markets in Alabama's Pulp and Paper Industry," *Rural Sociology* 61 (1996): 474–95; John Bliss and Conner Bailey, "Pulp, Paper, and Poverty: Forest-Based Rural Development in Alabama," in *Communities and Forests: Where People Meet the Land,* ed. Robert Lee and Don Fields (Corvallis: Oregon State University Press, 2005), 138–58; Glenn Howze, Laura Robinson, and Joni Fisher Norton, "Historical Analysis of Timber Dependency in Alabama," *Southern Rural Sociology* 19 (2003): 1–39.

2. Southern Center for Sustainable Forests, "Economic and Ecologic Impacts Associated with Wood Chip Production in North Carolina," July 2000, accessed July 5, 2009, http://scsf.nicholas.duke.edu/node/19.html.

3. Joshi, Bliss, and Bailey, "Pulp Mills and Public Schools"; Joshi, "Industrial Recruitment Policy."

4. Concerned Citizens of Rutherford County, "A Guide to Environmental Action Resources (GEAR)," 1997.

5. Concerned Citizens of Rutherford County, "Landowner's Help Guide to Low-Impact Forestry in Western North Carolina," Dogwood Alliance, Asheville, NC, 1999.

6. Concerned Citizens of Rutherford County, "Leadership Strategies and Tactics," 1998.

7. John Gaventa, *Power and Powerlessness: Quiescence and Rebellion in an Appalachian Valley* (Urbana: University of Illinois Press, 1980).

8. James C. Cobb, *The Selling of the South: The Southern Crusade for Industrial Development, 1936–1990* (Urbana: University of Illinois Press, 1993).

7

Environmental Justice from the Roots

Tillery, North Carolina

Mansoureh Tajik

Most rural communities in eastern North Carolina are underdeveloped and confront a multitude of environmental, economic, and sociopolitical problems linked to how local lands are used. Decisions about land use, however, frequently are made without local citizen input. Often unrepresentative of the local population and operating under the rubric of economic development, decision makers on local, state, or regional boards introduce and enact public policies that are heavily influenced by powerful economic interests and that often have perverse public and environmental health effects. While the authors and beneficiaries of such policies mostly live in locations far removed from the harm caused by their actions, local populations suffer. This disconnect between who decides and who benefits or is harmed by a given development policy has forced many rural communities to make a journey that begins with an underdeveloped economy and ends with the loss of any reasonable hope for development of a sound, healthy, or sustainable local economy.

Some local communities, however, have resisted loss of the economy and environment upon which their livelihoods and well-being depend. These communities have rebuffed unsound development through grassroots participation, formation of strong local community-based organizations, and collaborative relationships with university researchers. In some cases these local organizations have been instrumental in affecting relevant public policies by engaging in various policy-related activities, such as building effective partnerships, raising public awareness, and educating policy makers about critical issues.

This chapter presents a narrative of a partnership between Concerned Citizens of Tillery (CCT), a community-based organization in eastern North Carolina, and researchers in the School of Public Health at the University of North Carolina at Chapel Hill (UNC). It builds on results from a W. K. Kellogg Foundation–funded study conducted in 2004 as well as more recent communications with key community and academic partners to examine the community-based organization's roles and the research partnerships that had an impact on policies related to the spread of industrial hog operations in North Carolina. The chapter begins with a brief account of such operations in North Carolina, followed by a short history of CCT. It then explores the partnership that developed between CCT and one UNC researcher.

In exploring this partnership, the chapter draws on data obtained from a set of semistructured, open-ended interviews and focus group discussions with various partners and key community members. The key community partner, Gary Grant, and the academic partner, Steve Wing, offered the most in-depth look into the partnership, mostly due to the deep and expanded dimensions of their involvement. The focus group was conducted with key community members and longtime residents and addressed their participation and role in the policy-making process. On the policy side, additional interviews were conducted with two county commissioners who were actively involved in policy changes at the county level. The objective of the latter two interviews was to understand from the policy makers' perspectives the level of influence that CCT partnerships and activities had on specific local outcomes in regard to industrial hog operations. In addition, published articles, reports, photographs, video records, and documents produced and collected by CCT over the past twenty-five years also were examined as part of a larger study.[1]

Industrial Hog Operations in North Carolina

Between 1980 and 1997 the state of North Carolina moved from fifteenth to second in hog production among U.S. states, a position it continued to hold through 2009. This growth occurred with a significant national restructuring of farming practices in general that effectively transformed raising hogs from a family farm activity to industrial-corporate production. Owen Furuseth explains this transformation as an "explosion-implosion" phenomenon: at the same time that the swine population expanded rapidly (exploded), it collapsed within certain geographical bounds (imploded). In other words, the transformation resulted in the production of millions more hogs in very few, large corporate facilities while eliminating thousands of small farms throughout the state and region. This explosion-implosion pattern led to very high-density corporate hog production in the Black Belt of eastern North Carolina, which generated massive quantities of wastes that threatened groundwater and surface water. It also exposed surrounding populations and workers to potential environmental hazards, adverse health risks, and diminished quality of life.[2]

This explosion and implosion exhibited both geographic and population patterns. According to a U.S. Department of Agriculture (USDA) Economic Research Service report, four factors influence corporate location decisions: natural endowments, economic costs, business climate, and public policies (including environmental regulation). The report indicates that large farm operations may move to particular areas because of possibly less stringent environmental regulations: "Lax [environmental regulatory] structure can mean either no effort to enforce, or lack of institutional capabilities or financial resources to enforce. It may also mean an absence of perceived need for environmental regulation or enforcement. Locational shifts may involve moves between geographic areas, or clustering within a given area."[3]

Donnie Charleston explored economic and sociopolitical factors influencing the hog industry's location decisions and concluded that communities in economic distress were targeted for industrial hog production. In eastern North Carolina, communities in economic distress are those with the highest concentration of African Americans and are concentrated in the Black Belt counties. A high percentage of the population in these counties lives in poverty, which has made the growth of industrial hog operations an example of environmental injustice in general and of environmental racism in particular.[4]

Concerned Citizens of Tillery

Since it was founded in 1978, CCT has played an active role in community organizing, community mobilization, environmental justice research, and policy decision making in rural African American communities in Tillery and surrounding areas in eastern North Carolina. As declared in its mission statement, the organization's purpose is to promote cultural awareness and improve the social, economic, and educational welfare of citizens in Tillery and Halifax County through self-development. CCT promotes self-development by providing information to communities, participating in voter registration, promoting leadership, teaching organizational skills, and conducting educational activities such as workshops on issues of land ownership and debt control and programs on African American culture and heritage, as well as by providing necessary services, such as transportation and health care.[5]

CCT's active membership is 99 percent black and has a history of more than two decades of successful organizing. Over this time CCT has benefitted from sustained collaboration with university researchers as well as local, state, and national health, environmental, and government organizations. The organization's success is reflected in policy changes at local, state, and regional levels. Using its extensive grassroots support, CCT introduced the first county-level intensive livestock ordinance in North Carolina and pressed for groundwater education and monitoring programs. CCT also pushed for the adoption of county and state environmental justice proclamations, demanded citizen input on environmental regulation, and encouraged state-level programs to promote education and awareness regarding issues of environmental justice and racism. CCT recognized uncontrolled growth of industrial hog production as a threat and formed effective alliances aimed to counter the spread of hog operations in Tillery and southeast Halifax County.

The Community-Academic Partnership Begins

Building upon extensive grassroots support, in conjunction with collaborative efforts with the Halifax County Health Department, CCT became instrumental in encouraging the county to adopt policy measures to protect public health and the environment with the growth of industrial hog operations. As a result of CCT's extensive efforts, Halifax County was the first county in North Carolina to pass an intensive livestock operation rule, through its Board of Health, in 1992. In 1995 the partnership between CCT and the county health department was extended to include a research scientist, Steve Wing, from UNC. The result has been an effective partnership that successfully obtained funding from the National Institute of Health Sciences for the Southeast Halifax Environmental Reawakening (SHER) project.

The project included community-based participatory research, community education and organizing, and improved medical services, with the goal of identifying and addressing environmental justice issues in predominantly African American communities in rural eastern North Carolina. The partnership aimed to achieve the project's goals through a series of activities that included participatory community workshops, medical care provider seminars, environmental health consultation and support, community festivals, quantitative environmental justice analyses, a speaker's bureau composed of community members, and outreach to other communities. As a community-based participatory research project, SHER's research questions were those of the community, and the study design required community participation and active engagement throughout the process. Each component was designed to achieve specific goals. For example, workshops were designed to encourage presentations by community members about their health concerns, covering diverse issues from water contamination to exposure to agricultural chemicals. The medical care provider seminars aimed to help the area's health providers gain deeper understanding of the potential impact of the environmental contamination on their patients' health and be able to recognize environmentally related symptoms should they be present. Quantitative and spatial analyses of environmental justice issues provided documentation of the racial and socioeconomic characteristics of communities located near intensive hog operations. These analyses assisted with the framing of possible adverse health outcomes in terms of environmental justice principles and possible violations of these principles.

As a result of the SHER project and other CCT efforts and partnerships, in January 1997 the county commissioners passed an intensive livestock operation ordinance, making Halifax the first county in the state to have both its Board of Health and its county commission adopt such an ordinance. As one of the county commissioners stated in an interview, "Even though we had other folks that were involved, had it not been for CCT's involvement, I don't think we would have gotten as far along as we did [with the livestock ordinance]."[6]

Under the SHER project, CCT's executive director, Gary Grant, and the academic researcher from UNC, Steve Wing, focused on emerging environmental health and environmental justice issues. They were able to identify specific instances of environmental racism and demonstrate the need for a study of the impact of industrial hog operations on health and quality of life in the communities near such operations. Remaining committed to its mission of social change, CCT expanded many of its activities under the SHER project to help southeast Halifax County and other multiracial communities empower and educate themselves and others, including health professionals, students, scientists, and government officials, in areas of institutionalized racism, environmental health, and environmental justice.

In this process the partnership between Grant and Wing was one of equals who not only had common interests and values but who also shared research responsibilities. The quality of the sustainable partnership and shared responsibilities is best illustrated by Grant's recollection of a critical event in which Wing was called to testify in a hearing before the North Carolina House Agriculture Committee:

> Once he released the results of his study, he was called before the House Agriculture Committee in Raleigh. He then called me and told me, "WE have been called." So, I said, "What do you mean, WE?" He said, "Well, your name is on that study just like mine." The day we were to testify, I came back and told the group [community members] what was happening. . . . You see, with black people, we know what happens when somebody calls you into a formal setting. They are getting ready to take you out behind the barn and whip your . . . or to string you up. That is exactly what they had planned to do with Steve Wing that day. We had about 35 members of the community that showed up. When the legislators came into the room you could just see utter surprise on their faces: there is this room full of black folk. They were not able to do to him that day what they wanted to do because we were there.

Wing echoed the position of shared responsibility and commitment. Throughout his interview he used "we" in reference to the key players on the project and its related activities. When asked to define "we," he responded, "I am being general in the use of 'we' there to refer to the formal SHER project team, meaning CCT and its supporters." This attitude went beyond semantics. In documenting the roles of partners, the SHER project had both Wing and Grant as the coprincipal investigators. In publishing the results of the study and creating reports, both partners shared the authorship, jointly publishing papers in peer-reviewed journals, producing various other joint reports, and appearing jointly in several public presentations. Wing defined his role as follows: "I go along with CCT members to help give information or just be there to indicate that there is technical support for CCT to respond to community needs."[7]

As time progressed, the community-academic partnership was further strengthened by Wing's increased knowledge, positive attitude, and responsiveness to community needs. Grant contrasted this relationship with CCT's relationship with academic partners who had previously collaborated on a community health survey: "they [other researchers] had brought the assessment instrument to Tillery, North Carolina, and one of the questions on the assessment instrument was, How far can you hit a golf ball? No relevance whatsoever to Tillery!" The need for the researchers to be open and think critically about their education when collaborating with the communities was evident. Grant emphasized that "it is a real hassle to de-program the people [who] want to talk about community-based research not wanting to give up what the institutions have taught them." Reflecting a growing sophistication in how university research operates, under Grant's leadership CCT wants to see research protocols before they are turned into the institutional review board for human subjects, "so that we are sure you are saying what it is that needs to be said."

CCT's experience working with traditional environmental groups was complicated by similar insensitivities to the needs of rural African Americans in southeast Halifax County. In particular, the failure of such groups to understand how the history of slavery and institutionalized racism contributed to contemporary environmental racism created an enormous challenge in efforts to build effective working relationships. Traditional environmental groups saw industrial hog farming as an isolated issue, while members of CCT understood this threat in a far wider context grounded in social justice. Grant noted, "One of the things we learned in this whole process was that white people want to solve problems and black people want to solve issues."

CCT's relationship with the county health department changed over time, from collaborative to distant, due to a change in personnel. When the department was led by an African American woman, it and CCT shared a common understanding that targeting rural black counties for industrial hog operations represented a form of environmental racism and that the community's health issues could be understood only in the context of racism and social justice. After her departure, however, the new health director brought a new orientation to the department that did not address environmental racism or social justice components of public health.

Despite this setback, CCT was able to gain some sympathy from some members of the white community after one hog operation's cesspool spilled 25 million gallons of raw sewage into the Neuse River. This accident brought the whole issue of industrial hog operations and their handling of massive wastes onto the radar screen of people who would otherwise not have been too concerned. As Grant put it, "It got pig poop on all of the yachts and boats of the folk who never had to worry about the stink because they lived far enough away and thus [were] unaffected by the hog wastes' impact till then." Industrial hog farming in North Carolina and its impact on African American communities received additional publicity when Grant was interviewed for a segment of the CBS show *60 Minutes,* named "Pork Power," which was first aired in December 1997.

The Policy Process

Everyone interviewed for this chapter agreed that policy change was not the primary focus of the SHER project. Nonetheless, working to affect relevant policy measures became a necessary step in the process, and various community partners met frequently with government officials and participated in public hearings on industrial hog operations. Relationships with the media were also developed, and CCT gave awards to newspaper columnists who maintained fair and balanced coverage of community activities around important issues or who had taken the initiative to tackle tough environmental or social justice issues that were of public concern.

CCT's policy efforts grew out of research that demonstrated that African American and low-income communities bore disproportionate burdens from industrial hog operations. CCT's focus was on educating county commissioners and legislators. Over time CCT developed a political presence so that, according to Grant, politicians and elected officials "know if [they] want to be re-elected [they have] to play ball with us [the community]." They come "whenever [they are] asked to speak." The visibility and recognition of CCT and its efforts with the media (such as the *60 Minutes* segment) and Tillery's receipt of the prestigious international Healthier Community Award brought with them widespread positive exposure. Such exposure led in turn to an influx of funding that helped finance CCT's various activities.[8]

Grant credits the traditional environmental groups for getting the industrial hog issue on the table, but grassroots involvement of CCT also played an important role. Even so, when CCT made an attempt to use scientific evidence about the adverse impact of concentrated hog wastes on health and environment in other states, state legislators rejected the evidence because the studies were from Iowa and Nebraska and not North Carolina. As Grant put it, "That's when we realized hog poop smells different in Iowa and Nebraska than in North Carolina." It was then that the community started to realize it needed to conduct its own study.

Success and Challenges

CCT's influence was pervasive and led to small, unanticipated victories that cumulatively had a major effect. According to Grant, the victories made community members realize that they have the capacity "to achieve other goals." "Once rallied," for example, "the community was able to see and work on getting other things such as a fire district" for the first time in the history of the community. The success in getting a new fire district also led to other positive consequences, such as lowered insurance rates and "opportunities for 24 young men [to work] as volunteer firefighters." These positive outcomes, in turn, further boosted the community's confidence and capacity and emboldened them in their efforts to achieve other goals.

Members of CCT were persistent in attending meetings of the county commissioners. As a community member put it, "We kept going and going [to commissioner meetings] until it got done." Community organizing and petitioning to "make the government see they had to take action" and crossing the color line by "getting whites to go to Raleigh and complain too since we all use the same water" were also important.

Crossing the color line was a major achievement. One of the most important barriers to progress in Halifax County was institutionalized and individual racism. It seemed that "getting past racism is always an issue" and "when black people start hollering [about what is affecting their health and community], they are hollering as second-class citizens," Grant explained.

The long history of being treated like second-class citizens created an atmosphere of inertia due to fear or lack of awareness. This led to the partners "having to educate the whole community about the environmental issues and their impacts." The complacency of citizens who felt that they did not have the ability to change anything or who were discouraged from speaking out because they feared something might happen to them also was an important obstacle. Even as CCT gained influence, some community members feared losing their Social Security or medical care if they spoke up about environmental issues. As Wing explained, these fears may not be entirely unfounded:

> We generated a reaction in some quarters that we didn't intend. For example, the pork industry tried to obtain confidential research records from us. . . . We believe that it put the members of communities that worked with us and participated in our research in a compromised situation. Their confidential information could conceivably lead to something that would be a problem for them. These are communities where there has been intimidation, people's jobs have been threatened, there are people who carry weapons because they are concerned about the potential for violence. They have been verbally harassed. They are definitely vulnerable.

Government bureaucracy was another obstacle mentioned by both Grant and Wing. Government agencies are often very slow to respond to citizen concerns, largely due to industry's profound influence over local and state governments, elected officials, and even universities. Wing noted that "federal and state agencies which control policy work closely with industry so it's hard to have the same access needed to make change." With regard to universities, Wing noted that there were "close ties between the board of governors, [the] campus attorney and [the] pork industry."

Policy Outcomes and Beyond

Different partners had different views about specific outcomes of the collaborative research between CCT and Wing at UNC. Wing insisted that it was difficult to assess change and perhaps there needed to be "a longer time frame in evaluating effectiveness." He argued that many of the outcomes were more symbolic than substantive. To some extent, the ultimate victory still seemed elusive to some community members because, as one CCT member said, "Hog factories were still there with odors." The elusiveness of the ultimate goal seemed evident since, "despite research, outreach and education about environmental racism," there were still no increases in "fairness in the location of facilities."

Despite these cautious proclamations, there were both small and large tangible outcomes, the most important of which was passage of the intensive livestock ordinances that set limits on the spread of industrial hog operations in Halifax County. Certainly, these positive outcomes had followed many years of grassroots activism and community organizing and had built on successes in getting a county-level health rule and ordinance passed in April 1992, a four-year moratorium on any new or expanded farms passed by the North Carolina General Assembly in 1995, and a statewide moratorium on industrial hog operations passed in 1997. As one community member put it, "Without our efforts, I think they [hog operations] would have been all over Halifax now. I think what we did had a major role."

Commissioners in Halifax County and later the state of North Carolina adopted environmental justice proclamations in response to CCT's work. Numerous other outcomes, such as creation of the North Carolina Environmental Justice Network and efforts by other counties and citizens to set local limits on industrial hog operations also emerged as a result of CCT's efforts. CCT also was effective in getting the language of racism, discrimination, and environmental justice on the table where it had to be considered by county commissioners and other government officials.

The organizational efforts of CCT extended well beyond the question of industrial hog farming to include support of black farmers who sued the federal government over land loss caused by actions of the U.S. Department of Agriculture. CCT helped conduct some background work that led to the black farmers' success on land loss litigation. As

Wing put it, "We helped build the movement that was involved in this [land loss] litigation and which led to a settlement agreement in which black farmers were able to get some compensation for the discrimination that had occurred over decades."

Overall, the SHER project raised consciousness about environmental justice issues in general and industrial hog issues in particular, from county to regional to state and national levels and from legislators to academics to others in professional and public circles. Wing noted that the SHER report "generated newspaper articles [and] other media accounts that in turn increased awareness" and promoted the "discussion of environmental justice issues in the rural South" among the public. The establishment of the North Carolina Environmental Justice Network led to the creation of a coalition of communities across the state with the specific goal of raising consciousness around environmental justice issues. The network's mission is "To promote health and environmental equality for all people of North Carolina through community action for clean industry, safe work places and fair access to all human and natural resources. We seek to accomplish these goals through organizing, advocacy, research, and education based on principles of economic equity and democracy for all people."[9]

At UNC the partnership raised awareness by connecting issues of environmental injustice with public health. Public health graduate students who participated in the North Carolina Environmental Justice Summit requested and designed a community-driven graduate-level course, built around presentations from members of communities experiencing environmental injustice, in which students developed research to address the needs of communities. The consciousness-raising among the students and by the students cannot be underestimated. As Wing explained, "Students have contributed every year at the Environmental Justice Summits and they continue to participate in community meetings and have formed strong relationships with community members. They have played essential roles in research. We never would have accomplished what we did without strong support from students with a sense of idealism who are not totally indoctrinated into the system of self-promotion."

Grant expanded on these comments, noting that "students helped the community members understand and value the research component of the partnership and . . . they provided necessary and accurate information without fear and distrust. The students have learned that earning the community's trust is critical to community members' participation."

Based on interviews with participants in the SHER project, this chapter explores the struggle to maintain community quality of life in the context of expanding industrial hog farm operations in Halifax County, North Carolina. Members of the community tended to think in terms of "education" rather than policy change. As Grant noted, "All those issues were policy issues but we just looked at it as being education." Further, "African American communities do not set out to change policy. They set out to protect themselves. Maybe it eventually reaches that level [of policy], but to say that we are going to sit down and strategize on how we are going to change policy, no. That was not part of the plan." The community nevertheless did recognize some policy steps to be very important in order to "change the law" or "get existing laws that were there to protect [the public] be enforced." There was also an astuteness on the part of the community in framing the issue as a health problem. As such, the community put pressure on the county commissioners, "who were supposed to protect the health of their constituents," and framed their concerns "from a health perspective rather than from a farming or any other perspective."

CCT's academic partner, Steve Wing, was more skeptical of the true impact of the research partnership on public policy. He perceived the complex and institutionalized nature of the problems to require broader social change. Nevertheless, he stated that informing policy was "our responsibility" and therefore he "would do it again" in terms of trying to achieve more local, discrete, and immediate changes for the community while also working toward "broader social change." On the other hand, the two policy makers who were interviewed about CCT's role, the research partnership, and the degree of their impact on policy had quite a positive perspective. One lawmaker put it very bluntly by saying, "I don't know if CCT would agree with me or not but I have always said that we have an intensive livestock ordinance in Halifax County due to the efforts of CCT. They started it. I don't recall the county commissioners or the Board of Health in any way being involved until we were brought into the issue by CCT." Later in his interview he elaborated, "It is good to have organizations at the grassroots level that can see things that we might not see in the commissioner boardroom and to know that when they see it they are going to bring it to our attention and it will hopefully be addressed some way."

The SHER project expanded in scope, geographically and topically, under another National Institute of Environmental Health Sciences (NIEHS)–funded, follow-up project called Community Health and Environmental Reawakening, for two consecutive cycles, renewed once in 2000 and again in 2004, allowing the partnership between CCT and Wing to continue. The partnership has remained committed to the original, collective goal of the project to support the community fight over environmental injustices and to recover community environmental values. In addition, the sustainability and the strength of the project activities have been achieved through formation of coalitions with other progressive grassroots organizations in North Carolina.

Notes

1. For more detailed discussion of the larger context behind this case study project and its methodology, see M. Minkler and M. Tajik, "Environmental Justice Research and Action: A Case Study in Political Economy and Community-Academic Collaboration," *International Quarterly of Community Health Education* 26 (2007): 213–31; M. Minkler, V. Breckwich, M. Tajik, and D. Peterson, "Promoting Environmental Justice through Community-Based Participatory Research: The Role of Community and Partnership Capacity," *Journal of Health Education and Behavior* 35 (2008): 119–37.

2. USDA, National Agricultural Statistics Service, "Hogs and Pigs," 2003; USDA, National Agricultural Statistics Service, "Quarterly Hogs and Pigs," 2010; O. J. Furuseth, "Restructuring of Hog Farming in North Carolina: Explosion and Implosion," *Professional Geographer* 49 (1997): 391–403; R. Meadows, "Livestock Legacy," *Environmental Health Perspectives* 12 (1995): 1096–100; T. Ciravolo, D. Martens, D. Hallock, E. Collins, E. Kornegay, and H. Thomas, "Pollutant Movement to Shallow Ground Water Tables from Anaerobic Swine Waste Lagoons," *Journal of Environmental Quality* 8 (1979): 126–30; M. Tajik, M. Muhammad, A. Lowman, K. Thu, S. Wing, and G. Grant, "Impact of Hog Odors from Industrial Hog Operations on Daily Living Activities," *New Solutions* 18 (2008): 193–205; S. Wing and S. Wolf, "Intensive Livestock Operations, Health, and Quality of Life among Eastern North Carolina Residents," *Environmental Health Perspectives* 108 (2000): 233–38; L. Forshell and I. Ekesbo, "Survival of Salmonellas in Composted and Not Composted Solid Animal Manures," *Journal of Veterinary Medicine* 40 (1993): 654–58; K. Donham, "The Impact of Industrial Swine Production on Human Health," in *Pigs, Profits, and*

Rural Communities, ed. K. Thu and E. Durrenberger (Albany: State University of New York Press, 1998); K. Thu, K. Donham, R. Zeigenhorn, S. Reynolds, P. Thorne, P. Subramanian, P. Whitten, and J. Stookesberry, "A Control Study of the Physical and Mental Health of Residents Living Near a Large-Scale Swine Operation," *Journal of Agricultural Safety and Health* 3 (1997): 13–26.

3. USDA, "Environmental Regulation and Location of Hog Production," *Agricultural Outlook,* September 2000, 22.

4. D. Charlston, "Feeding the Hog Industry in North Carolina: Agri-Industrial Restructuring in Hog Farming and Its Implications for the U.S. Periphery," *Sociation Today* 2 (Spring 2004), accessed January 1, 2012, http://www.ncsociology.org/sociationtoday/v21/hog.htm; S. Wing, D. Cole, and G. Grant, "Environmental Injustice in North Carolina's Hog Industry," *Environmental Health Perspectives* 108 (2000): 225–31; S. Wing, G. Grant, M. Green, and C. Stewart, "Community Based Collaboration for Environmental Justice: South-East Halifax Environmental Reawakening," *Environment and Urbanization* 8 (1996): 129–40; A. Ladd and B. Edwards, "Corporate Swine and Capitalist Pigs: A Decade of Environmental Injustice and Protest in North Carolina," in "Global Security: Beyond Gated Communities and Bunker Vision," ed. R. Gould and P. Sutton, special issue, *Social Justice* 29, no. 3 (2002): 26–46.

5. CCT, "Concerned Citizens of Tillery 25th Anniversary," *Tillery,* October 2003.

6. Wing et al., "Community Based Collaboration."

7. Wing et al., "Community Based Collaboration"; Wing, Cole, and Grant, "Environmental Injustice."

8. Minkler and Tajik, "Environmental Justice Research and Action."

9. North Carolina Environmental Justice Network, accessed September 2, 2011, http://www.ncejn.org.

8

The Incineration of Chemical Weapons in Anniston, Alabama

The March for Environmental Justice

Suzanne Marshall, Rufus Kinney, and Antoinnette Hudson

Anniston, Alabama, lies in the southernmost reaches of the Appalachian range, where the mountains merge with the Deep South's old cotton belt. Here in the 1870s entrepreneurs from Britain and the northern United States founded a private company town to produce iron. Later Anniston became a New South industrial city, attracting workers such as African American sharecroppers from the Black Belt of Alabama, whites from the highlands, and European immigrants. During World War I two newcomers arrived—the chemical industry, in the form of the Theodore Swann Company; and the military, at Camp McClellan—and provided jobs. In 1929 Swann manufactured the first polychlorinated biphenyls (PCBs), a seemingly miraculous flame retardant used in electrical transformers and other industries. Monsanto Company bought Swann in the mid-1930s and continued PCB production. With the advent of World War II, McClellan was raised to fort status, and a new military facility, the Anniston Army Depot, was constructed west of town. Over the years waste streams from the military and industry silently contaminated the land, air, water, and bodies of Anniston citizens.[1]

Some people suffered more pollution than others, depending on their proximity to the company plant and the bases. Anniston was divided by race and class. Noble Street, the main business thoroughfare until the early 1940s, ran north-south. To the east lay the Chocolocco Mountains and the elite and middle-class white residential neighborhoods. African Americans, due to Jim Crow segregation, settled mostly on the west side across the railroad tracks, with some black neighborhoods southeast of town. The Swann/Monsanto plant sat just outside the Anniston city limits, the Anniston Army Depot was on the outskirts of the black community, and Fort McClellan and its firing ranges lay to the north of Anniston, where poor and working-class whites also lived. When Swann and later Monsanto (now Solutia) began PCB production, the neighborhoods of Sweet Valley and Cobbtown, situated just across the street from the facility, endured severe contamination from water discharge as well as air pollution. Ultimately, no one escaped the toxic contamination, and PCBs are now ubiquitous in the environment in Anniston.[2]

In 1995, after the PCB contamination became known, residents noticed bad smells; stinking, oddly colored water in the creeks; skin problems; breathing difficulties; and other maladies, but they did not complain. The pay from the corporation and the lack of any warnings about possible industrial hazards subdued questioning or protests. Workers handling PCBs were known to suffer from chloracne, a skin ailment, and from liver problems, but knowledge of that was not widespread. Monsanto did not warn the workers or the community, and by the late 1960s it began actively covering up its pollution. In 2003 health effects were revealed in a lawsuit settled out of court, but in the meantime the PCBs continued to flow.[3]

In the early 1960s Cold War era a lethal new threat came to the Anniston Army Depot, although few people knew it at the time. The army depot became a storage site for some of the nation's chemical weapons, including mustard gas, sarin (GB), and VX nerve agents. Stored in underground bunkers in a remote section of the property, the munitions sat waiting to be used. No public alert system was established to warn of an accident, and no plans existed to destroy the stockpiled weapons in an environmentally safe way. No one questioned this either, mostly because residents were completely ignorant of the threat in their community. If one did seek answers, officials stated that the bunkers were safe and that the Cold War demanded patriotic support for the good of the nation.[4]

In the 1980s, after an international treaty banned chemical weapons, the army visited all eight U.S. storage facilities and announced to the interested public that incineration would destroy the chemical weapons. Citizens at the sites expressed concern about the weapons, the method of destruction, and the lack of democratic involvement they had experienced. People at each site eventually organized local grassroots groups to educate the public, question and monitor the army, and advocate for alternative disposal technologies. Those small groups created a coalition called the Chemical Weapons Working Group (CWWG). Based in Kentucky, they collected information, coordinated actions, lobbied for alternative technologies, and unified the movement. The CWWG also reached out to Russian citizens' groups working on chemical weapons issues. Additionally, the CWWG and state groups made alliances with other local, state, regional, national, and international environmental, social justice, and related organizations. Linkages with such diverse groups provided additional expertise, strategy suggestions, educational ideas, and research sources as well as assistance with media relations and funding. Allies also extended moral support and encouragement during the long and difficult struggles.[5]

In the mid-1990s various organizations working on chemical weapons disposal and PCB cleanup began to consider the issue of environmental racism and justice. The term "environmental racism" was coined in the late 1980s by Benjamin Chavis of the United Church of Christ Commission for Racial Justice, who was involved with a toxic landfill fight in a predominantly poor, African American community in Warren County, North Carolina. Essentially, environmental injustice has come to mean that minority and poor people are subject to pollution more than most and often get the cleanup last, if at all. Environmental justice means that all citizens, regardless of race, income level, or social status, have an equal right to clean air, water, soil, and food. Members of the local CWWG group in Anniston decided to investigate and press the issue of environmental racism and justice in Anniston. What follows is an account of and reflection on the efforts from three local leaders who were involved in the movement against the incineration of chemical weapons.[6]

How Academics and Other Residents Got Involved

In the sections that follow, Suzanne Marshall, Rufus Kinney, and Antoinnette Hudson each describe in their own words their involvement in chemical weapon demilitarization and related issues in Anniston.

Suzanne Marshall

In July 1992 I moved to Anniston to take a job in the History Department at Jacksonville State University and soon became involved in the chemical weapons issue. I saw fliers posted around the town and campus about meetings of a group called Families Concerned about Nerve Gas Incineration (Families Concerned), and at first I tried to ignore them. They sounded ominous, and I could not believe I had unwittingly moved to a town with such a horrendous stockpile of weapons. How could I have been so stupid? Eventually, I decided to attend a meeting and asked if I could observe the group and do oral interviews in anticipation of doing research and an article on grassroots organizing. The group welcomed my idea but asked me to be the secretary since I'd be taking notes anyway. I couldn't refuse. Later I helped gain 501c(3) status for another community organization, Serving Alabama's Future Environment, worked more closely with the CWWG, and attended its annual conference in Washington, D.C.

At one of the CWWG annual conferences Melissa Tuckey, Elizabeth Crowe (both CWWG staffers), Evelyn Yates of Arkansas, and I began to informally discuss the environmental justice issue in Anniston and at all the other sites. We believed it was an issue that the CWWG ought to address formally. Melissa began writing a grant to get research funds. At the same time I received a call from Cassandra Roberts, who needed research done for her Sweet Valley–Cobbtown Environmental Justice Society, recently formed after knowledge of PCBs hit the community in West Anniston. Apparently, Monsanto was arguing that the chemical industry had been built before the Sweet Valley and Cobbtown neighborhoods arrived. Thus the people who had suffered PCB contamination should have realized the dangers and avoided living there. The attorney hired by the group also needed evidence of people's knowledge of the company, the pollution, and the health and environmental effects over the years. I volunteered my time to do oral interviews with community residents and archival research to gather information. This work clearly showed that the neighborhoods had preceded the industry's arrival by nearly a decade, and Monsanto quietly dropped that line of argument.

Research from the project and additional information culminated in a 1996 report, "Chemical Weapons Disposal and Environmental Justice," which was used to educate the public, the media, and our political officials. The report revealed that Anniston's African American population made up 44 percent of the town, in a state where 25 percent of the population was black. The share of African Americans in Anniston was 3.7 times higher than the U.S. average of 12 percent, according to the 1990 census. The poverty rate in the town stood at 24.0 percent, nearly twice the national average of 13.2 percent. The Anniston Army Depot, where the incinerator was being constructed, was close to the black west side and near the historic all–African American Hobson City, with its approximately one thousand residents. Pockets of poor whites and working-class people of both races lived near the depot, and citizens in surrounding areas were virtually ignorant of the incinerator and its potential for problems.[7]

Furthermore, the study showed that a majority of the nation's stockpile sites were in poor, minority communities and that these people stood to suffer a disproportionate impact when the incinerators were burning. The army's own March 1995 "Final Screening Risk Assessment" for the Anniston, Alabama, incinerator listed scores of unpronounceable toxins plus dioxins, furans, vinyl chloride, heavy metals such as lead and mercury, low levels of the nerve agents GB and VX, and to top it off, more PCBs—all of which would be constantly emitted from the stacks during the incinerator's operations. For a community already poisoned by PCBs and other industrial contaminants, an incinerator dumping more pollutants seemed almost criminal and certainly illogical. Why clean up the Monsanto PCB mess if more would be spewed out the army's incinerator stacks? The combination of the existing PCB contamination and the potential pollutants that the chemical weapons incinerator would emit appeared to be a double insult. Also, as the full extent of the PCB contamination became public thanks to Community Against Pollution, we were convinced that Anniston was a classic environmental justice case.[8]

Part of my work as a scholar was to read academic books and journals that covered environmental hazards, toxins, environmental justice, grassroots organizing, and health issues. We collected these documents to serve as a storehouse of information to use with the press in making our case against incineration and for cleaning up PCBs. *Rachel's Hazardous Waste News,* published by the Environmental Research Foundation and edited by Dr. Peter Montague, another scholar-activist, presented scientific information about hazardous substances and other topics in a simple, accurate, documented way. We learned that people living near hazardous waste sites were at increased risk for cancers including leukemia, birth defects, heart problems, neurological problems, respiratory ailments, and skin disorders, to name a few. I had heard of such suffering in my oral interviews, and it almost seemed as if the articles had been written for us and about us.

On June 19, 2000, *U.S. News and World Report* published an article about Anniston and other towns dealing with hazardous chemicals. Specifically, the piece focused on children and how PCBs and toxic contamination might contribute to learning disorders and the increase in learning disorders in the United States. The reporters talked to Jeanette Champion and other activists and residents. In our talks with reporters, we provided the most accurate information and insights that we could, with the goal of publicizing our cause and informing the local community—blacks and whites, poor and affluent—about toxic pollution, PCBs, chemical weapons, and the potential harm to human health and the environment.[9]

In our never-ending effort to ally with other organizations to help educate the community, Serving Alabama's Future Environment (SAFE) sponsored an environmental justice workshop led by Dr. Robert Bullard, an expert and scholar-activist from Clark Atlanta University. It was held on the west side in the black community, a place some white SAFE members, reflecting an ugly remnant of Anniston's racist past, refused to go. However, those who attended learned about environmental racism and injustice, its history, how it affected communities, and how it was operating in Anniston among blacks and poor, working-class whites. The experience helped community members see the need for united action across race and class barriers.

In another alliance, Sweet Valley–Cobbtown Environmental Justice Society, the Southern Organization for Social and Economic Justice, SAFE, Families Concerned, and students and faculty from Jacksonville State and Auburn University administered a citizens' public health survey to current and former residents of Cobbtown and Sweet Valley. We met at the local church and interviewed families about their health and the history of toxic exposure they had endured. The stories of diseases, cancers, and pain moved everyone involved and heightened our awareness of the effects of toxic pollution and its local environmental and health costs.

We then held another bridge-building effort, a community dinner, at the Anniston City Meeting Center to bring local black and white citizens together to learn about environmental racism. The dinner attracted only about fifteen attendees. We were frustrated by the apathy but understood that many people had busy lives, feared the chemical weapons issue, and were in a state of denial about the whole toxic mess. Who could blame them? I often wished I'd never heard about it.

During this time we began to reach out to national organizations. I was already a member of Sierra Club, as was Rufus Kinney. I had also attended a Highlander Research and Education Center workshop in New Market, Tennessee, where I met many activists from across the country, including John McCown, who had recently become the southeast regional environmental justice director for the Sierra Club. He agreed to give a talk to our groups and the public. I then contacted the chair of the Alabama state chapter of the Sierra Club, Peggie Griffin, and offered to get involved on toxic issues. I wound up being elected to the Executive Committee and was able to make the chemical weapons issue and PCBs an area of interest. Another activist, Aaron Head, an African American working on landfill issues, and I became cochairs of the new Environmental Justice Committee. From then on the Sierra Club became heavily active at the state and national levels on this issue; we then helped organize a group for our region named the Coosa Group of the Sierra Club.

We also forged an alliance with the Coosa River Basin Initiative (CRBI), headquartered in Rome, Georgia, an organization that had dealt with PCB contamination from an old General Electric facility. Jerry Brown, the CRBI founder, recognized that people in northern and western Georgia were downwind of the proposed incinerator, and he wanted to fight it. Beth Fraser, CRBI's director during these years, recognized and supported the environmental justice work we were doing. CRBI worked with us, and we got involved in some of their projects as well and learned that mutual assistance builds stronger alliances, which may, eventually, lead to successes. Moreover, this was the first time a neighboring, "downwind" state group joined the CWWG effort.

During these years I became more and more publicly known as an activist. At first I had limited my work to background tasks, research, and writing. I dreaded any public notice or controversy, but of course it came anyway. I often ended up going on television or radio, being quoted by reporters (not always accurately), testifying at hearings, and marching in our protest actions. At the same time I was working toward tenure, finishing my first book, and teaching nine courses a year. During one busy winter I landed in bed with pneumonia, a clear sign to slow down a bit.

Another event, more worrisome than pneumonia, was a purported job threat directed at Rufus Kinney and me. One of our SAFE board members, a very reliable, socially connected person, reported that he had learned we would be fired if we did not "shut up about the incinerator." Both Rufus and I were sole providers for our families, I had not been tenured, and Rufus was not in a tenure-track position at all. We talked about it, wondered how serious it was, and worried. I tended to cave in to my fears around three o'clock in the morning on a regular, sleepless basis. Ultimately, I had a supportive department chair and got tenure and all my promotions. Rufus kept his job, too. My other negative experience occurred during a job search in which I was told in confidence that the hiring committee was concerned about my activism, resulting in no job offer—admittedly, a disappointment. On the positive side, however, my second book, which culminated in my promotion to full professor, was a direct outgrowth of my activism and studies of grassroots environmentalists. I chose to openly write as a scholar-activist and embrace that definition of my professional work, whatever the consequences.

During these same busy years, Rufus Kinney initiated a collaboration with the civil rights organization the Southern Christian Leadership Conference (SCLC). At its founding, Families Concerned's governing board had included black and white members, one of whom was Edward Wood, a member of the Seventeenth Street Missionary Baptist Church, pastored by the Reverend Nimrod Q. Reynolds, a cofounder of the SCLC and an Anniston civil rights activist. Wood learned that Reynolds knew of and took seriously the concept of environmental justice, and Families Concerned periodically met with Reynolds and sent him materials about the issue to share with his congregation. I gave several talks at his church about PCBs, chemical weapons, and environmental racism. Rufus also built on this earlier contact, and Antoinnette was a member of his congregation.

Rufus Kinney

My first memory of the anti-incineration movement was my attendance at a public meeting on the issue in June 1992 at the old Anniston City Meeting Center on Gurnee Avenue. The meeting was sponsored by a group called Families Concerned about Nerve Gas Incineration. I went there tentatively supporting incineration and hoping not to get involved. The place was packed with an angry crowd of over four hundred, most of them quite vocally unhappy about the army's proposed incinerator. Observing the proceedings, I tried to take the army's side in my mind. However, within the first ten minutes it was revealed that the groundbreaking and site preparation had already begun without legal permits and that, contrary to the announced plan of building incinerators at all eight stockpile sites in the continental United States (a ninth site, at Kalama Atoll in the Pacific, was already hosting a prototype facility), the army was seeking funding for the upcoming fiscal year for only two sites: Tooele, Utah, and Anniston, Alabama. The Utah incinerator was already well under construction, with Anniston clearly next in line. There was talk at the meeting of a western regional incinerator in Utah and an eastern one at Anniston.[10]

These revelations gave me that sinking feeling that is familiar to enlightened citizens living in backward places, the sensation of being had and "here we go again"—good old, stupid old Alabama letting itself be used badly by powerful interests, in this case the most powerful of them all, the military-industrial complex. The weight of it hit me right then. I knew that it was going to be a long, uphill struggle and that I would have no choice but to engage in it if I was going to be able to live with my conscience, the reluctant activist who either joins the battle or knows he will have to endure the self-loathing that accompanies inactivity in the face of a real threat to community, family, and self. My instincts proved right. Twelve years later, I am writing this piece while planning an anti-incinerator event! Thus I learned in the early years of the struggle a fundamental lesson that most long-term activists eventually learn: burnout comes early and often, apathy sets in quickly, yet one must persevere in the face of dwindling numbers and declining interest. But in the summer of 1992 the immediate prospects for the community, as it turned out, were good. Local movement leaders did such an excellent job of initially rallying anti-incineration sentiment in Anniston that the movement quickly won an eighteen-month moratorium on construction. Funding was denied for Anniston for the 1992–1993 fiscal year.

By the start of 2000, however, many original leaders as well as rank-and-file supporters had moved away or dropped out of the movement. This left a core of about a dozen activists, all white. We needed to reconnect with Anniston's African American community, which was, by the mid-1990s, learning that it had been hard hit with PCB contamination from the local Monsanto plant. Awareness of environmental justice issues was rising in the community, as Suzanne discussed. We began to realize that Anniston was a classic environmental justice case in progress, and the chemical weapons destruction program also appeared to be an environmental justice problem. Seven of the nine sites scheduled for incinerators, for example, had "a greater percentage of minorities and/or people living below the poverty level in the affected population than the national average, and the sites [had] a history of being the home of polluting industries."[11]

Although the army intended to put incinerators at all nine sites, strong opposition resulted in four of the sites being allowed to install an alternative technology, neutralization, in place of burning. Neutralization uses low temperatures and low pressure and has no toxic emissions. It is significant that the *only* two sites that did not have "a high percentage of people of color or low income populations"—Newport, Indiana, and Aberdeen, Maryland—were the *first* two to be designated for neutralization. Eventually Pueblo, Colorado, and Richmond, Kentucky, were also officially slated for neutralization after years of activists' work. Thus five of the seven sites that have a high percentage of minorities and poor people have incinerated or are incinerating chemical weapons, while the only two that do not have a high percentage of people of color or low-income populations were the *first* two chosen for neutralization. By any reasonable definition, that is the living embodiment of environmental injustice.[12]

Anniston has the largest at-risk population of any of the stockpile sites. Indeed, its metropolitan area is one of the larger ones in Alabama. Thirty-five thousand people live within a five-mile radius of the incinerator, 70,000 within a nine-mile radius, and over 120,000 within twenty miles. There are people whose backyard fences border the incinerator complex property, less than a mile from the burning—Ground Zero, as we call it—and these are neighborhoods, not scattered rural homes.

The media covered the issue extensively. For instance, the cover story in the June 19, 2000, issue of *U.S. News and World Report,* titled "Kids at Risk," featured Anniston. The city also has the dubious distinction of being rated dead last among ninety-six small cities by *Forbes,* which commented, "With the worst overall salary growth as well as the lowest overall technology industry concentration, it's not shocking to see this metro ranked last overall. It also has the fifth-worst score for job growth.

In addition to their weak economy, a local plant has been found guilty of poisoning the community's water with toxins for the past few decades." Things were not going well for Anniston in previous years, either. A *Birmingham News* editorial cartoon in November 2003 summed it up well, depicting a sign on the edge of town reading, "Welcome to Anniston, home of the Anniston Army Depot: Hold your breath!"[13]

To make matters worse, the incinerator is located a short distance off the southwest border of the city—and the prevailing winds blow east and northeast 75 percent of the time, directly over most of Anniston as well as the other communities in Calhoun County: Saks, Weaver, Alexandria, Jacksonville (where I live with my wife and two boys), and Piedmont, near the Georgia line. This huge complex now comprises three incinerators, one each for chemical agents, metal parts, and energetics. Millions of taxpayer dollars were spent on a fourth incinerator, the dunnage incinerator, which was built and then scrapped before the complex ever began operations, a huge waste of public funds. It is one of the world's largest incinerator complexes and will be burning for ten to twelve years even if all goes well and there are no significant delays. Pollution from the stacks will settle on a city that is already severely contaminated by PCBs from Monsanto and other industrial polluters. The 2003 settlement of a class action lawsuit against Monsanto brought several million dollars to be divvied up among some thirty-two hundred beleaguered Annistonians, white and black, who live on the west side of town. But they never got their health restored, and since August 2003 the incinerator has been dropping more PCBs on this devastated community.

One of the litigants in the successful lawsuit against Monsanto was Jeanette Champion. In her mid-fifties, Jeannette is white, from a working-class background, and until recently, a lifelong resident of West Anniston. Jeanette was among the most active and determined incinerator foes of all the West Anniston residents, and her motives are clear in her story in the *U.S. News and World Report* article:

> For more than 40 years, the family shared the big house and two trailers a mile from the Monsanto chemical plant, on the west side of Anniston, Alabama. In time, the 18 of them learned to put up with the rotten-cabbage odor that wafted through town. The plant, after all, is what stood between many resi-

dents and poverty. Besides, there were family troubles: Jeanette Champion . . . is nearly blind and has what she calls a "thinking problem." Her 45-year-old brother, David, can't read or write. Her 18-year-old daughter, Misty Pate, has suffered seizures and bouts of rage. Misty's 15-year-old cousin, Shane Russell, reads at a second-grade level.[14]

I recently sat down with Jeanette and asked her to talk about her opposition to the Anniston chemical weapons incinerator. She spoke at length and at times with emotion, comparing the incinerator to the experiments research institutions do on animals: "I felt they made monkeys out of us. I grew up in Anniston all my life. I was sick all my life. On my daddy's side of the family, everybody died with cancer. His liver was destroyed by PCBs." Jeanette noted that her father never drank. She said that only two people in her extended family have lived beyond the age of fifty-seven and that both of them have had chronic health problems. She added that such problems are endemic to her community:

> I can just go down every street in my community and tell you one person in every house that has died of cancer. Here we are with all these PCBs in our bodies and all our health problems watching all our families die—then they come up with the incinerator to start burning chemicals in the incinerator. I will always be against it because we don't know what kinds of chemicals are coming into our bodies and when we're dead and gone our children—what kind of consequences are they going to be facing? I mean, it's not been a happy life for us—not me, none of my family it's been a happy life for, not none of my children, and I don't want my grandchildren to go through what we went through. I want an end put to it, and the only way you can do that is to get the air clean and just get it out. Stop it.

Speaking further of the incinerator and particularly of the manner in which the citizens of West Anniston are being used, Jeanette continued,

> I did everything in my power to try to stop this incinerator from starting up. We're already exposed to chemicals. Why did they

want to finish us off? Just because people see this thing burning every day and they're getting these rockets finished here, nobody knows what they're doing to somebody's blood while they're doing it. That's why I always thought they wanted to put it here, because this incinerator's doing away with stuff that has PCBs in it. Then they're going to say, "Well, hey—we'll put that incinerator here because these people are already infested with it and they can't blame us because they already got it." Because we're already contaminated, who are you going to lay the blame on?

Jeanette, a person of strong faith who believes that God helps those who help themselves, attended numerous meetings, participated in marches (one where she was a powerful featured speaker), traveled to Montgomery to present her case to the Alabama Department of Environmental Management, wrote letters, put out thousands of fliers, and did all the other things, big and small, that dedicated activists do. At first she advocated for shipping the stockpile to an uninhabited location for disposal, and later she came to support on-site neutralization. Shortly before the incinerator started up, Jeanette's granddaughter Trinity, whose mother, Misty Pate, was a lifelong resident of West Anniston, was born with all her internal organs on the outside of her body except her heart and lungs. Jeanette prayed for a miracle. After two successful surgeries, the first of which was on the day of Trinity's birth, the doctors were preparing to graft pigskin to cover the large hole from which Trinity's external organs protruded. According to Jeanette, the night before the grafting surgery

I was praying and when I went to sleep that night, God showed me that He was going to take his Hands and close her stomach up. He showed me in a vivid dream—it was just His hands closing her stomach up. The doctor told us after the surgery—he said, "I can't understand this, but when we started doing that surgery it was like something just took her little tummy and just pulled it straight together." He said he had never seen that happen before. They never had to use the pigskin and her stomach and belly button look normal. When you're close to God, He's going to show you stuff. He said He wouldn't ever let you walk alone.

At this point in the interview I asked Jeanette to comment on how she has reconciled her faith in God with the fact that after all we had done to stop the incinerator and after so many years of truly dedicated effort on our part, the incinerator was up and operating anyway. Jeanette replied,

> God said He lets it rain on the just and the unjust alike. He don't show no difference in the just and unjust, but on Judgment Day, that's where He'll step in. Our efforts were not in vain—no they were not. If you'll read in Psalms 56 and 11, He says He takes every tear that you shed and He stores them up in a bottle and He writes them down in a book of remembrance, so He knows every reason why. And He don't write them down just for Him to scan through. He writes them down for Judgment Day. Every tear that you've ever shed and every reason why is stored in a bottle.

After all was said and done with the incinerator controversy, Jeanette took definitive action on one matter that she did have control over. She used funds from her settlement in the Monsanto litigation to buy a home in Jacksonville and has rarely visited Anniston since.

While Jeanette Champion's story is that of a courageous white person who helped lead community opposition to the incinerator, her efforts were matched by equally courageous blacks. The need to work with the African American communities of West Anniston was pressing by the spring of 2001, with the army's upcoming grand-opening ceremonies slated for early June. I thought that the idea for a ribbon-cutting ceremony was asinine. So Families Concerned, SAFE, and CRBI proposed a counterdemonstration and march to the gates of the incinerator complex for June 8. Our ribbon *burning* turned out to be one of our most successful actions incorporating the principles of environmental justice. I called the Reverend N. Q. Reynolds and asked him to take part in the protest, and the minister agreed.

I will never forget how tense I was as I drove with my wife, Carolyn, and two children, Bryan and Shannon, to Morrisville Road that morning. I was afraid no one would show up. It was cloudy and looked like rain. No one else was there when we arrived at Shady Acres Trailer Park, our starting point. I feared the worst. But soon the sun came out and people poured in, including CRBI's Mitch Lawson and Matt Jones, with a huge sign, a fifteen-foot-tall walking puppet, noisemakers, and great enthusiasm. Activists carried signs expressing their views: "Welcome to Death Valley," "Don't Poison My Children," and "Mommy, When Can I Go Outside Again?" Just as we were about to start, Reverend Reynolds drove up. He was experienced and committed to environmental justice and led us in prayer. Then we followed him for half a mile in the heat and humidity to the gates of the incinerator. As the group assembled, Reynolds gave an eloquent speech pointing out the environmental injustices of PCBs and chemical weapons disposal in Anniston. I suggested that the army and government officials inside the gate celebrating should move into one of the vacant trailer parks near the depot and "maybe then they'd start taking this whole thing a little bit more seriously." No public servants attended the ribbon cutting or other scheduled "festivities." Hearing about our march beforehand, the governor, local congressman, and both senators stayed away, even though all had been invited by the army. The news coverage of our grassroots effort was all good, a positive achievement despite the loss of having the incinerator built after years of opposition.

After the march Reynolds invited me to attend a meeting at his church, Seventeenth Street Baptist, the following evening. It turned out to be a gathering of the Calhoun County chapter of the SCLC. I learned that the national conference of the SCLC would be held in Montgomery in August, and Reynolds encouraged me to join the SCLC and attend the conference. The group would express its concerns about the weapons and PCBs to the National Board of Directors, on which Reynolds served as recording secretary. I eagerly agreed to this idea and made plans to go to Montgomery that summer.

At the national conference Reverend Reynolds and I presented the board with an anti-incineration resolution that had been drafted by Craig Williams, national spokesperson for the CWWG. The resolution passed unanimously. It called for a halt to incineration and a retrofit of the facility for a safer alternative technology, like the stockpile sites in Maryland and Indiana—sites with more affluent, whiter populations—were getting.

In Montgomery I also met for the first time another civil rights leader from Birmingham, the Reverend Fred Shuttlesworth. I had known of and admired him for decades as an icon of the Civil Rights Movement. He was one of its most unsung heroes until the 2001 publication of Diane McWhorter's Pulitzer Prize–winning book, *Carry Me Home.* Shuttlesworth's physical courage on the front lines of the struggle is legendary, yet he is friendly, engaging, and modest—and a powerful, inspiring speaker. His energy makes you doubt that he is in his ninth decade. I asked him to come to Anniston to address the incinerator and PCB issues there. He agreed. To emphasize their commitment, several other SCLC National Board members, including Bennie Roundtree and Phil Higgs, both North Carolinians, joined Shuttlesworth and Reynolds. They left the meeting in Montgomery and drove two hours in the rain to Anniston to join local protesters at a rally in Zinn Park against toxic pollution, chemical weapons incineration, and racism in the city schools. In an interview with a local television station after the rally Reverend Shuttlesworth stated, "Pollution knows no color and is no respecter of persons. . . . I was real proud to see the white people who were here today and I said if more white people worked with their black sisters and brothers, we'd soon get over most of the problems in this country." Crossing the boundaries of race resulted in a continuing relationship between environmental and civil rights activists in Anniston and, more broadly, in the chemical weapons disposal movement nationally.[15]

Following this event Reverend Reynolds and our organizations worked well together on the incinerator and PCB pollution issues. I've always been something of a hero worshiper, and when I learned that Reynolds was a cofounder of the SCLC with Martin Luther King Jr. and others, he really became one of my heroes. Only through Reynolds were Families Concerned, SAFE, and the CWWG able to bring the full power of the SCLC to ally with our cause.

At the time of the SCLC conference Reynolds used the term "environmental racism" in referring to the situation in Anniston. The local paper, the *Anniston Star,* a rabid supporter of the army's incinerator, criticized Reynolds for using the term because large numbers of working-class whites as well as blacks live on the west side of the city, where all the polluting industries have operated over the years. The *Star's* editorial brought rebuttals from Elizabeth Crowe of the CWWG and from me, in which we defended Reynolds from what we saw as an unfair and mean-spirited attack. There may be more than one valid definition of racism, but among them there is no definition more valid than disproportionate impact, and the fact is that in Anniston the vast majority of the African Americans live on the west side of town, while a considerably smaller percentage of whites do. Also, it is worthy of mention that most of the best educated, most affluent whites, including the editors of the *Star,* live on the east side. Thus Reverend Reynolds's use of the term "environmental racism" was appropriate.[16]

The next major project that Shuttlesworth, Reynolds, and I worked on together was a planned September 2002 march for environmental justice to be held in Anniston. This time almost the entire Board of Directors of the SCLC was involved and in attendance at the event. Antoinnette Hudson, the SCLC Youth, and Calhoun County SCLC, along with the CWWG, Families Concerned, SAFE, CRBI, the national office and several state chapters of the Sierra Club, and international organizations like GAIA (Global Alliance for Incinerator Alternatives) joined efforts to bring the plans to fruition. On a hot Sunday afternoon in early September hundreds arrived to march, over 350 by our count, with great press coverage, including a front-page photo and feature story in the Sunday *New York Times.* One of the most significant things about the march was the number of blacks and whites protesting together in a town that once had been infamous for ugly racism—a Freedom Riders' bus had been burned there in the 1960s.[17]

Accompanied by Antoinnette, I arrived at the Birmingham airport to pick up Reverend Shuttlesworth the day before the march. For fear of getting in an accident with this Civil Rights icon on board, I drove so slowly that finally, in exasperation, he said, "Man, you're going to get us in a wreck if you don't speed up." Somehow we made it in spite of my nerves, and in fact he was delightful company. I pumped him with questions about the old movement days, and he said, "Sometimes I had to push Martin to get him to do certain things." Impressive. It isn't every day that one gets to spend quality time with a living legend of the Civil Rights Movement. Antoinnette and I remember the experience as a genuine honor. Recently the Birmingham, Alabama, airport was renamed after Shuttlesworth, and I am so proud to have known and worked with him. Sadly, Reverend Shuttlesworth died in October 2011.

The march was preceded by a formal press conference at the Anniston City Meeting Center. Reverend Abraham Woods of Birmingham's SCLC gave the march invocation, and veterans of the 1960s Civil Rights Movement acted as marshals, assisted by the local SCLC Youth. Well organized, the crowd set out for a mile-long walk from the meeting center on Noble Street through the heart of Anniston's black business district on West Fifteenth Street to the Martin Luther King Jr. Pavilion at Zinn Park. SCLC organizer Reverend Fred Taylor led the energetic chanting that characterized our march, which was attended by some forty different groups from Alabama, the Deep South, Kentucky, Ohio, Utah, California, and Oregon. Twenty-five students from Piedmont High School, about twenty miles north of the city, marched also. As master of ceremonies, I opened the program: "Welcome to the new civil rights movement of the twenty-first century, and this one is starting out with blacks and whites together!" Indeed, the mix of blacks and whites marching together for safe destruction of chemical weapons and environmental justice was, to me, the greatest thing about that event. Hopefully it will set the stage for future cross-race cooperation and social change in our city and state and beyond.[18]

Among the inspiring speakers were Craig Williams of the CWWG, who emphasized that "pollution is a violent crime, threatening our health and our children," and SCLC president Martin Luther King III, who said, "A nation is judged by how it treats its most precious resource, its children. We must protect our environment." Reverend Shuttlesworth led us in singing "The Battle Hymn of the Republic" and said, "If one person dies of pollution, a little bit of me dies, too." State senator and Alabama SCLC president Charles Steele said, "We must support each other's issues." That day we heard powerful messages, and our program ended with a hilarious but disturbing street theater performance by the young people of the CRBI of Rome, Georgia. By all accounts, the day was a major success.[19]

Antoinnette Hudson

I had been aware of the chemical weapons incinerator issue for quite some time, but I was a busy mother, student, and caretaker of my elderly parents, which took all of my time. In 2000 I became involved after listening to Suzanne Marshall, Rufus Kinney, and others on the news and at school. They spoke of the dangers of incineration and the problems with PCB pollution. Their knowledge and passion inspired me to help in any way that I could.

After becoming involved I was asked to help organize a march to protest the incinerator, raise awareness of PCBs, and call for environmental justice. The organization of such a protest required time, contacts, and foot soldiers who were willing to go into the different communities and inform people about the event and its purpose. As a member of the Calhoun County chapter of the SCLC and the mother of one of its youth members, I asked the young people to spend a Saturday passing out leaflets—door to door. Jessica Elston, Toccara and Tonarra Welch, and my son Marcellus Hudson stepped forward and took on the task.

On the Saturday before Labor Day weekend we gathered along with Suzanne Marshall and Rufus Kinney at the Seventeenth Street Baptist Church. We divided up the neighborhoods and set off in pairs to walk and hand out our information. It was a sunny, hot, humid morning, but everyone was enthused about the project. We all went to our assigned streets and stuck the leaflets in doors, and if someone was on the porch or out washing the car, we stopped to talk to them if they were willing to listen. We walked the neighborhoods for more than four hours. Later some of us would leaflet mailboxes from our cars to speed the process and alert more people.

During our canvassing, we learned that many people we encountered knew only what the local paper, the *Anniston Star,* wrote about the issue. The paper favored the incinerator project and argued that there was no danger, it would be easy to evacuate the city, and citizens would be protected and not suffer any harmful injuries in case of an accident. Some of the SCLC youth reported meeting people who said they'd never heard of the incinerator issue or PCBs. After a half day of work, we felt we had at least informed people about the issues and given them a different perspective. We hoped they would respond by attending the march and rally. To reward the SCLC volunteer youth, we went out for pizza and relaxed in the air conditioning.

To reach more people, I turned to the pulpit. I knew that in order to contact most of the African American community, the churches would have to become involved. Historically it has been the church that we have turned to for help, whether for spiritual or secular matters. In Anniston the Seventeenth Street Baptist Church has been the most influential. It was founded in 1880 and is located near the heart of the African American community, at West Seventeenth Street and Cooper Avenue in West Anniston. The church's congregation took pride in its many members who were employed by the school board as teachers and in its nurses, doctors, dentists, and lawyers. The church was also home to widows, unemployed people, and blue-collar workers, all of whom felt the sting of segregation and inequality. To combat segregation, the congregation often sought strong, well-educated ministers. For instance, in 1939 the church called a young man from Montgomery, Dennis Comer "D. C." Washington. Not only was Reverend Washington an effective pastor to his flock, he was also very active in the civil rights issue. Shortly after arriving in Anniston, he began a campaign to get the members of the church registered to vote. During the famous Montgomery bus boycott, he traveled to that city to lend his support. His dedication and activism earned the respect and loyalty of the congregation and paved the way for his successor, Reverend Nimrod Q. Reynolds.[20]

Seventeenth Baptist called Reverend Reynolds to the pulpit in 1960, and he quickly became a committed preacher and an activist in the community and the Civil Rights Movement. He cofounded the Southern Christian Leadership Conference and helped establish the local Calhoun County chapter in Anniston. Often he put himself in harm's way to test the newly passed desegregation laws. He will be remembered most for leading the fight to desegregate the Anniston Public Library—an act of great conviction and bravery. It was also an act that resulted in pain. He was badly beaten by segregationists who hated the changes of the time and hated him for forcing them to accept a political system and society that were ending a way of life that they considered their birthright based on skin color. Gradually, the white power structure begrudgingly accepted that African Americans were part of the community.[21]

I served as a sort of liaison between Reverend Reynolds and the environmental groups with which I was involved. I could call Reverend Reynolds or visit his office and relay messages, get his advice, and coordinate the march planning. Reynolds was very busy as national secretary of the SCLC, a full-time minister, and the husband of a wife who was ill. He gave us his full support, and we carried out the nuts and bolts of the event. I contacted all the African American churches in town by phone and asked each minister to participate in the march and to encourage his members to do the same. Although most were eager to get involved, some were not. To get them on board I asked Reverend Reynolds to use his influence, and he did. I also talked with friends, neighbors, and relatives to spread the word. Of course, the SCLC at the county, state, and national levels contributed enormously to our project, as Rufus has explained above.

We also needed the press to pay attention to our event and our messages. To assist in that effort, I lined up a number of people for a *New York Times* reporter, Rick Bragg, to interview. He had done a very good article a few years before on the Sweet Valley–Cobbtown PCB problems and was familiar with local issues due to that experience. He was also a native of rural Calhoun County. Suzanne Marshall, Rufus Kinney, and I met Rick one afternoon, drove him on the "toxic tour" we had developed over the years, and took him to the West Anniston homes of a retired African American dentist and African American teacher so he could talk with them. He also did some of his own investigating. One of his interests was how elderly African Americans living close to the incinerator site felt about their safety. Later, at the time of the 2002 march, an article by Bragg and another reporter appeared, along with a photo of the march itself. Many other news programs and newspapers also covered the events. The success of the march was a combined effort of the CWWG, the SCLC, many volunteers, and the research and education that Suzanne and Rufus provided.[22]

The help of academics was very important to communities such as Anniston. First, they were able to gather and interpret the hard-to-find data that were needed to sustain the protest against the incinerator and Monsanto; second, academics increased community protestors' confidence in their ability to lead. Because of the participation by academics, most of the people directly affected by the PCBs and the incinerator in Anniston felt they were not alone in their fight, and a bond of trust grew between the community leaders and the academics of Jacksonville State University. The trust that developed was possible because Suzanne and Rufus let the people of the community know that whatever they had to say or whatever they felt was important and worthy of consideration. Suzanne and Rufus made themselves available for community meetings, whether they were in a public place or someone's home. The community leaders saw them as part of the struggle and as part of the community, not as faculty members of a university.

Although Suzanne and Rufus won the trust of the community, some community members did not have the same respect and trust for the U.S. Army or the federal government. Reverend Carlos Woodard, executive vice president of the local chapter of the SCLC, was very disappointed with how the army and the U.S. government handled the issue of the incinerator. During an interview, Reverend Woodard said, "In my opinion, I do not think the army was interested or listening to what we had to say about the incinerator. Their so-called safety programs are inadequate, especially for people living in this high-risk area, the Pink Zone. They should have honestly considered a safer method since our community is already sick from all the contamination from the PCBs and since so many of those people living closest to the Anniston Army Depot have been infected by the PCBs."[23]

Reverend Woodard was not happy with the way Anniston has been treated by the military, and he believes the march was a success. According to Reverend Woodard, "Education is the greatest tool we have in letting people know that the incinerator is a very dangerous element in our community. SCLC will continue to fight for what is right, to bring about some kind of change, and to educate people just in case the worst happens." All who participated in this effort agreed that the many hours and days of hard work had paid off with lots of press coverage and with both African Americans and whites attending the march.[24]

Reflections by Rufus Kinney

The basic idea of exploring the subject of academics who are social activists is quite appealing to me, first, because I am one, and second, because I do not know of any such study being undertaken in the past. My main observation is that having spent twenty-six years as a college English teacher at two universities in Alabama, I have seen very few activists among the large number of academics I have known. Early in my career I posed a question to a more experienced colleague: Why do so few university professors get involved? I'll never forget his answer: "Didn't you know? Most college professors are scared to death to take a public stand on any controversial issue. They hide in their ivory towers and are among the biggest cowards you'll ever meet."

That was in the early 1980s. I recalled the campus unrest of the 1960s, and it seemed to me that professors everywhere were activists in those days. My own religion professor, who was also my undergraduate mentor, was active in the Civil Rights Movement. But come to think of it, there weren't many others, even though my professors, virtually without exception, were excellent teachers and scholars and wonderful human beings. Nor were they a bunch of conservatives. A clear majority of my professors were moderates and liberals, and I would never think of calling them cowards. Yet in general I do recognize some validity to what my colleague said.

As an academic and activist this has been a source of long-standing frustration to me. I have often felt that if we are going to teach John G. Woolman, Emerson, Thoreau, and Frederick Douglass—and admire them—then it is incumbent on us to live their message in the present. If democracy needs to be reinvented, let's be the ones to reinvent it—we who have specialized knowledge of the best that has been thought, written, researched, and put into action in our country.

My students would know from my reputation that I am very sincere about this, and I might note that opportunities to discuss the incinerator have come up fairly frequently in some of my classes. I might also add that the administration of Jacksonville State University has never once interfered with my activism. The academic freedom I have enjoyed for over twenty years at Jacksonville State is one of the things I admire most about the university. In fact, the current president invited me to be a guest on his weekly radio program to give the opposing view. Let us not forget that discussing, debating, and sharing ideas is the cornerstone of a functioning democracy, and universities and university faculty should function with this key principle in mind. In my freshman composition class, for instance, students are required to write expository essays on current issues. Similarly, in my speech classes current issues are frequently debated and used as subjects of informative and persuasive speeches. In my American literature survey courses a good deal of the material directly relates to issues involving both the history and the meaning of democracy. It is not a stretch to discuss the incinerator from time to time in such classes.

Notes

1. Suzanne Marshall, "Chemical Weapons Disposal and Environmental Justice" (unpublished manuscript, Berea, KY, 1996).

2. Suzanne Marshall, "Even the Houses Die: The Poisoning and Demise of Sweet Valley, Alabama," *Tributaries: Journal of the Alabama Folk Arts Council* (1998): 56–68; Nancy Beiles, "What Monsanto Knew," *Nation,* May 29, 2000, 1–5.

3. Marshall, "Even the Houses Die."

4. Marshall, "Chemical Weapons Disposal."

5. Marshall, "Chemical Weapons Disposal."

6. Robert Paehlke, ed., *Conservation and Environmentalism: An Encyclopedia,* Garland Reference Library of Social Science, vol. 645 (New York: Garland, 1995).

7. Marshall, "Chemical Weapons Disposal."

8. Commander, U.S. Army Chemical Demilitarization and Remediation Activity, "Final Screening Risk Asessment, Research, Conservation, and Recovery Act, Part B, for the Anniston Chemical Demilitarization Facility," Anniston Army Depot, Anniston, Alabama, RA No. 39–26–1399–95, Aberdeen Proving Ground, MD, March 1995, table 1.

9. Sheila Kaplan and Jim Morris, "Kids at Risk: Chemicals in the Environment Come Under Scrutiny as the Number of Childhood Learning Problems Soars," *U.S. News and World Report,* June 19, 2000, 47.

10. Marshall, "Chemical Weapons Disposal."

11. Marshall, "Chemical Weapons Disposal."

12. Marshall, "Chemical Weapons Disposal."

13. Kaplan and Morris, "Kids at Risk"; "Special Report: 5 Worst Small Places," *Forbes,* May 9, 2002, accessed June 19, 2010, http://www.forbes.com/2002/05/09/bestplaces.html; Scott Stantis, editorial cartoon, *Birmingham News,* November 22, 2003, C2.

14. Kaplan and Morris, "Kids at Risk."

15. Diane McWhorter, *Carry Me Home: Birmingham, Alabama, the Climactic Battle of the Civil Rights Revolution* (New York: Simon and Schuster, 2001); "SCLC Leaders Speak at Anniston Rally: Resolution Opposing Chemical Weapons Incineration in AL Adopted Unanimously at National Convention," *Common Sense,* September 2001, 1; ABC News, "Incinerator Protest," segment broadcast August 7, 2001, WBMA, Birmingham, AL.

16. "Environmental Racism? Flawed Argument Is a Barrier to Resolution" *Anniston Star,* August 9, 2001, A4; Elizabeth Crowe, letter to the editor, *Anniston Star,* September 7, 2001, A4; Rufus Kinney, letter to the editor, *Anniston Star,* August 28, 2001, A4.

17. Rick Bragg and Glynn Wilson, "Burning of Chemical Arms Puts Fear in the 'Wind,'" *New York Times,* September 15, 2002, A1.

18. Joe McCary, incinerator rally videotape, 2002, copy in Rufus Kinney's possession.

19. McCary, incinerator rally videotape.

20. Harold Washington, interview by Antoinnette Hudson, 2005.

21. Washington interview.

22. Bragg and Wilson, "Burning of Chemical Arms."

23. Carlos Woodard, interview by Antoinnette Hudson, 2005.

24. Woodard interview.

9

Expertise and Alliances

How Kentuckians Transformed the U.S. Chemical Weapons Disposal Program

Robert Futrell and Dick Futrell

In 1984 the U.S. Army's Program Manager for Chemical Demilitarization (PMCD) declared the existing U.S. stockpile of chemical weapons obsolete and announced plans to incinerate the weapons in the eight communities that housed them. Before proceeding with this plan, the army held a public hearing in each of the eight communities, but few residents attended. Madison County, Kentucky, was an exception, where more than two hundred curious citizens came to find out what the army had in store for them. They got no clear answers. What the army intended as a perfunctory hearing to begin the incineration program sparked fears in local residents, who began to organize against incineration.

The controversy that began at that first hearing has now gone on for more than two decades. For much of the dispute, the relationship between citizens and PMCD was adversarial. Public meetings continually devolved into confrontations between the public and army officials and their experts. Citizens wanted to know how safe incinerating the world's most deadly substances in their community would be. Would it affect their health and the environment? What if there were an accident? Are there alternatives to incinerating the weapons? They came to believe their concerns mattered little to PMCD. They faced a bureaucracy committed to incineration, with army officials and their technicians all conveying the same message: Just trust us. We're the experts.

But many citizens did not trust the army and organized to fight the army's plan. They lobbied politicians and regulators, marshaled experts against incineration, and strategically wielded sophisticated technical arguments about the human and environmental impacts of burning the deadly agents. Eventually they forced the army to back off its plans for incineration in Madison County, Kentucky, and pursue safer, more environmentally sound ways to neutralize the chemicals.

How did Madison County activists become powerful players in such a complex political and technological dispute? This chapter draws on documentary analysis, participant observation, interviews, and conversations with activists and officials done periodically between 1991 and 2008. We describe how citizens have been doggedly persistent in interjecting their opinions and perspectives against incineration at various political levels. They have also been adept at collaborating with scientists and others to produce technically sound and scientifically defensible claims against the incineration project. They have developed a broad set of alliances among activists, academic scientists, technicians, and engineers, as well as lawyers, regulators, lobbyists, and legislators. Their experiences over the course of the dispute have coalesced into forms of knowledge and a quality of expertise held only by the activists, which now legitimate them as indispensable players in the U.S. chemical weapons disposal program.[1]

Chemical Weapons Disposal: The Controversy

Safely destroying chemical weapons is an exceedingly complex technical, social, and political task. The chemical compounds used in the weapons are among the world's most lethal substances. In pure form they are odorless and colorless, and minute amounts can kill within minutes. They are among the most feared military weapons, but they have rarely been deployed in actual battles. Most of the weapons in the U.S. stockpile have been stored in earthen bunkers, unused for decades.

The weapons include rockets, land mines, artillery and mortar shells, bombs, spray tanks, and bulk containers of nerve agent. Agent stored in bulk containers simply needs to be drained and the compounds neutralized. However, rockets are loaded with chemical agent packed close to fuses, explosive charges, and rocket propellant. Destroying them requires a complex and risky process of separating the explosives and propellants from the chemical prior to destruction. Incineration adds the risks of a high-temperature, high-pressure combustion process and carries the possibility of a catastrophic explosive accident. Even when the incineration process functions normally there may be long-term health risks from the release of persistent toxins such as dioxin produced during the burn.[2]

These risks are coupled with a great deal of social and political complexity. Foremost, people are very afraid of deadly toxins such as chemical weapons. In *A New Species of Trouble,* Kai Erikson observes that chemical toxins "clearly have a special place on the human list of horrors. . . . [They are] furtive, invisible, unnatural. In most forms it [a chemical toxin] moves from the interior, turning the process of assault inside out and in that way violating the integrity of the body. . . . Toxic poisons provoke a special dread because they contaminate, because they are stealthy and deceive the body's alarm systems, and because [depending on their concentrations] they can become absorbed into the very tissues of the body and crouch there for years, even generations, before doing their work."[3] Add to this concerns about how (or if!) the toxins can be handled safely. The price of destroying toxic chemicals by any means is also enormous, and delays in the process have increased costs by hundreds of millions of dollars. Treaty obligations and deadlines set by the International Chemical Weapons Convention also loom over the U.S. disposal program.

In February 1984 the army announced its plans to incinerate chemical weapons stored in Madison County with a small, one-inch advertisement on the classifieds page of the local paper. The ad referred all interested citizens to a "scoping meeting concerning the destruction of chemical munitions at the Blue Grass Army Depot." It was the sort of announcement that is easy to miss. But a local reporter at the paper spotted it and called friends to ask what they knew of chemical weapons at the depot. She found that "no one knew a thing, but they were plenty interested so we all called other friends and within the week we had sparked some curiosity in the thing. We were going to the meeting." And go they did. More than two hundred citizens packed into the depot's small, crowded cafeteria, a far cry from the scoping meetings the army held at the seven other storage sites, where only a handful of residents had attended.[4]

But the Blue Grass Army Depot, with its history of secrecy, accidents, misinformation, and denials of wrongdoing, had eroded its standing in the county. According to an activist, many were stunned to hear that the depot in their backyard had more than seventy thousand chemical weapons, much less that they would be destroyed there. "To say we were surprised is an understatement. We were shocked that they [chemical weapons] were even out there. . . . No one had any clue we were living with those things, a mile from the middle school, communities, people living all around. It's scary. Then they say, 'Oh, by the way, we have all these weapons out here, they're old and leaking and dangerous so we're going to burn them.' Talk about a jolt. It was a little hard to take and we had to figure out what was going on."[5]

Expecting this to be yet another perfunctory meeting, officials seemed wholly unprepared for a large turnout. The army billed the meeting as an opportunity for public input, then had its technicians speak about their plans for more than two hours in almost undecipherable technical language. When citizens were finally given the floor they asked straightforward questions: How safe would incineration be? What toxic residues would be left over from burning the weapons? What would happen in the case of emergencies? What long-term health risks did incineration pose? PMCD officials appeared unprepared and could not answer many of the questions citizens raised. They repeatedly fell back on the uninspiring message to "trust us and everything will be fine."

This message did not allay concerns. As one attendee explained, "Going into that meeting . . . a lot of us were skeptical about the plan, but that didn't mean we were necessarily opposed to it. But they came in, treated us like children, as if we didn't know a thing. Then that little lady asked them the simplest question—What's left over after the weapons are burnt? They couldn't answer. That's about the time when we started thinking a little harder that this might be a really bad idea." Another citizen at the first meeting recalled that "it wasn't a hot, fireball meeting. It was a group assembled, asking very reasonable questions, and it was obvious that these guys didn't have the answers. They didn't come prepared [and] the impression of the group was that these guys didn't know what they were talking about. That meeting was the beginning of the concerns."[6]

Learning and Playing the Game

Local citizens quickly began to organize. After the meeting an eclectic group of residents from the county's two main cities bordering the depot, Richmond and Berea, began gathering under the name Concerned Citizens of Madison County (CCMC). The core group included bankers, college professors, doctors, lawyers, carpenters, environmental and civil rights activists, artists, and musicians. They wanted a voice in decisions on the project and believed they would have one. The first army meeting had been to initiate the programmatic environmental impact statement (PEIS) for the disposal program. Federal regulations require public participation in the development of environmental impact statements so that local views are included in the analysis of environmental and social impacts of the project, although the regulations do not specify what the exact nature of participation is to be. Madison Countians at the meeting had hoped to give meaningful input on decisions; they instead experienced a highly controlled, adversarial process in which the army marginalized and delegitimized them.

Between 1984 and 1988 army officials held a series of public meetings for the PEIS. CCMC wanted to ensure the citizens would have a voice in PMCD's decisions. But locals soon concluded that the army was only going through the motions of public involvement to meet their legal obligations, with no real intent to meaningfully involve them. The army controlled information about the project, and its relationship with citizens was largely mechanistic and dismissive. According to one CCMC member, "In the early period . . . the community was getting more and more concerned that a decision had already been made. The whole thing was very frustrating . . . because things weren't getting more clarified but . . . more obfuscated, if anything." Another recalled, "They would waltz into every public meeting with their cadre of engineers and staff acting like we were stupid hayseeds with no chance of understanding them. We were the ones asking questions that they couldn't or wouldn't answer with anything more than a 'Don't worry about the details. We'll take care of them.' They were like a parent scolding a kid who keeps asking why something is the way it is saying, 'Because I said so.' That kind of answer is just not acceptable."[7]

Activists tried to play a numbers game. They felt that if they could turn out large numbers of local citizens to the meetings to raise pointed questions about the project, then the army and elected officials would take notice and bring them in as participants. "I know we felt, at first, that if we could get the word out about this deal [the disposal plan] and get people to stand up, confront the army, especially at those scoping meetings, then they'd get the message. You know, power of the people, turn 'em out and they'd cave. That's the democracy tack, right? Well, the army is obstinate. One way, one-sided. They didn't cave. We learned that fairly quickly."[8]

As the conflict spiraled, some in CCMC realized that numbers alone would not win the day. They broke away to form a new group, Common Ground, and began to closely inspect the rationale underlying incineration.

> We wanted to be versed as much as possible in the details of the plan so when we faced them [the army] again, we could point to the specifics of the plan and say, "We don't think this will work" or "This seems a little too risky." I mean, it was like we were playing on their turf and we thought if we wanted them to listen we had to try to speak their language . . . to play their game. At least that's the way we thought about it in the beginning. . . . The problem was, we thought they would listen.[9]

Deconstructing the technical and scientific language of the army's reports was daunting, even though some members of the groups were experts in health sciences, social sciences, and engineering. The two groups also received help in deciphering the technical data from researchers at Eastern Kentucky University and Berea College. Together they identified deficiencies in the army's plans and strategized about how to present these at the army's public meetings.

> If you go back and look at these public meetings between '84 and '88, what you'll see is an average Joe like me getting up and saying whatever, followed by Dr. So and So saying whatever from the medical field and let's say an engineer getting up, then John getting up, then an economist getting up and then another activist. We mixed it that way on purpose to create a legitimate image of the integration of the common citizen and this pool of experts in different fields all basically sending the same message . . . to give it that diversity, credibility, speaking with one voice kind of thing—the average person, the housewife and the nurse, the activist and the M.D.[10]

By 1988 Common Ground and CCMC had become very adept at mobilizing hundreds of citizens for public meetings, raising criticisms about the incineration plan, and lobbying officials. In fact, most Kentucky politicians at every level had come out against chemical weapons incineration in Madison County. These efforts delayed the program but did not change it. In 1988 the army released its final PEIS with its incineration plans unchanged.

The decision was a blow to CCMC and Common Ground but not their last chance. PMCD soon announced a second environmental impact statement phase, called the site-specific EIS, or SSEIS, which would focus on impacts for each site individually instead of lumping them all together as in the 1988 assessment. Activists hoped that this phase would show how unworkable incineration was for Madison County, especially given how close the depot is to neighborhoods and schools. Instead, PMCD declared that the new study would not reassess incineration but instead would assess the best location on the depot to build the incinerator.

Common Ground activists began a new, proactive effort to challenge the science of incineration. Responding to advice from a congressional staffer, they also began a search for alternatives to incineration technology. Activist leader Craig Williams recalled, "This staff guy for [Senator Mitch] McConnell said, 'You can say no all you want, but if you don't have something to replace it you're not going to get anyplace.' He's the one that created that concept in our organization that you just can't say no. That you have to say no to something and have something to replace it or else. . . . You know, everybody is saying no about something."[11]

They also made some organizational changes. In 1990 Common Ground members organized the nonprofit Kentucky Environmental Foundation (KEF) to coordinate the Kentucky protest and support the activism that had emerged at the other disposal sites around the nation. In 1991 they drew activists from the other sites into a political coalition they called the Chemical Weapons Working Group (CWWG).

Instead of waiting and reacting to the army's public meetings, Kentucky activists organized their own public meetings, one of which drew several hundred people to hear international experts on incineration criticize the army's program. KEF/CWWG also worked with local engineers, chemists, environmental and social scientists, and incineration technicians to prepare a formal position paper titled "The Citizens' Solution," which systematically detailed technical arguments against incineration and listed possible alternatives. They presented the paper to PMCD in an April 1991 meeting that drew more than a thousand people. "It was the first time that the citizens put together their views in a very aware kind of way [and] dealt with the alternatives [to incineration] that are available according to data from Greenpeace and others," a KEF staff member recalled. "It was very empowering. We were getting better at playing them in their own game. Of course the question is, to what effect?"[12]

Between 1991 and 1994 KEF/CWWG also used their technical arguments for alternatives to incineration in renewed lobbying efforts with federal legislators. Their efforts, combined with massive cost overruns and delays in PMCD's incineration program, gave Congress grounds to divert millions of dollars originally set aside for the incineration program and force the army to study alternative technologies. But again, the army concluded in early 1994 that it would proceed with incineration.

That might have been the last straw, if not for two crucial revelations that amplified citizens' claims and brought new federal scrutiny of the incineration program. In late 1994 the army admitted that it had overestimated the deterioration rate of the chemical weapons stockpile by more than a hundred years. This was a major blow to PMCD's push for incineration, which they had long justified with claims that the munitions were breaking down, they would pose a grave threat of leaks and explosions within a decade, and incineration was the only technology that could destroy the weapons in time. Craig Williams summed up the worries of many when he asked, "If the army can't be correct in a simple mathematical problem, how can we expect them to oversee such an immensely complicated and dangerous project? Either they're totally incompetent or this is part of a larger pattern of deception. Either way, it stinks."[13]

The second revelation came from Steve Jones, a highly commended safety officer overseeing the prototype chemical weapons incinerator being tested at the storage depot in Tooele, Utah. Jones found more than a thousand safety-code violations and fifteen components of the facility that would be rated as "failing deficiencies during an Army inspection, [including] program management, inspection program, abatement plan, hazard analysis, safety training, respirator protection program, accident/incident reporting, monitoring program and seven others." There were even incidents in which chemical agent was vented directly into the atmosphere, something citizens had long worried about. The allegations piqued concern among citizens and legislators at each disposal site. The army rejected Jones's statements and quickly fired him, but later audits by the army and independent firms found his assessments to be accurate. An audit by Science Applications International Corporation listed 3,013 separate hazards at Tooele. An investigation by the Army Safety Center into 119 of Jones's allegations confirmed over half of them. A study by the army inspector general listed numerous deficiencies in safety, training, and reporting rules; violations of standard army procedures; and failure to capture and relay to Tooele "all lessons learned (in particular environmental) from [prototype] operations and design." Overall, the inspector general found "inherent environmental problems associated with the design and operation" of the Tooele facility.[14]

In the wake of these allegations, KEF/CWWG organized rallies, press conferences, and town meetings in each community near the chemical weapons stores to publicly denounce the incineration program. In Madison County more than four hundred people marched through downtown Richmond. Responding to these pressures, the army and the House Armed Services Committee began investigations, which again delayed the program. The delay gave citizens added time to speak with legislators and their staffers, and they began lobbying to have the disposal program taken out of PMCD's control. Craig Williams explained, "We knew that we had to get it out of [PMCD's] hands. It's the only way of changing things. They were committed [to incineration] and there was no turning that around. They wanted nothing to do with the public, with their ideas, with anything that compromised their mandate to destroy the weapons and do it by incineration. The only way to get them to stop and listen was through Congress, because they control the mandate and they control the budget. Take away the mandate, stop the money, things happen."[15]

Congress responded in 1997 by creating a new program, the Assembled Chemical Weapons Assessment (ACWA), to evaluate and demonstrate at least two technological alternatives to incineration, for use in Kentucky and Colorado.[16] By separating ACWA from the army branch overseeing incineration, Congress alleviated some of the citizens' deep suspicions about the project. Craig Williams explained, "We were able to argue effectively that the program should be moved out of their hands because they are so committed to incineration in the first place and because they did such a lousy job in the first phase. . . . It's a tried and true fact that the army's incineration people can't be trusted to be open to citizens. We've strengthened [the citizens'] position by being able to pull this off at a different level of the bureaucracy." Responding to citizens' calls for more participation, Congress mandated that ACWA make collaborative decisions that included input from military officials, regulators, scientists, and citizens.[17]

These changes produced constructive, open dialogue and a wide-ranging study of alternative disposal technologies in a public involvement process called the Dialogue on Assembled Chemical Weapons Assessment. The dialogue involved citizen delegates from all eight chemical weapons disposal communities as well as state regulators, Department of Defense staff, U.S. Environmental Protection Agency staff, and representatives from national activist organizations. In face-to-face, consensus-based meetings, they developed the technical and social criteria for assessing new technologies in just three months and gave input at each stage of testing. In 2003 the dialogue selected neutralization as the destruction technology for Kentucky and Colorado.

Legitimacy through Expertise and Alliances

Legitimacy lies at the root of this conflict. By legitimacy we mean the acceptance of citizens as worthy contributors and active support for them to carry out that role. Citizens should be treated as knowledgeable participants with constructive questions and sound ideas about how chemical weapons will be dealt with in their community. Government agencies should create opportunities for citizens to be meaningfully involved and should provide them resources; they should partner with citizens rather than fighting them. In the army's eyes citizens had little claim to legitimacy, and so they were not meaningfully involved in decisions. PMCD had a mandate to destroy the weapons. They saw the risks of chemical weapons incineration as technical problems for technicians to solve. They gave the impression that citizens could not understand the technical issues and were incapable of offering constructive input, a common perception in technological disputes. They treated citizens as obstructionists who stood in the way of their fulfilling orders, and so they limited meaningful citizen involvement. The question, then, is how did citizens earn the legitimacy to become powerful players in the dispute?[18]

One of the most remarkable features of the citizens' efforts is simply how long they have been at it. As KEF's John Capillo explained, "One of the things we've been successful at is to have a presence that outlasted the expectation of the bureaucracies." Indeed, few protests endure more than two decades with the persistent vigor of Common Ground, KEF, and CWWG. Fatigue, burnout, uncertainty, and limited resources stand in the way of citizen persistence. These issues have certainly challenged citizen-activists in the chemical weapons dispute. Activists felt that PMCD knew this and played a holdout strategy many times, expecting to "just weather the storm [of opposition] and it would be gone in a year and a half. Delays are partly because of how bureaucracies work, but partly because it has also been one of their strategies. I mean, 15, 20 years later the army is saying . . . 'All we have to do is, if we get this under the table, those guys they won't last.' They don't know the issue, don't know the history, then we're still around turning up information that makes them red in the face. They don't get it. We're here and ain't going anywhere."[19]

Fear, grounded in what many refer to as their "commonsense intuitions," drove their diligence. "At its root, this whole thing is driven by the sense that this is crazy. Our common sense that told us it's probably not a good idea to burn the most lethal chemicals on the planet in the middle of a populated area. But yet you have this bureaucracy saying this is fine. It didn't make sense then, and certainly doesn't now."[20]

But the activists did not persist on intuition alone. They sought experts to clarify the risks and realities of incineration. John Capillo explained, "There's the distinction between scientific knowing and intuitive knowing. . . . We were able to empower citizens to know what they knew. Susie says, 'You're going to burn this stuff and make all this stuff come out the stack? That doesn't make sense.' Well, experts that are with us say, 'That's right and you're right in what you know.' I think that's the most critical part of the relationship between academics and activists. To play around in the area of what assumptions you bring to the issue and change some of those assumptions, strengthen sensibilities."[21]

The experts that activists connected with throughout the dispute legitimized their intuitions by lending credibility to positions taken against army technicians. Activists used this feeling of credibility as a driver for their continued fight, in spite of the many obstacles they faced. Craig Williams observed,

> The professors, the technical experts, all the folks with letters
> behind their names, credentialize and give substance to the

commonsense intuition. So you get people from EKU [Eastern Kentucky University] and Berea College and so on, these people came into this thing early on . . . so many people from way back, still engaged in this thing. They brought different types of expertise into the discussion that kind of propped up and gave security to the people's basic intuitive knowledge which said, "This is crazy." And that is critical at the activist level of things . . . where Susie or John says, "Wait a minute, this doesn't sound right," and there's a chemist also saying you've got something there. It's a feeling that their commonsense instinctual perception of what's going on is credible at a higher level. That's important for keeping folks engaged.[22]

As the controversy developed, citizens were forced to focus on crafting complex technical arguments against incineration in Madison County and using those arguments to lobby officials at all governmental levels, including Congress. They required constant information about political activity in Washington, D.C., and the Kentucky legislature, changes in the army and ACWA, and changes in the technical landscape of chemical waste disposal. Staying abreast of these issues fell to a small cadre of activists who formed KEF and CWWG to act as a watchdog over the program and advocate for local concerns. As John Capillo said, "It's a political job with a scientific vernacular. One of the things that we have been able to do is grab this commonsense knowledge of the people and, with the help of others, fuse it with science and make it part of the decision-making process with PMCD, ACWA and Congress."[23]

Citizen Experts

The most persistent KEF/CWWG activists have been involved in the dispute for more than twenty years. Through their unique and invaluable experiences, they acquired a blend of knowledge and communication skills that only they possess. Many parties in the dispute, including legislators, regulators, and even army officials, have great regard for their brand of expertise and draw upon it frequently. Below we describe this expertise as a combination of several interconnected dimensions: holistic knowledge, issue memory, vernacular translation, and the ability to cultivate alliances. These dimensions of expertise legitimized KEF/CWWG activists as influential players in the dispute.

Holistic Knowledge

KEF/CWWG members possess holistic knowledge of the dispute. By this we mean that the depth and breadth of their experiences in the dispute give them a perspective that no other individuals or entities have. Their understanding encompasses technical issues of chemical weapons disposal, the web of political interests and power relations across the bureaucracies involved, and the sociocultural issues shaping community concerns about the project. This knowledge is based on years of self-training from within the dynamics of the dispute and is a critical addition to credentialed forms of expertise that have so dominated debates on the issue. As Craig Williams said, "We've been the eyes and ears for the communities. We know this issue through and through because we've been living it. It's not easy, but it's what we do. Somebody's got to do it and we've been doing it for 20 years now."[24]

Bureaucrats, regulators, political officials, scientists, media, and others recognize the activists' knowledge as legitimate. They use it as a resource to fill out their own understanding of the dispute's history and how it bears on the specific problems on which they are working. Craig Williams explained,

> Many people in power, whether it's inside the Pentagon, the army, on Capitol Hill, local elected, not that they always agree with us, but they now look to us as a pool of knowledge about a broad array of everything having to do with this program or this effort. It amazes the hell out of me when I think about it. Now that doesn't mean that they necessarily come to us with an engineering question, although they might, and if we didn't know it we'd get one of our experts to educate us to give them the answer. So they would still look at us as a source. Clearly, the media, nationally, comes to us about everything having anything to do with this issue, whether it's Iraq or [Madison County], or whatever. It's all the time, "Well we were told you were the experts." And they use that word. You're the experts in the chemical weapons treaty. You're the experts in chemical weapons disposal. You're the experts in the health effects of chemical weapons. I mean all this stuff. So over the years there is a perception in a large group, whether they're military, legislator, whatever, that consider us experts.[25]

They are also considered the experts on public opinion. Legislators, the army and ACWA officials all look to KEF/CWWG to give them the pulse of public opinion on chemical weapons disposal or how they might react to program changes. KEF's Elizabeth Crowe observed, "We're asked a lot about what the public thinks. A lot of times it'll be in the form of the question like, 'Well what will the public have to say about changing this or delaying that?' and we can kind of say, based on 20 years of dealing with folks, 'Well here's how they'll feel about it.'"[26]

There is no straightforward formula for developing this knowledge. It comes solely from intimate daily involvement in the issue. It demands getting your hands dirty "down in the weeds," as Craig Williams likes to say. Sociologist and CWWG member Dick Futrell compared it to KEF/CWWG being in the flow of a big, shifting, multichannel conversation and trying to gauge each party's interests and aims and match them to their own agenda. He said, "A lot of that [holistic knowledge] has come from being on the phone talking with these other people, kind of a conversation with lots of different other people and that's the way your training or learning has occurred . . . in this real large and varied kind of conversation."[27]

This conversation spans a wide range of public arenas and bureaucratic channels, which poses big challenges for activists, who need to understand the standpoint each entity comes from. "They all speak a different language," Craig Williams explained. "Everybody speaks a different language and they are all coming at this thing from their own interests or the particular part they've been mandated to do. Part of the reason why many people feel that we know more about this issue than anybody in the country is that we're dealing directly, constantly with all these groups. And we probably do [know more], because we know where everybody's coming from because we're talking to everybody at the same time . . . juggling all these balls at the same time and understanding which one's falling where."[28]

Issue Memory

Their holistic knowledge is closely tied to their extensive issue memory—the capacity to recall a broad swath of past actions and experiences over the history of the controversy. Memory and recall is critical in this dispute, given PMCD's attempts to control the program by changing budget priorities to favor its aims, reasserting already-refuted claims about risk and/or safety, or bypassing congressional requirements in order to move forward with incineration. Over the course of the controversy PMCD has also tried to institute ideas that citizens and Congress have categorically rejected, such as transporting the weapons to another storage site for disposal. KEF/CWWG members are able to recall and track a running record of ongoing technical and managerial problems, broken promises, budgetary changes, congressional requirements that go unheeded, and other mishandlings of the disposal program, which they use as ammunition in their political battles. Legislators, media, and others tap into this knowledge frequently.

No other entity in this dispute commands this type of expertise, knowledge, and memory, in part because of the extremely high turnover rate among army and other government personnel involved in the disposal program. Very few army administrators and legislative personnel have participated in the program continuously from its early stages. Additionally, each organization with a role in chemical weapons disposal is highly compartmentalized, focused on a limited part of the problem, and not expected nor able to preserve a holistic understanding or memory of the project; likewise, on the public side, attention to the issue waxes and wanes for most citizens. It seems that only KEF/CWWG activists have a truly comprehensive sense of the issue through its twenty-four-year history.

Vernacular Translation

Holistic knowledge and issue memory contribute to the skill of "vernacular translation"—the ability of these leading activists to initiate and broker conversations that cross many different areas of expertise and authority. This is a crucial skill for expressing citizen interests throughout various bureaucratic realms, as well as translating so-called government speak or the language of technical experts to the public. Scientists, technicians, bureaucrats, legislators, and academics possess specialized, compartmental knowledge and power. KEF/CWWG staff translate what they learn from each into a common language, or an "issue vernacular," which helps people with different standpoints understand each other and how their interests are tied together. Dick Futrell observed, "What I've seen happening in the conversations that KEF/CWWG has with people with really specialized, narrow expertise on specific issues in the disposal program is that KEF/CWWG is in the midst of that flow, talking to engineers, chemists, lawyers and so forth and pulling all that diverse information together. There's a real unique skill at pulling all those things together, working with these narrowly trained experts and administrators, learning so many more angles and ways to translate, mediate, shape between experts, between public, between legislators, and so forth . . . [KEF/CWWG's] varied forms of expertise comes out of that conversation."[29]

The combination of holistic knowledge, issue memory, and vernacular translation gives KEF/CWWG activists an invaluable set of skills and knowledge. KEF's Lois Kleffman reflected,

> I really think that's the value of where we are. We have all this experience in this issue. We're linked into experts which means that we can make statements that we know can be backed up by the scientific knowledge of other people who have supplied it to us. That gives a further validation to what we are saying and that's enabled us to have a reputation of being . . . you know we don't say things that we can't back up. So that's been a real value. The powers that be now tend to ask our opinion and are always talking to Craig [Williams] who himself has this immense range of background knowledge and a way of communicating it so that regulators or whomever can use it, understand where we're coming from and even where others are coming from and why, and then use it. What we know, what we've put together, is important. . . . It may not win the day in any one instance, but we're part of the mix and there's been some movement over the years.[30]

Cultivating Alliances

KEF/CWWG members' reputation as expert, trustworthy, and valuable contributors to the issue positioned them to build an informal alliance network that has produced new forms of political leverage in the dispute. This is a network of individuals with positions in organizations stretching across large, multifunction bureaucracies, such as ACWA, PMCD, Congress, universities, environmental organizations, and private industry. Most of these relationships are not with entire bureaucracies but with people embedded within the various layers and levels of these organizations. This creates a horizontal web of communication that cuts across the organizational hierarchies and specific mandates of any one group involved in the issue. The network involves activists, bureaucrats, scientists, technicians, engineers, academics, lawyers, regulators, lobbyists, and legislators. It is held together not by any official mandate but by trust and interest in safe chemical weapons disposal. Expertise in this alliance network spans the technical, social, and political issues, including incineration and alternative technologies, risk analysis, emergency planning, worker safety, environmental protection, and regulatory rules.

KEF/CWWG helps to bridge these otherwise disconnected actors, creating a context for these varying interests to communicate and act collectively on the disposal issue in ways not otherwise possible without the activists' mediation. Dick Futrell explained, "I think what is really important is what this group [KEF/CWWG] has done . . . to ferret out and find people who've been in different bureaucracies who are trying to do their job fairly and well . . . making those contacts in the official world and pulling them together to talk to one another, to go beyond the bureaucratic parts they're contained or constrained in, to make changes." KEF/CWWG is the master link in a chain of experts and administrators with power to shape the disposal program. This alliance network links interests that intersect on certain issues at particular times, where a flow of information from a specific set of participants can push safe disposal forward. By connecting people and groups to one another and helping them see their common interests, they create a new, albeit unofficial, collective actor—the alliance system—which has produced new advantages for the anti-incineration movement.[31]

As the master link in the alliance network, KEF/CWWG activists have crafted a position from which to leverage citizens' interests by introducing information and posing arguments that reflect community concerns. For instance, their relationships with government insiders periodically result in access to confidential information about the program, which they use to expose technical and managerial problems in the program and drive the issue into "the higher echelons of political power where the final shape of the program is decided."[32]

Leveraging this alliance system was instrumental in creating the ACWA program and the dialogue process as an alternative to the PMCD-supported incineration program. Congress approved ACWA in large part because KEF/CWWG was able to understand, translate, and link the interests of local citizens, congressional legislators, alternative technology firms, state and local authorities, EPA officials, and others concerned about the incineration program. As they talked to people with various interests in the issue, they began to construct numerous rationales for shifting authority on chemical weapons disposal to a new entity that would be more responsive to local citizens.

One of the most important rationales was to counter the immense cost overruns in the program tallied by PMCD's push for incineration. As they spoke simultaneously with legislators and firms developing alternatives to incineration, they realized the power of the "money pitch," and it became a core strategy. John Capillo explained,

> In terms of the power networks at this juncture we built a coalition with yet another powerful group—technologists that are in the game to make money who have enough lobbying clout to sit in the office with Senator McConnell or whomever and say, "We've got the technology. You know we can spend the bucks in your district. And, you can go back to the Appropriations Committee and tell them it's cheaper than incineration." That brought the technologists into the issue, the alternative technologists, on our side. So it became Bechtel Corporation and neutralization against EG&G Corporation with incineration. We were able to exploit that part of the corporate world that wanted to get into the program. Money is the motivator with the firms and with Congress. We helped them see the carcass of incineration lying on the side of the road and they started circling. We tried to push that along.[33]

The strategy worked, as Kentucky's U.S. senator Mitch McConnell used the arguments to pass legislation that funded the ACWA program.

The ACWA dialogue process led to new alliances. KEF/CWWG's involvement led them to develop a new degree of familiarity with and trust in firms developing the new technologies and scientists helping to evaluate them and, most importantly, to develop a partnership with the ACWA leadership. Unlike PMCD managers, ACWA's director Mike Parker recognized that KEF/CWWG's technical and political expertise made them an important ally in ACWA's mission. They developed a sense of mutual trust and respect for one another. As a dialogue participant explained at the time,

> There's a real sense of back and forth trust developing. Almost trust, anyway. At least starting to believe each other, work with each other. That development is really different from what's been going on in the last decade. The Army versus citizen thing that has been really characteristic just isn't there with this. Everyone is very concerned about building a kind of relationship and atmosphere in which we can do things together. It's from a change in personnel. It's from a change in process. It's from a change in attitude. There's a whole new dynamic going on that is really different.[34]

Collaboration replaced conflict. Craig Williams observed, "People are just beginning to realize that this kind of program [i.e., ACWA] is really a way to get something done. That's the bottom line. We also have a common objective, which allows us to create this framework through which we can work. So we have a collaboration of folks from all the various entities represented in ACWA coming to the dialogue [meetings] and singing the same song . . . and without a lot of strife, all because of a rather simple change in how decisions are to be made."[35]

Although the ACWA process produced outcomes embraced by all participants, the road to getting the alternative technologies up and running in Kentucky and Colorado has not been smooth. Continual wrangling over money and timelines in the Department of Defense and Congress has repeatedly delayed the program, a trend that has continued as this book went to press. Much of this wrangling has come as the Pentagon has tried to shift funds from ACWA to cover cost overruns in the incineration program. KEF/CWWG has thwarted each attempt by constructing paper trails on these maneuvers, with information culled from their alliance network of sources inside the Department of Defense, its contractors, and other agencies. Craig Williams explained that their sources have different reasons for coming to them with information. Some see the delays as a safety problem, others see it as a "profit problem," and others see it as "an ethical problem because the DoD basically lies about what it's doing. We're a point of contact for all these people and their interests because we're trusted to do the right thing with the info."[36]

In short, KEF/CWWG acts as the master link connecting people and ideas in their alliance network. They are central to brokering relationships because so many parties see them as citizen experts on the social, political, and technical complexities of chemical weapons disposal. Involvement in the alliance network has helped KEF/CWWG envision new ways to solve the disposal dispute and create the opening to do it. By mediating the conversation among the wide array of players in the conflict, they have become the experts who best understand the technical possibilities of alternatives, how to translate and argue for them, and how the arguments will play best in the bureaucracies that control the fate of chemical weapons disposal.

Citizens' efforts in Kentucky have produced a technically safer and more socially acceptable resolution to the disposal dilemma. Nonincineration plants are now scheduled to be built in Kentucky and Colorado. This success is limited, though, as sites in Utah, Oregon, Arkansas, and Alabama are incinerating their weapons, despite technical and operational problems that plague the plants. Vigilant activists watch operations at each site closely.

Citizen resistance emerged from direct experiences with an army that was unresponsive to their concerns. Their frustrations grew as their expectations collided with decisions that often conflicted with citizen desires and were imposed with little public deliberation. Only by bringing many of PMCD's claims about incineration into question and making them politically salient at various political levels were they able to interject their standpoint into the process.

The degree of influence these activists have carved out is, on the one hand, impressive and hopeful. It demonstrates that there are openings in government bureaucracies to exploit and opportunities for lay citizens to become players in even the most complex technical and social decisions. On the other hand, it is discouraging that it takes such extreme effort to break into bureaucratic decision-making processes, much less to gain the type of leverage needed to create change for the common good.

Collaboration with academics and other experts created experts out of the citizens themselves. Their dogged persistence in challenging incineration led to interaction with a range of experts knowledgeable about different aspects of the issue. They drew on academics, political specialists, legal experts, and others to build a specialized understanding of chemical weapons disposal that no others in the conflict can claim. Their holistic knowledge, issue memory, and skill of vernacular translation earned them the legitimacy from which they built the informal alliances so crucial in leveraging their challenge to chemical weapons incineration. If the past is any indicator, they will need to continue building their expertise and activating their alliances to keep safe disposal in the forefront of the U.S. chemical weapons program.

But persevering as a powerful political player requires a delicate balance between bureaucratic politics and community action. KEF/CWWG's efforts to increase their power and legitimacy in bureaucratic politics can take them away from community contact. They must work hard to ensure they represent the public's interests. As Elizabeth Crowe said, "We try to play it big without losing the community focus that anchors the activist effort." She continued,

> There is a danger in getting seized up in being experts in the power circles and not giving enough time or connection to the grassroots community. Yes, you know what you know and you can speak this language and you're a player, but make sure to keep connected. I think that's one of the challenges for us. We have such a level of success in some of these areas and are a player and are called upon repeatedly by the media and elected officials and people writing the regulations who are saying, "What do you think about this or that?" We have to make sure that in our expertise that we're still bringing along people from the community and doing what we can on that level, while knowing that the changes we want as a community require us to play ball at this other level, with other powers. You have to do both.[37]

This would not be such a problem if there were institutionalized decision-making processes that, from the start, stressed meaningful citizen collaboration rather than exclusion. A much different public might have emerged if initial conditions had nurtured participation instead of constraining it. A big challenge that this case highlights is how to create decision-making frameworks that, from the start, legitimize strong citizen involvement even for the most complex technological decisions.

Notes

1. Robert Futrell, "Framing Process, Cognitive Liberation, and NIMBY Protest in the U.S. Chemical-Weapons Disposal Conflict," *Sociological Inquiry* 73, no. 3 (2003): 359–86; Robert Futrell, "Technical Adversarialism and Participatory Collaboration in the U.S. Chemical Weapons Disposal Program," *Science, Technology and Human Values* 28, no. 4 (2003): 451–82.

2. National Research Council, *Disposal of Chemical Munitions and Agents* (Washington, D.C.: National Academy Press, 1984).

3. Kai Erikson, *A New Species of Trouble: Explorations in Disaster, Trauma, and Community* (New York: W. W. Norton, 1994).

4. *Richmond Register,* February 8, 1984; CCMC member, interview by Robert Futrell, December 19, 1992.

5. CCMC member, interview by Robert Futrell, December 27, 1992.

6. CCMC member, interview by Robert Futrell, December 28, 1992; CCMC member, interview by Robert Futrell, June 7, 1994.

7. CCMC member, interview by Robert Futrell, July 14, 1994; CCMC member, interview by Robert Futrell, July 19, 1994.

8. CCMC member, interview by Robert Futrell, December 20, 1994.

9. Common Ground member, interview by Robert Futrell, December 28, 1994.

10. Craig Williams, interview by Robert Futrell, July 27, 2004.

11. Craig Williams, interview by Robert Futrell, July 12, 1995.

12. KEF staff member, interview by Robert Futrell, May 8, 1995.

13. Craig Williams, interview by Robert Futrell, August 9, 1994.

14. "Incinerator under Fire: Safety Questions Swirl at a Facility Designed to Burn Chemical Weapons," *Tooele Transcript Bulletin,* September 9, 1994.

15. Craig Williams, interview by Robert Futrell, August 4, 1997.

16. See Defense Authorization Act, PL 104-208, sec. 8065.

17. Craig Williams, interview by Robert Futrell, August 4, 1997.

18. Richard E. Sclove, *Democracy and Technology* (New York: Guilford, 1995); Frank Fischer, *Citizens, Experts, and the Environment: The Politics of Local Knowledge* (Durham, NC: Duke University Press, 2000).

19. John Capillo, interview by Robert Futrell, May 31, 2005; Craig Williams, interview by Robert Futrell, May 27, 2004.

20. John Capillo, interview by Robert Futrell, May 27, 2004.

21. John Capillo, interview by Robert Futrell, May 27, 2005.

22. Craig Williams, interview by Robert Futrell, May 27, 2005.

23. John Capillo, interview by Robert Futrell, May 27, 2004.

24. Craig Williams, interview by Robert Futrell, July 27, 2004.

25. Craig Williams, interview by Robert Futrell, May 17, 2004.

26. Elizabeth Crowe, interview by Robert Futrell, May 27, 2004.

27. Dick Futrell, interview by Robert Futrell, May 27, 2004.

28. Craig Williams, interview by Robert Futrell, May 27, 2004.

29. Dick Futrell, interview by Robert Futrell, May 27, 2004.

30. Lois Kleffman, interview by Robert Futrell, May 27, 2004.

31. Dick Futrell, interview by Robert Futrell, May 27, 2004.

32. John Capillo, interview by Robert Futrell, August 4, 1997.

33. John Capillo, interview by Robert Futrell, May 31, 2005.

34. Dialogue participant, July 30, 1997.

35. Craig Williams, interview by Robert Futrell, July 8, 1998.

36. Craig Williams, interview by Robert Futrell, May 27, 2005.

37. Elizabeth Crowe, interview by Robert Futrell, May 27, 2005.

10

Headwaters

A Student-Faculty Participatory Research Project in Eastern Kentucky

Alan Banks, Alice Jones, and Anne Blakeney

The Headwaters Project began as part of an Appalachian Regional Commission (ARC) project being carried out through the Consortium of Appalachian Centers and Institutes. This consortium project grew out of a reciprocal desire between academic regional studies centers/institutes and the ARC to envision ways to work more closely with citizens in the Appalachian region, especially those living in counties classified by the ARC as "distressed." Over a three-year period, the ARC hosted several discussions between ARC staff and center directors from a variety of institutions in Appalachia. With the guidance of Dr. Ron Eller, then Whisman scholar at the ARC, these discussions led to a working draft of the vision, goals, and objectives of the group. Then, at an October 2000 meeting held at East Tennessee State University, the group agreed to conduct a project on each campus and asked current Whisman scholar Dr. Jean Haskill to prepare the proposal for funding from the ARC. The project challenged each institution to create a course that was place-based and participatory in nature. Each course was to address a single question: How do we build sustainable futures for Appalachia?

While each institution approached the question in its own way, the projects followed agreed-upon guidelines set down by the consortium. Faculty and students were to: (1) work in an ARC–designated distressed county, if possible; (2) employ a participatory approach where feasible; (3) focus on one or more of the ARC's strategic goals; and (4) present a final report to ARC staff in Washington, D.C., at the end of the semester.

To support this ambitious endeavor, the ARC provided travel funds for all participating faculty and students to attend two meetings: a meet-and-greet strategy session in September at East Tennessee State University's campus in Johnson City, Tennessee, and a miniconference in Washington, D.C., in November 2001, where students presented their reports to consortium participants and ARC staff. Another grant, from the Kentucky Flex-E-Grant Program, administered by the Kentucky Department for Local Government, provided travel assistance and overall support for our Headwaters Project at EKU.

Letcher County is home to the headwaters of the North Fork of the Kentucky River. Despite the breathtaking beauty of the Kentucky River and its tributaries, the river system has suffered for nearly a century from the impact of timber, mining, and other industrial operations. The area is also marked by a lack of regulator zeal and infrastructural support to improve water management. Residents rarely swim or fish in the North Fork nowadays, and parents tell us they don't let their children near the water for fear of sickness. Kentucky historian Thomas Clark put it this way:

> Now in this sophisticated scientific age the Kentucky River is burdened with an obscene amount of physical and chemical pollution. . . . In flood season and out, its channel is littered with plastic jugs, cast-off automobile tires, discarded household appliances, and even an occasional over-age highway department truck. After every high-water stage, trees and bushes are left adorned with litter intimately related to motherhood—plastic diapers. . . . Far more burdensome than diapers [however] are the countless tons of silt which wash down regularly from the stripped highland coalfields. . . . Grim telltales of the changes in mining procedures upstream are the ever-rising high-water marks which bank dwellers paint on bridge piers, the walls of homes and stores, and even mark on the outer limits of cornfields and meadows.[1]

The Kentucky River flows from the mountains of southeastern Kentucky northwest through the rolling topography of central Kentucky to join the Ohio River near Carrollton. More than 700,000 people live in the basin, and roughly 620,000 rely on drinking water supplied by water directly taken from the Kentucky River, its tributaries, and reservoirs located in the region. Within this large area there are numerous sources of contamination, including point and nonpoint sources, which threaten the water quality of the Kentucky River and the stability of communities within the water basin. According to the *Kentucky River Basin Status Report,* the major environmental problems in the North Fork watershed include habitat degradation, runoff, and siltation from mining, timber, and agricultural operations; illegal dumping; and pathogens from un-treated sewage—especially from "straight pipes" that connect toilets directly to streams—which have forced a "no bodily contact" swimming advisory for eighty-six miles of the upper reaches of the North Fork. Other threats to human and river health include contamination from leaking underground storage tanks, old landfills, and hazardous waste sites.[2]

Recognizing the importance of water issues, especially in a headwaters area, many residents of Letcher County welcomed our students and agreed to serve as members of a citizens' advisory council to support and guide what eventually became a three-semester project. Their partnership was, and continues to be, remarkable. Encouragement and letters of support from local leaders were instrumental in securing the funding necessary to sustain the project. For Letcher County residents, it was an opportunity to tap into the resources of the university to address one of the major environmental challenges facing them in their efforts to build a viable and vital future for their children. Their input was real. They helped set the agenda, write the syllabi, and guide us throughout the project. For us, it was an opportunity to transform the classroom, moving it off campus to provide real-life research skills, service learning opportunities, a better understanding of the riches of the region, and lessons in the importance of citizenship. It was also an opportunity for us, as one resident put it, "to put the 'E' back into Eastern Kentucky University." This partnership continues as students have moved on to other projects in the area.

Project Overview

From the start, the purpose of the Letcher County Headwaters Project was to expand Letcher County's civic capacity by developing tools that would help citizens and community leaders better understand and monitor how land use decisions—from straight-piping household waste to large-scale mining and timber activities—affect water quality, which subsequently affects public health, the natural environment, and the economy of the county. In response to citizens' suggestions and student interests, the emphasis on water quality and public heath increased as the project evolved.

Put simply, the Headwaters Project has been a participatory research project in which students and faculty work closely with a community advisory board to:

1. review the historical developments that have led to water quality problems in the North Fork of the Kentucky River;
2. develop community-based tools to help citizens address their concerns;
3. develop an integrated geographic information system (GIS) that community members can use to visualize water quality data, identify problem areas, and compare the potential impacts of different development options;
4. develop additional tools such as easy-to-read graphs and/or spreadsheets and community surveys that would help community leaders, activists, and others better understand and use the data that are regularly collected by various state agencies and by Watershed Watch volunteers; and
5. identify and publicize residents' concerns about water quality, public health, and community sustainability.

The Headwaters Project evolved as a three-semester teaching and research partnership that started during the fall 2001 semester and continued through the fall 2002 semester. Two of the three classes were team-taught, and each focused on different aspects of the problem, allowing students to stay with the project for more than one semester without redundancy if they chose to do so. During the three semesters more than thirty students participated in the project, and several were with the project for more than one semester. More than half of the students were from the region, and there were two international students, one from Cameroon and the other from Brazil. One graduate student completed her master's thesis based on data collected in the project, and others are working toward this goal.

Similarly, Letcher County has expanded its emphasis on clean water. With EPA funds, the county has hired a full-time water basin coordinator, and additional funds have been secured to expand water lines, improve sewage treatment capacity, and develop and implement alternative waste disposal technologies—an important step toward eliminating the nearly eighteen hundred straight pipes in the county. Local resident, advisory board member, and Appalshop filmmaker Herb E. Smith put it this way:

> Over the past 12 years, the people of Letcher County have been working to solve problems related to the lack of good water. The legacy of bad or non-existent water, sewage systems and the problems with current coal mining practices have left us facing a large mess that has overwhelmed previous efforts. EKU's Headwaters Project came at just the right time. The documentation in the project report has provided an important tool for building the case for making systematic change. We are laying new water lines now. Thanks for all of your good work. You have shown the way for a university to be a partner with county government and with local citizens.[3]

What follows is a brief summary of the three phases of the Headwaters Project.

Phase One:
The Historical Context and Mapping Project

During the fall 2001 semester a total of sixteen students enrolled in a course titled Social Change in Appalachia. In the first few weeks they were introduced to the principles of participatory research and prepared for their first visit to Letcher County. Their basic assignment for the semester was to focus on the first four of the five project goals listed above. Students were divided into teams with specific tasks and responsibilities. With moral and financial support from the university, the class was team-taught by Alan Banks (sociology) and Alice Jones (geography). While each instructor worked with students and all classes were taught jointly, Alice deserves special credit for her role as project director for the GIS portion of the project.

If there was one thing that residents of Letcher County residents told the students over and over again, it was that water quality is a complex problem that needs to be understood in the context of Letcher County's history. If environmental problems like contaminated water were simply a result of technological malfunction, they repeated, it would be relatively easy to fix the problem, using best management practices to build a nonpolluting and sustainable foundation for future growth and progress. Because Letcher County sat at the headwaters of the Kentucky River, residents were particularly aware that any serious pollution problem most likely had local origins. Put simply, they recognized that the environmental challenges currently facing them were more than technical. They were the consequence of human decisions made over the past hundred years in individual households, businesses, and governmental units within and outside the area.

The place to begin, they repeated, was with the emergence and growth of the coal industry. The central role of coal mining in southeastern Kentucky in the early years of the twentieth century is reflected in a cursory look at the number of miners as a share of the local population. Calculating male mine employees as a share of all male gainfully employed workers, for example, shows the striking dependence of wage earners on the mines. In Bell County in 1930, miners formed roughly 44 percent of gainfully employed male workers; in Perry County, 53 percent; in Harlan County, 75 percent; and in Letcher County, 65 percent.[4]

The Historical Context

In the 1930s coal camps, or company-controlled communities, provided miners in southeastern Kentucky with their everyday needs. Workers rented houses, all of similar shape and size, from the coal company. Buildings such as hotels and schools were often constructed in some of the better towns. Most towns had a church, which was important to the coal companies because it gave the town "respectability." The church was usually nondenominational and constructed by the miners themselves. Each town had a company store where the miners could spend their paychecks for items such as clothing and groceries. The miners' wages were often paid in script that generally was not interchangeable with other coal camps' script. This meant it could be spent only at the miner's employer's businesses. As a result, miners' paychecks ended up going right back to the company they worked for.

Urban planning and waste disposal in these coal camps was often rudimentary. Most towns had neither sewage systems nor onsite solid-waste treatment facilities. For the most part, those who did have indoor plumbing ran "straight pipes" from the house to the creek bed to discharge raw waste and sewage. Solid waste was often disposed of in dry branches or constructed trenches near houses, where materials would rest until the next rain washed them downstream and out of sight. This legacy set the precedent for the future. Even today nearly 70 percent of the households in Letcher County are without city water, and approximately eighteen hundred homes still use straight pipes.

Like other coal-mining communities, Letcher County had highs and lows, but the nature of competition in the industry led to variations that were much more extreme than usual. While the Great Depression saw coal production decline between 1930 and 1935, World War II boosted it again to unprecedented highs. Following the war, mergers of coal companies and the mechanization of coal production caused mining employment to drop while production continued to increase. This led to out-migration, which became an important issue in the 1950s, when Letcher County lost more than forty percent of its population. People left in search of better jobs, health care, and education for their children. The loss of this sizable portion of the productive population, along with the potential tax base that left with them, compounded the difficulties facing this resource-rich but infrastructure-poor county.[5]

Our students came to realize that coal production continued to be an important component of the economic livelihood of many local residents during the 1990s, but it is also clear that the role of coal as a staple industry and the sole foundation for growth and development continues to diminish. Occupational shifts in Letcher County can also be seen from 1969 to 1999. Employment in mining in Letcher County reached a high of nearly thirty-two hundred workers in 1977, and mining was clearly the largest occupational category through the late 1980s. Since then other employment categories have increased in relative importance, as growth in service, retail trade, and government occupations has changed the overall composition of the labor force. The number of miners working in Letcher County fell to less than a thousand by 1999.[6]

One thing is certain. There is enough coal in Letcher County to provide economic activity for the next thirty-five years and more, but if current employment trends and trends in mechanization continue there may be fewer and fewer jobs for area residents and greater environmental devastation, which will likely undermine alternative development strategies and erode the local tax base. Building a sustainable future for this county, with its majestic scenery and concerned citizens, will require abandoning the old approach of depending on a single or master industry to provide economic sustenance for residents. It will require a focused, comprehensive, well-funded, and serious plan to develop new, smaller, and more innovative endeavors that provide stable and well-paying jobs. Filling the economic void left by the decline in coal employment will require reversing the environmental problems caused by a hundred years of neglect. It will require serious efforts to rebuild and extend existing waterworks and sewage systems as well as renewed efforts at restoration of the North Fork of the Kentucky River. If new opportunities do not arise, the area's citizens will, once again, be forced to migrate to other areas, abandoning the region for good.

The Mapping Project

At present, water quality data for the upper North Fork of the Kentucky River is fairly easy to come by. The major sources of pollution are well known—siltation and chemical loading from mine sites and faulty wastewater treatment (straight pipes, failing septic systems, and community wastewater facilities).

In 2000 the federally funded PRIDE program (Personal Responsibility in a Desirable Environment) provided funds for a focused sampling effort in the North Fork by Kentucky River Watershed Watch volunteers. The subsequent report, issued by the Kentucky Water Resources Research Institute, echoes these same water quality concerns: failing wastewater treatment/package plants, straight pipes, failing septic systems, illegal dumps, and mining operations.[7]

The 2001 *Kentucky River Basin Assessment Report* provides detailed information about the impaired waters identified by the state in its biannual report to Congress required by the Clean Water Act. The assessment report ranks all 102 subbasins of the Kentucky River watershed as high, medium, or low priority, depending on their level of degradation or the threat of degradation. Nearly all of the North Fork's watershed was ranked "high" on this list, with sources of pollution identified as "straight pipes and failing septic systems, contamination from runoff in heavily settled areas, modification of streambeds or removal of vegetation, and siltation resulting from logging, mining, construction, or other activities."[8]

The difficulty, then, is not always the availability of data but rather the form and usefulness of that information. The 2000 *Kentucky River Basin Assessment Report* and the *Kentucky Basin Management Plan* are both available online, presumably to facilitate access by community members and other interested citizens. But public availability and public accessibility are not necessarily synonymous. Admirably, the reports are arranged geographically, but their sheer size makes them tedious to navigate. The management plan's section on the North Fork alone is a forty-eight page PDF document that, while attractive and official looking, contains only referential statements about water quality—referring the reader back to the assessment report for more specific information about impairments and sources of impairment. Yet when a reader checks the assessment report, the information is presented in tabular form that can be confusing at best or, at worst, complicated to the point of being meaningless. While such tables are the norm in scientific and academic communities, they can be confusing and intimidating to even the most well-meaning and interested citizen or public official who wants to understand water issues in his or her community. Although the data are complete and accurate, they leave many questions for the ordinary citizen: What is fecal coliform, and why is it being measured? What are the critical levels above or below which the measurement is of concern, and why? Where are the sampling sites?[9]

To address the needs of Letcher County citizens and officials, one of our original project objectives was to develop an integrated GIS that community members could use to visualize water quality data, identify problem areas, and compare the potential impacts of different development options. We also wanted to develop additional tools, such as easy-to-read graphs, to help community leaders, activists, and other citizens better understand and use the data that are regularly collected by various state agencies and by Watershed Watch volunteers.

To start to meet these goals, three students in the fall 2001 class were designated as the GIS/data visualization team. Together they developed a series of preliminary graphs and maps to convey existing water quality information in visual form. Graphics can paint a picture that shows how sites compare with one another and can highlight extreme water quality values across sites. Horizontal lines can, for example, provide a baseline reference of the standards set for either drinking water quality or stream quality to assist community officials and citizens in evaluating sampling results. Often a brief text box can be included to explain why the given water quality parameter—oxygen levels, fecal coliform, conductivity, heavy metals, and so on—is an important measure of water quality and/or public health. Given data displayed this way, the average citizen or county official with no expertise in water quality can easily interpret the results of a sampling effort.

Maps can also convey a great deal of information quickly, by providing the locations of sampling points and of such things as straight pipes, wastewater treatment systems, and other potential problem sources, such as mine sites or other industrial and agricultural operations. Maps can therefore help link reported water quality and contaminant levels with possible sources of that contamination—namely untreated or improperly treated human household wastewater. Assembling the GIS to produce such maps involves first gathering standard map layers (e.g., roads, county boundaries, rivers, and watershed boundaries) and then inputting (or obtaining) other relevant field data for separate map layers. Roads, county boundaries, watershed boundaries, and stream channels map data can be obtained from readily available websites, while wastewater information can be obtained from various watershed groups or state agencies. During the fall 2002 course students accompanied Watershed Watch volunteers to each of the sampling points and recorded the latitude and longitude with a handheld global positioning system (GPS) unit. Later, the results from this effort were added to a spreadsheet that included GPS coordinate points to map and show water quality results from this sampling effort.

In short, when presented together, the graphic and mapped information can convey a great deal of very complicated information in a way that is easily understood by citizens and decision makers. During the semester our GIS students developed a series of maps and graphs to communicate the basic water quality parameters of concern in Letcher County in a citizen-friendly format. All of the water quality data were taken directly from sources that are available to the public, but we believe that our format made the data much more accessible than the original sources from which they were drawn.

Phase Two:
A Survey of Health Care Professionals in Letcher County

Early in our conversations, local residents expressed grave concerns about the quality of water and its effects on health. Based on these concerns, we made arrangements in the fall of 2001 for three students to spend a weekend in Letcher County asking residents about local water quality. Some initial responses included:

- I'm tired of water being such a central issue in my life.
- I don't know if the vegetables I plant are safe to eat.
- People know the water's bad so why dwell on it—we need to find solutions!
- We buy our water.
- My kids know they have to scrub off after coming indoors if they were out near the stream.

Water quality data from the first phase of our project indicated that residents' concerns were legitimate. Fecal levels, in many cases, were off the charts. Sediment and dissolved minerals data suggested that normal recreational and household use of water was not supportable. When mapped, state water quality data revealed that only a small segment of rivers and streams in the county would support normal aquatic life and allow swimming. We therefore turned to the relevant health agencies to determine whether these concerns were borne out by incidences of waterborne disease.

What we discovered is that data collected by these organizations are aggregated and reported in such a way that it is virtually impossible to tie specific conditions to water quality. When we mapped county-level data on cancer obtained from the Kentucky Cabinet for Health Services, for example, the results were not particularly revealing—and in fact, they suggested that Letcher County fared fairly well when compared with other eastern and central Kentucky counties. In a fall 2001 interview an official with the Kentucky Division of Water suggested that there are at least two reasons that it may be difficult to link health statistics to documented water quality problems. First, short-term conditions—nausea, cramps, and diarrhea, for example—either are not reported or may have causes other than water quality and therefore are not reported as water-quality-related conditions. Second, for the purposes of county health statistics, long-term conditions that might indicate a link between health and water quality (rectal cancer, for example) are reported in broader categories (overall cancer rates) that may mask the linkage with water quality. Breaking out these conditions to report them in more detail could be too expensive or time-consuming for both state and local health agencies. The official also suggested that failure to establish a causal link between health and water quality may not be unintentional; it is possible, he said, that health statistics are reported the way they are in part because industries and local officials do not want certain incidence rates known by those who are affected by them.[10]

On the one hand, then, we had substantial anecdotal evidence from our local citizen advisory committee and from conversations with residents that the county has serious health problems associated with water quality. On the other hand, none of the state or local agencies monitoring and collecting health information could provide information that clearly linked the incidence of disease with water quality.

This was a crucial time for our EKU research team and for the local residents with whom we were working. Our students had to ask themselves some very important questions: Were the state and county health data—published by reputable agencies guided by state and federal regulations—incorrect, incomplete, or deliberately misleading? If incomplete, then was it the agency's responsibility to compile a more thorough set of data, or should average citizens concerned about the relationship between water quality and health be responsible for seeking further information they can't find at their local or state health departments? Or had we perhaps entered our investigation with a bias that there *must* be a strong relationship between water quality and health, and were we therefore inappropriately scrutinizing valid and reasonable health statistics for relationships that simply weren't there?

To pursue these questions, five students from the fall 2001 Social Change in Appalachia class and two additional students signed up to continue the Letcher County project during the spring 2002 semester. After considerable discussion within our group and with our citizens' advisory council, we decided to survey health care professionals in Letcher County to resolve some of the contradictory information we were finding regarding the connections between clean water and human health. Starting early in the semester, students and faculty at the center:

- Visited Letcher County to talk with our citizens' advisory council about the best way to proceed with the survey.
- Designed and secured approval to distribute a quantitative survey to health care practitioners in Letcher County.

- Notified administrators at local health care facilities about our plan to bring the surveys to Letcher County and asked them to help us deliver and collect them in a timely fashion.
- Delivered surveys on the morning of Friday, February 8, 2002, and picked them up later in the afternoon. (Business reply envelopes were provided for those who could not finish them the same day.)
- Statistically analyzed the results of the survey.
- Assembled a posterboard and PowerPoint presentation to show the results of the Headwaters Project to date, including historical information, water quality data, maps and charts, and health care survey results.
- Held several public hearings, including one at the Cowan Community Center in Letcher County (May 2002).
- Discussed several recommendations to promote sustainable economic development in the Kentucky River watershed and the state as a whole.

We distributed 122 surveys to local health care workers, mainly doctors and registered nurses, in Letcher County. In the 73 that were returned, the vast majority of health professionals agreed that:

- Water quality was a serious issue for the health of Letcher County residents.
- Current water treatment practices were less than effective.
- They had recommended that their patients use bottled water.
- Specific ailments were traceable to impaired waters.[11]

Overall, there appeared to be great concern among health professionals about water quality in Letcher County. In addition, while only 25 percent of healthcare professionals who had lived in Letcher County for less than a year considered there to be a problem with drinking water, over 90 percent of those who had lived in the county for over a year saw it as a problem. This seems to strengthen the argument that a problem with drinking water exists. As medical professionals became more familiar with their surroundings and the health problems of residents, the percentage of those who saw drinking water as a health issue increased.

When asked to rank the possible sources of contamination in the

Kentucky River, Letcher County medical practitioners identified failing septic systems as the greatest or a great source of pollution, followed by surface or deep mining, petroleum extraction, pesticide runoff, and other waste-generating industries. While these results are tentative, it is interesting and instructive that the answers of health care professionals parallel those of citizens, whose firsthand accounts are presented next.

Phase Three:
The Listening Project

In spring semester of 2002 the opportunity to continue the Headwaters Project or to establish a new line of place-based pedagogy was opened to all faculty associates of the Center for Appalachian Studies. Anne responded with a proposal to alter her course, Providing Health Care Services in Appalachia, by focusing it on the possible impact of poor water quality on health and human activities or, in other words, "human occupations." She defined human occupations as those things that *occupy our time each day*—the *things we have to do* in order to maintain ourselves (cooking, eating, bathing, cleaning, working, etc.) and those *things that we choose to do* to bring meaning to our lives (leisure, recreation, hobbies, expressive or artistic occupations, etc.). This course examined the connection between human occupations and local water quality and was team taught by Anne (occupational therapy) and Alan (sociology). Alice (geography) continued to provide valuable input on the project.

Following two public meetings and one with our citizens' advisory committee in August 2002, we were asked to go directly to the people of Letcher County. Advisory members suggested a listening project, in which students would listen to citizens' accounts of their experiences with water. At the August meeting, the community advisory board supplied us with an initial list of phone numbers of people they thought would be willing to talk to students. They also provided input on a set of interview questions that were being developed. Finally, the set of questions and necessary consent forms were submitted and approved by our university's institutional review board mid-September.

The goal of the listening project was to collect and transcribe a minimum of thirty interviews from citizens across Letcher County in order to record how their health and human occupations were affected by water quality. At the beginning of fall semester 2002 we actively recruited students for the graduate and undergraduate course. Faculty associates of the center supported this process by encouraging students across disciplines to enroll. Fourteen students enrolled: eight graduate students (six from the master's in public administration program and two from occupational therapy) and six undergraduates, from occupational therapy, English, sociology, psychology, and pre-med. At the first class meeting we presented students with an overview of the previous work done on the Headwaters Project and an outline of the design for this field research course. Because course requirements were heavy, including at least four weekends of travel plus transcribing and coding the interviews, we asked students to carefully consider their decision before making a commitment to begin the class. To provide an incentive, we reminded them that a trip to Washington, D.C., and an opportunity to present their findings to the Appalachian Regional Commission would conclude the course.

During the first month of the course we trained the students in the ethics and strategies of conducting, transcribing, and coding interviews. Then, over three nonconsecutive weekends during the fall, students conducted forty interviews with forty-five adults ranging in age from eighteen to eighty. Prior to entering Letcher County, they had divided into self-selected teams of two for the field research activities. Following each weekend in Letcher County, students participated in debriefing sessions on campus in which they shared their individual experiences, and collective impressions began to emerge. This served as a way to track information being collected and allowed students the opportunity to clear up questions about any part of the research process. It also allowed for reinforcing effective interview techniques.

Because the semester's activities were compressed due to the need to be in Washington, D.C., in mid-November, students and faculty were able to complete only a preliminary analysis of the information obtained. Four main themes were identified from the forty transcribed interviews: water's effect on health; environmental degradation; loss of business and recreation opportunities; and individual and collective solutions and adaptations.

Water's Effect on Health

All interviewees believed that their water or the water of friends and family members was contaminated. Those who believed that they had "good water" from wells located at high elevations with no mining operations above them expressed fears of losing access to this water. Everyone knew of individuals whose well water was ruined by mining operations. Thus, those who believed that they currently had "good water" expressed anxiety over the potential loss of this resource. The following quotes reflect citizens' experiences and beliefs about Letcher County water and their health:

- My sister went to a friend's house and actually got hepatitis from the water in the well.
- Whole families are sick. They can't afford bottled water. . . . The doctor said water is making them sick.
- When I was drinking the water, I'd wake up with a bad taste in my mouth . . . and got sick from it. It tasted like rotten eggs, smelled like rotten eggs, and when you drink it, and burp it up, that's the taste you get.
- They're putting us in the grave, really. My wife's health has gotten worse. My brother's health . . . has gotten worse, mine has gotten bad. It's just worry, worry all the time . . . about the water. . . . It's just completely changed our lives.
- We've seen tons of areas [in the county] where there's been disease. . . . I have an article . . . that talks about this area as one of the unhealthiest places in the state.

Environmental Degradation

The interviews also demonstrated a collective sense of loss regarding the environment. Over and over, people spoke about the days when streams were "crystal clear" and the water was clean enough for swimming, playing, fishing, bathing, and drinking. People were not opposed to coal mining as an industry; however, they were opposed to contemporary strip-mining methods that resulted in major environmental degradation. They spoke about how blasting during the strip-mining process cracked underground aquifers, resulting in the contamination of many wells and the loss of "good, clean water." The following quotes are indicative of the frustrations apparent in the transcribed interviews:

- I went to run water in the tub. It was first black, like off coal, and then it came out all rusty lookin' stuff. Well, you come out of the tub worse than you went in. I took it to Standard Laboratory . . .

and they got back to me a few days later and said, your water is twenty-one percent sulfur and iron, and six percent grease and oil.

- About fifteen years ago, there was a petroleum dealer in Whitesburg who cleaned his [gas] tanks with . . . some solvent chemical and dumped it in the river. . . . And . . . all our drinking water is taken from the North Fork of the Kentucky River.
- I'm . . . concerned now with sediment in the river, from . . . mountaintop removal. . . . On a real rainy day . . . the river gets muddy; [the water company] has to shut down till the river clears. They have to flush that intake system until it will intake water again.
- With this strip mining and mountaintop removal . . . water don't flow like it used to.
- Well . . . for years now . . . we have laws on the books . . . that's supposed to keep people from . . . dumping fuels out, dumping oil out, and doing all this stuff. But none of this . . . is being enforced . . . so . . . we still have . . . loads of pollutants reaching our river systems.
- The coal company . . . put the septic systems in, and the houses close together; nobody ever checked to see if the system would percolate. So the crap ends up running directly into the river, the creek, or whatever. It eventually goes right into the water we drink.
- I think our biggest water problem is not knowing what's in the water.

Loss of Business and Recreational Opportunities

Citizens believed that Letcher County could not hope to attract new industries or increase tourism until the water quality was improved. This included cleaning up the sources of drinking water, cleaning up streams for recreation purposes, and improving the infrastructure that serves both the water and sewage treatment systems. In addition, students were struck by the collective sense of grief expressed over the loss of outdoor recreation. County residents did not expect easy access to museums, theaters, ethnic restaurants, or coffee houses, as would be typical in urban environments. However, in a rural setting, where one expects to find opportunities for fishing, swimming, hiking, camping, and so on, local people were deeply saddened by the loss of these opportunities in their home communities. Thirty-seven of interviewees indicated that children are not allowed to swim in local rivers, creeks, or lakes. Additionally, twenty-four indicated that children and youth are not allowed to fish locally. Adults who do fish throw the fish back into the water rather than eat them. The following quotes represent this theme:

- There won't be no factories here; I don't see that ever happening. . . . It's produce the coal, get the severance tax money, and get our goods out of our ground, the fuels, and the heck with the people and the heck with the nation.
- Tourists aren't gonna come to a dump, a junk hole, or a cesspool. So, if you're going to attract tourists, you're gonna have to clean up your house.
- All this silt and stuff that's going into the streams, it's killing fish and wildlife.
- We try not to get in the lake. There is some iron that runs from that mine . . . so even fish don't like to live in it very much. Minnows can't make it. I guess the pH is bad.
- I wouldn't eat a fish out of this river if you stacked 'em up here in bucketfuls because it's contaminated.
- It kind of goes along class lines. The poor people go ahead and enjoy water sports and things in the lakes here without really constantly paying attention to non-touch advisories. . . . Somebody who is affluent . . . stays away from those things and chooses other places. . . . The poor can't just say: "Let's go somewhere else to have fun."
- We used to fish in the creek behind my house, until you would see the dead animals rotting in the water, so we don't fish there no more.
- We used to picnic on the river. . . . We would go there camping and fishing. . . . I wouldn't camp now if someone held a gun on me.
- I've had my kids go down to the lake . . . and I've noticed . . . they develop little bumps on their skin.

Individual and Collective Solutions and Adaptations

The final theme that emerged from the initial analysis of the interviews centered upon the actions that local people had taken to address problems with their water. Students were particularly struck by the fact that people had not simply given up in despair. Instead, county residents took a variety of actions to resolve their problems. These fell into individual acts and adaptations that people did every day and collective actions in which people joined forces as they attempted to support county- and region-wide change. Individual actions were often costly to people, again highlighting the need to know more about what the poorest residents of the county do in the absence of resources. Students agreed with those citizens who told us that it is impossible to attain a sustainable future unless the very real problems surrounding water are addressed. The following quotes offer examples of both the individual and collective strategies that residents of Letcher County pursued:

- Our water is good, after we got salt filters and potassium filters and chlorinators, and then we got just the regular final sediment filters, just before it goes into the house.
- Our water runs through a salt filter, a potassium filter, and a reverse osmosis system.
- Well, yes, we've got a lot of stuff we do without. I'm on a fixed income. . . . It's tight. . . . I can't pay bills. I'm in debt head over heels. . . . It takes, in a month's time, probably $300 or $350 for the water and filters.
- A lot of people still filter their city [municipal] water.
- I believe the day will come when water will be more important than coal. You can't drink the coal.
- I am a member of KFTC [Kentuckians for the Commonwealth] and we're fighting [for] this water act, about these strip miners polluting the streams, dumping over the hills, and throwing waste and stuff in water, so I'm fighting.
- Community groups have been extremely helpful to me . . . the State Preserve and Nature Conservancy . . . the County Judge [Executive]. . . . KFTC has also been extremely supportive as a community resource group.
- It's a team effort in the community; everybody's trying to help solve these problems.

The Headwaters Project demonstrates several challenges and benefits in collaborative teaching and research. Among the challenges is the need for strong administrative support at all levels of the university.

This support is especially important where interdisciplinary centers are just emerging on a campus. As at any higher-education institution, many faculty at our university still question the value of interdisciplinary studies. Without the support of the university administration in establishing the Center for Appalachian Studies, there would have been no mechanism for faculty to come together and teach across disciplines as we did.

However, while our departments were also supportive of our involvement in the project, our department chairs lacked any mechanism to attach official credit to our workload when we were coteaching these classes. Sometimes this meant that teaching a Headwaters Project course was an overload; other times, chairs reduced a faculty member's "official" workload, internally handling the department's accountability for credit hour production. An institution with more experience in interdisciplinary teaching might have a better system in place. In addition, officially "cross-listing" courses for program credit hours for different majors sometimes takes time in an academic bureaucracy. In many academic settings faculty who are committed to interdisciplinary teaching will be challenged just as we were in breaking new ground to work out the structures for teaching across disciplines.

Because of the support we received from our university and department we found that the benefits of collaborative teaching and research far outweighed the challenges for both faculty and students. As each class of students entered and exited the Headwaters Project, they developed a sense of being part of something more significant than completing program requirements and credits for their majors and undergraduate or graduate degrees. Engaged in mapping, surveying, or interviewing, university students benefited from seeing their individual work as part of the larger project. They also learned valuable information from the students who had gone before them and those who were still part of the project.

Like our students, we have seen the value of linking our work across time and disciplines. When the mapping project began under the direction of geography and sociology faculty, there was no way of predicting that a year later the maps would provoke further investigation and discussion of health and human occupations under the direction of occupational therapy and sociology faculty. Each faculty member in the project has benefited from the work of others. Just as the students felt part of a larger whole, we feel that there was a greater value than the sum total of our individual work. And although some of us have never taught together in a classroom, we feel that we have worked together as members of a team. We have learned a great deal from one another. For us, this has generated professional growth and excitement that we could not have achieved by teaching exclusively within our own disciplines. From the very beginning our center has fostered this type of collaboration, overriding any sense of "territoriality." Our center provides a space for faculty to come together as respected colleagues where we can pursue our work both individually and collaboratively. It is within this environment that the Headwaters Project emerged and developed across time and disciplines.

Notes

A version of this chapter with maps and other graphics first appeared in *Journal of Appalachian Studies* 11, nos. 1 and 2 (Fall 2005): 104–32.

1. Thomas Clark, *The Kentucky* (Lexington: University Press of Kentucky, 1992).

2. *Kentucky River Basin Status Report* (Frankfort: Kentucky Division of Water, 1997).

3. Herby Smith, e-mail to Alan Banks, April 18, 2005.

4. U.S. Bureau of the Census, *Fifteenth Census of the United States: Population,* vol. 3, pt. 1 (Washington, D.C.: U.S. Bureau of the Census, 1930), 902–11, table 11.

5. Tim Collins, Ronald D Eller, and Glen E. Taul, *Kentucky River Area Development District: Historic Trends and Geographic Patterns* (Lexington: Appalachian Center, University of Kentucky, 1996).

6. U.S. Department of Commerce, *Regional Economic Information System, 1969–1999* (Washington, D.C.: Economics and Statistics Administration, Bureau of Economic Analysis, U.S. Department of Commerce, 2001).

7. L. Ormsbee and E. Zechman, "Letcher County Water Quality Assessment" (Kentucky Water Resources Research Institute, University of Kentucky, 2001).

8. *Kentucky River Basin Assessment Report* (Frankfort: Kentucky Division of Water, 2000).

9. *Kentucky River Basin Assessment Report* (2000); Kentucky Water Resources Research Institute, University of Kentucky, *Kentucky River Basin Assessment Report* webpage, accessed September 7, 2011, http://www.uky.edu/WaterResources/Watershed/KRB_AR/INDEX.htm.

10. Lee Colton, interview by Amy Marshall, 2001.

11. Alan Banks, Alice Jones, Anne Blakeney, and students, "The Headwaters

Project: A Collaborative Teaching/Research Project between Citizens of Letcher County, Kentucky, and the Center for Appalachian Studies at Eastern Kentucky University" (report, Center for Appalachian Studies, Eastern Kentucky University, 2003), accessed September 7, 2011, http://www.appalachianstudies.eku.edu/projects/headwaters/report.pdf.

11

Social Theory, Appalachian Studies, and the Challenge of Global Regions

The UK Rockefeller Humanities Fellowship Program, 2001–2005

Betsy Taylor, Lynne Faltraco, and Ana Isla

From 2001 to 2005 several interdisciplinary programs at the University of Kentucky (UK) sponsored a fellowship program for Appalachian activists and international scholars working to build strong communities. Over three years the program awarded seventeen fellowships to scholars and citizen leaders who are at the leading edge of global innovation in new models for partnership among communities, academics, and governments in community-centered and participatory planning. Fellowships were equally divided into two tracks—one for activists working in the Appalachian region, another for scholars from the Southern Hemisphere, or "the global South."

Worldwide, local communities face similar problems as economic globalization hits. Global markets pull jobs and capital around the world at dizzying speeds. How can communities protect their economic, cultural, and ecological health when jobs, young people, and natural resources keep heading over the horizon? We believe that people engaged in local struggles in widely scattered places are capable of envisioning new solutions to these global problems, but they need spaces where they can come together to learn from each other. Our dream was to use the resources of a public land-grant university to create these kinds of spaces. This dream became the UK Rockefeller Humanities Fellowship

Program, titled "Civic Professionalism and Global Regionalism: Justice, Sustainability and the 'Scaling Up' of Community Participation," with the central goal of bringing people together from around the world to connect the dots between their struggles.

Reflecting this spirit, this chapter was written collaboratively. Two of the coauthors were fellows with the Rockefeller program. Lynne Faltraco, who is a key leader in the citizen movement against mega–chip mills and has advocated for a sustainable forestry that builds vibrant, equitable rural communities in Appalachia, was an activist fellow from western North Carolina. Ana Isla was an academic fellow, looking at the narrow environmentalism of "sustainable development" programs in mining, biotechnology, ecotourism, and carbon sinks in Central America. Originally from Peru, she is now based in Canada. The third coauthor, Betsy Taylor, was one of three UK faculty codirectors of the fellowship program (along with Wolfgang Natter, geography and social theory, and Herbert Reid, political science and Appalachian studies). Betsy starts this chapter with an overview of the program and then discusses some of the lessons learned, with a focus on what might be useful to academics trying to plan similar programs. Ana then talks broadly (theoretically) about some of the challenges and possibilities for building solidarity between the global South and global North. Finally, Lynne provides some practical advice on how communities can make use of universities.

The Rockefeller Fellowship Program: An Overview

The Rockefeller fellowship program arose out of a concern that too much in community-academic partnerships is one-way—focused more on changing communities than on changing academics. Too many academics think of public service as outreach, as if the resources and wisdom are on campus and need to be taken out. Our program emphasized what the folklorist Mary Hufford calls "inreach"—bringing a diversity of public concerns into the heart of campus life to shake up the academic status quo and to make university resources directly available to activists.

Inreach creates spaces within campus life where community and scholarly voices can come together in equal and mutually enriching ways to build common purpose and to connect ideas with action. After many years of working on community-academic collaborations out in communities, the fellowship organizers wanted to start a program that could bring the community perspective and community leaders onto campus.

If there is one phrase that summarizes what we were trying to do, it is to build conversations across communication gaps. We had learned that the best way to ask the best questions and come up with good answers is to get many voices and perspectives in critical dialogue with each other. At the heart of our fellowship program was the hope that it could break down some of the divides that make it hard to have good conversations. We wanted to bridge divides between activists and academics, the global South and the global North, activists who work on single issues (culture, forestry, water, economics, labor, and others) and those trying to build multi-issue coalitions, and different disciplines and specializations, especially the big divide between the humanities and the sciences.

The program demonstrated, with great success, that a research university can be used as a site in which to create a hybrid public space, designed to break down the above barriers. Regional analysis and action was central as a strategy for understanding globalization. Regional analysis keeps one close to local realities while enabling useful comparisons between different parts of the world. Activist fellows struggle with global impacts as rural Appalachian economies collapse when textile mills or timber or coal jobs flee, illegal drugs move in, and youth move out. As our conversations deepened, however, the phrase "there are many Appalachias" recurred. The parallels—with the ethnic minority Middlebelt in Nigeria, the Seven Sisters in northeastern India, Indigenous Andean communities, and others—were striking.

At the heart of this program were the fellows themselves. Each fellow came to UK's Lexington campus for a three- to six-month residence to accomplish a project of his or her own design. Over three years, the UK Rockefeller Humanities Fellowships attracted a remarkable group of seventeen fellows. Each year we had four to seven fellows, with the fellowship money equally divided between activists and scholars. The fellows were astonishingly prolific—producing popular education manuals, multimedia productions, and scholarly publications of all sorts as well as developing rich new partnerships and networks.

Anybody who knows about social and environmental justice movements in Appalachia over the past twenty years will recognize names of many of the eleven activist fellows as well as the citizen organizations they represent—including the Highlander Center (Tennessee), Kentuckians for the Commonwealth, Appalshop (Kentucky), Concerned Citizens of Rutherford County (North Carolina), and ACENet (Ohio). The six international fellows have done distinguished work as scholars, journalists, and public intellectuals on how to build democratic collaboration among communities, academics, media, and government to promote equity, democracy, or ecological stewardship. Our international fellows came from diverse interdisciplinary scholarly institutions: the Madras Institute of Development Studies, the Centre for Policy Research, and the Asian Development Research Institute, all in India; Ahmadu Bello University in Nigeria; the University of Western Cape in Zimbabwe and South Africa; and Brock University in Peru and Canada.

A central concept was that democracy must be built across multiple scales simultaneously. The program was designed to link local, regional, national, and global levels of public action, discourse, and imagination. It built rich social bonds and allowed for debates and collaborations among our very impressive fellows and across the diversities they represented. The fellows participated in dozens of public forums, field trips, and discussion groups created by the program, which attracted hundreds of local citizens' and civic organizations, representatives of Appalachian social change groups, students, scholars, culture workers, journalists, and interested others. These crosscutting civic webs and conversations culminated in a powerful wrap-up conference in spring 2005 that brought fellows back to campus.

The wrap-up conference demonstrated the commonalities underlying the many differences within our group. Our program cultivated conversations about the global resonances of seemingly local struggles. For instance, there was a striking dovetailing of themes on the "Globalization and Inequality" panel in our wrap-up conference, an area in which, on the surface, issues might look disparate. Amelia Kirby, an activist fellow from Appalshop, a very creative media collective in eastern Kentucky, opened the panel by talking about the growth of privatized prisons in Appalachian communities desperate for steady jobs in a collapsing rural economy, the global prison industry, prison abuse, and racism. Ana Isla talked about her research in Central America on globalization, ecotourism, neoliberalism, and U.S. military and drug policies, examining displacement of local communities and informal economies particularly damaging to women. Joan Robinett, an activist fellow from Kentucky (see chapter 3), looked at her current work with a community-driven listening project in Harlan County on illegal drug abuse and other issues of civic revitalization and collective trauma, part of another Rockefeller-funded community arts project collaborative with Southeast Kentucky Community and Technical College. Herbert Reid, codirector of the project, closed the panel talking about North-South inequality, corporate globalization, and the myth of progress.

Dramatic interconnections and resonances emerged among these seemingly different topics. There were direct connections among the global jobs crisis; projects promising jobs and prosperity; large amounts of public money leaving local economies and profiting global industries; government corruption, civic distrust, and the undermining of local economies; globalization and the growth of the drug and sex trades; environmental damage; loss of local knowledge; threats to family structure; inflammation of identity clashes of class, race, and gender; detention, surveillance, and insecurity; human rights abuses linked to inequality, police violence, and militarization; and cycles of trauma, violence, displacement, denial, and forgetting. These linkages were sometimes quite specific—as in direct connections (of people, institutional culture, and management models) between military detention practices abroad and the privatized prison industry in the United States. In a recent book Herbert Reid and Betsy Taylor discuss these linkages in detail, drawing on examples from the UK Rockefeller fellowship program and from community-based struggles in many parts of the world.[1]

The impacts of the program flowed out from a "campus around the world" as the fellows took their projects back to diverse efforts to reclaim and reimagine community, democracy, justice, and ecological sanity. There were seven types of direct impact from our fellows' projects. First, some fellows helped create new public spaces to empower the disempowered or bring diverse political actors together into new alliances and public action. Second, some fellows worked to nurture counter publics and alternative civic networks to create the civic preconditions for new social movements or alternative institutions. By "civic" we mean those informal webs and networks through which citizens engage each other in their real, everyday lives to try to work together for the common good. Third, fellows enlarged existing or created new spaces of imagination to steward memory and imagine new futures and solidarities—in art, storytelling, drama, critical journalism, documentary film, and music. Fourth, many fellows created alternative educational media and popular education tools (citizen manuals, films and shows, and workshops). Fifth, several fellows continue to serve on important government advisory boards (national and provincial) or to testify to legislatures on pressing public issues. Sixth, several fellows have been directly involved in electoral politics or citizen lobbying. And last, seventh, fellows continue to work for institutional transformation of academia, expert organizations, journalism, or regulatory bodies.

Likewise, the program had strong impacts on students. Fellows reached many hundreds of students through guest presentations in classrooms and in several dozen campus and public forums sponsored by the program as well as during field trips hosted by grassroots Appalachian social and environmental organizations. At least a dozen graduate students were directly shaped by the fellowship program. Each year the UK faculty codirectors taught an advanced, transdisciplinary graduate seminar that created a forum for resident fellows and students from many disciplines to put academic social theory on globalization from below into dialogue with perspectives and voices emerging from transnational civil society and activist literatures about corporate globalization. More than seventy faculty members actively participated in discussion groups, roundtables, field trips, and presentations.

Reflections from Betsy Taylor, Program Codirector

The UK Rockefeller Humanities Fellowship was a good beginning, but we were definitely going against the grain of academic life. We learned a lot about the institutional barriers to civic professionalism and community-based research. Some of the lessons learned from our mistakes and difficulties may be useful for anyone interested in building similar programs. Looking through the eyes of the community activist fellows, we could see how strange a university is, in many ways bureaucratic and alienating, with faculty under wearying time and work pressures. Mentoring and community building were important to ameliorate the tendencies toward coldness and bigness in university life.

There were large differences in worldview among all involved. For instance, some of those coming from the global South were struck by how disconnected U.S. media and citizens seem to be from on-the-ground realities elsewhere.

To bridge radically different worlds, it was crucial to cultivate critical reflection, openness, and trust in our events and conversations. After some trial and error in the first year, we settled into a system that worked well. The codirectors met with each fellow upon arrival to share food, plan, and build relationships. Each fellow was paired with a codirector who coordinated his or her mentoring and support systems. Different fellows expressed quite different needs. Mentoring included regular (usually weekly) meetings between fellow and assigned codirector; access to advice about people and resources on campus so that the fellow could independently make connections; social events to bring people together; formal reading and discussion groups that included faculty and graduate students with relevant interests and met weekly to discuss the fellows' ongoing work, brainstorm ideas, and share readings; and screenings or presentations of the fellows' films, manuals, and projects for critique and discussion. Fellow-to-fellow learning and debate was crucial. We selected the location of their offices to maximize collegial exchange with like-minded people. In addition, regional citizen organizations generously provided crucial mentoring, hospitality, and networking, especially the Highlander Center and Appalshop.

Activists were hungry for this time to reflect, for freedom from crushing scarcities of money and time, for insulation from the demands of people in need and the pressure of immediate problems demanding practical solutions, and for time to concentrate and go deeper. While it was exciting, it was not easy to transcend differences between global South and North and activist and academic. Differences in language took constant work and will need much more work. Differences in perspective and ideology took time. One of the best parts of the fellowship program was that it provided time in which to build conversations, empathy, and trust—bringing people together in ways that were personally compelling, rich, and often transformative.

This program was possible only because of many preceding years of scholarship and civic professionalism that self-consciously built intellectual and collegial connections across disciplines and with grassroots civil society. It demonstrates that formal programs for transdisciplinary collaboration and place-based scholarship are essential to larger societal goals to nurture public scholarship. The UK Rockefeller Humanities Fellowship Program was a project of the UK Committee on Social Theory, received crucial staff support from the UK Appalachian Center, and had close intellectual links with UK Appalachian studies, environmental studies, geography, and other units with strong interdisciplinary orientation. The advisory board included three regional civic leaders and thirteen senior UK faculty from anthropology, English, geography, philosophy, political science, and sociology.

By almost any measure, our program had remarkable successes. However, there were areas where we came up against deep structural problems. Many activist fellows, for example, face daunting financial scarcity, despite their splendid credentials. There are just not enough jobs out there for people doing truly grassroots work. We believe that there are glass ceilings for grassroots activists if they do not follow narrow professionalizing and specializing paths and hypergroom themselves for donors. For the codirectors this program took more time, work, and care than the typical academic program, leading us to wry recognition of what academic status and reward systems cannot see. We learned a lot about the ways in which universities are like outsized ships that do not easily turn. Yet the joy of the work and our comradeship with one another compensated for the lack of professional recognition.

Reflections from Ana Isla, Fellow, 2002

To start with I will borrow from Cherríe Moraga and Gloria Anzaldúa some thoughts to locate myself. I was born in the rainforest of Peru, but I am living in Canada. Living in Canada, as a Canadian citizen, I am the "other" (for Canadians) but at the same time I am the "them" (for Latin Americans). Latin America is my land, and Canada is my country. I do not feel that I have been a traitor to the geopolitical borders that divide nations of people. My sense of place is on the American continents. Because of that I do not have borders, and all the issues of the American continents are my issues. I have a large space to span, from Patagonia through Argentina and Chile to the Northwest Territories in Canada. I must inhabit many *mundos* (worlds). I have been bridging all these as I go back and forth, showing that whether the "discoverers or imperialists and their children" want it or not, we are all in symbiotic relationship, and we live in a state of deep interconnectedness.[2]

In my academic work I identify with eco-feminism. Eco-feminism elaborates on nonwage women's household work that is often not recognized as work and links it with peasant and Indigenous peoples' subsistence production, which subjects them to underpayment, nonpayment, discrimination, and exploitation. Most women's, peasants, and Indigenous peoples' households combine income from various sources, one of which is their subsistence activity. According to Maria Mies, Veronica Bennholdt-Thomsen, and Ariel Salleh, all of these groups are producers directly concerned with provisioning—the production and maintenance of food and life. They are exploited by capital, not through wages but through their product, which is taken from them with little or very low compensation. These colonized areas are ruled by violence through acts such as rape and domestic violence in the case of women, genocide of Indigenous people and peasants, and ecocide of nature.[3]

Here is an example on how this framework operates in Latin America. Since the 1950s, when the Cold War and Latin American economic development coincided, the United States reorganized Latin American social relations into a money/power dynamic backed by military dictatorships. As a result, millions of South and Central Americans were killed or forced into exile. Following the debt crisis of 1982 neoliberal economic development further reorganized all our ways of being. For those of us who survived, this is like the Auschwitz experience for the Jews, because over the span of two decades (1970–1990) the Cold War and economic development killed more than 1 million women and men, wage workers, nonwage peasants, and Indigenous people. Since the 1990s the establishment of numerous "truth and reconciliation commissions" in Chile, Argentina, Brazil, Guatemala, El Salvador, and Peru, among others in the region, speaks volumes about this tragedy. Since 1990, with the environmental crisis, the political ecology of sustainable development has used conservation as another instrument of colonization and subjugation of Latin America's natural resources and women's, peasants,' and Indigenous people's work. As biodiversity and women's nonwage labor make up the support system that local communities use for survival, the war on subsistence rights expands destitution. Consequently, sustainable development, with its emphasis on economic growth and narrow environmentalism, increases global monetary transactions while destroying local life systems and dispossessing millions of local community members, and global warming proceeds unimpeded.[4]

Women and men in the North and South have more in common than they think. Policy makers in the North and local elites in the South are passing the costs of economic growth to nonwaged poor women, peasants, Indigenous peoples, and nature. Consequently, in both the global North and South societies and cultures are disintegrating. Despite that, both empowered and dominated women and men are very well equipped to take up the case for themselves and other living beings. It is not just Latin American lives and livelihoods at stake here; the natural environment is equally being decimated.

Reflections from Lynne Faltraco, Fellow, 2003

In 2003 I participated in the Rockefeller Humanities Fellowship Program at the University of Kentucky. My own project was titled "Bridging the Gap—A Resource Manual for Local Rural Communities," and it gave me the opportunity to develop a manual that could be used throughout the Appalachian region. The manual was an effort to spotlight expertise and skills in various academic communities and thus to help make the talent available in academia more accessible to rural communities. It sought to bring academics and citizen activists together through this shared resource. I've come to realize over the years (see chapter 6) that universities have many resources and a vast body of knowledge that potentially can be invaluable to community members. University expertise and factual data can help communities build credibility while acquiring knowledge themselves; this in turn empowers local communities and helps them solve problems of environmental integrity and sustainability. While there are so many things I wish I had learned years ago, now I realize that education and knowledge promote power for all citizens by putting issues into some sort of perspective. And while academics have access to resources and both empirical and theoretical knowledge, citizens have real life personal, community, and organizing experience as well as other forms of professional and issue-oriented expertise that can also contribute to building understanding, building alliances, and taking action.

In compiling the manual I partnered with faculty from the Department of Forestry at the University of Kentucky, attended classes, and participated in classroom activities in the anthropology, forestry, political science, and sociology departments. Talking about my personal experiences in community-based work provided students and academics with a citizen perspective on rural communities. In my talks I encouraged those in forestry to look beyond statistics on "board feet" of lumber and consider the human element. To my surprise, some of them had never thought about community before! This established a new connection, and I believe my participation provided students and academics with different methods for addressing community- and forestry-related issues. Through this process, I believe I started to help bridge the gap in one small measure between universities and communities. Universities and their forestry departments, which are entrusted with the job of educating and training young adults in forest management, need to perhaps better link the timber industry with surrounding neighborhoods, especially when there are repercussions from building a wood-processing facility in a particular community.

Through interviews with university faculty I started to compile a resource manual to help connect university faculty with community leadership. Often academic resources are not available to communities, and it was my view that these resources needed to be more accessible. The purpose of the manual was to collect scholars' contact information, a brief biography, fields of expertise, education, experience, research interests, types of classes taught, membership in professional organizations and honorary societies, honors and awards, consulting experience, experience serving as a resource for citizens, and community activities. The last two are very important for citizens and community activists and were highlighted within the manual. If an academic has a history of being involved with citizens and community activities, citizens are more likely to feel that the academic may have a vested interest and genuine concern for his or her neighborhood and community. It is my experience that university faculty who have a history of working with communities tend to have a better ability to understand and appreciate the struggles and challenges that so many communities endure.

So how would a citizen use this manual to access and potentially partner with university faculty members? Let's say a community group was dealing with bad timbering methods that were adversely affecting local water quality. The community group would be able to use the manual's index to identify community-oriented academics who have conducted related research and have expertise on timbering, water quality, and best management practices. They could also find contact information for university faculty and staff, allowing them to call or e-mail to schedule a time to talk.

The manual also explains how to get the most from working with university personnel. It advises that preparing and prioritizing a list of questions in advance will lead to a more productive initial meeting and also show respect for the other person's time. The manual even suggests that sending an e-mail or note of acknowledgement after the meeting may lay good groundwork for follow-up conversations and possible partnerships and collaborations down the road. Finally, there is also a section on other resources available to citizens, including information on various agencies, citizen contacts, consulting firms, organizations, and publications.

My fellowship resulted in the distribution of this resource manual to community-based and nongovernmental organizations, citizen activists, academics, agency officials, industry representatives, private landowners, loggers, legislators, and the media throughout central and southern Appalachia. Communities were encouraged to pass "Bridging the Gap" on to other organizations, activists, and concerned citizens. Community by community, this could create and develop a platform to share myriad resources and knowledge that could help communities.

In my view and experience, it is often difficult for citizens to access accurate and easy-to-understand data to support their campaigns. One of the pitfalls of working in the grassroots arena is that corporations and other power brokers tend to demean citizens by saying that they are not experts and cannot possibly understand the science and technology behind the decisions that citizens are questioning. They often justify this by launching into a technical jargon that few community residents can understand. Yet when sympathetic academics, other experts, and citizen activists come together, there is the potential for new methods and models to evolve that generate a more democratic and more participatory dialogue that can help move us forward toward more sustainable and livable communities.

Knowledge empowers the community to put industry, science, and technical jargon into critical perspective. Let's face it, many community people tend to learn not from books and professional literature but from their own experience. They tend to build their strategies mostly by trial and error. Yet many times when a community finally realizes, for example, that a chip mill or other extractive industry is being built in its neighborhood, it is often too late to reverse the decision.

This fellowship project provided me with the opportunity to compile a resource manual that perhaps could be used by communities throughout the region to help citizens identify possible effective partners earlier on in their own struggles and organizing activities. I thought that spotlighting the expertise and skills of academics who are sympathetic to communities, community-based research practices, and participatory methods could help other partnerships to form. Developing long-lasting, respectful relationships and partnerships can help build sustainable rural communities. It can help local citizens define and democratically take back their neighborhoods and quality of life and achieve environmental sustainability.

Some Final Thoughts

We believe that it is crucial to build new models of partnerships between activists and academics to grapple with the depth of problems that we face in the twenty-first century. Our knowledge systems have become hyperspecialized and disconnected from reality. In real life, problems and solutions are multicausal. However, our traditional university system is itself like a huge extractive industry that mines data, sorts them into specialized categories, and then sucks them out through disciplinary silos that deposit information far away from the reality of real communities. Community members usually understand that their problems and solutions are holistic. Local knowledge tends to see the connections among economic, cultural, political, civic, and environmental challenges and opportunities. Joan Robinett, one of our UK Rockefeller fellows from Harlan County (see also chapter 3), often talks about the importance of "connecting the dots" between issues. It is almost impossible, however, for government agencies and academic experts to connect the dots between issues. The great Kentucky essayist and poet Wendell Berry talks about "one-eyed experts." Too many experts and government bureaucrats are well trained to close their eyes to the complexity of real life—focusing only on the small area in which they specialize.

Once the Humpty Dumpty of real life has been shattered into specialized issues, it can be impossible to reassemble. Knowledge becomes displaced and disconnected from real beings and communities as they actually exist over time. How can a community make informed decisions about what path to take? What is a community to do when it faces the backside of factories headed to China or politicians courting the money (or bribes) of chip mills, toxic waste dumps, pork-fed highways, mountaintop removal, oil rigs, and so on? How can community members evaluate the forces that are coming at them? How can they clarify what they want and know? How can they decide democratically what they want their community to be like in one hundred years? How can local communities build translocal solidarities and alliances?

Communities and academics need to find more powerful models for building partnerships. We believe that such partnerships are crucial to reclaim and rebuild our knowledge system so that it connects better with our policy system. Healthy government policy must be community centered. It should emerge from democratic debate among citizens—especially those directly affected by issues or those most at risk. It should be able to connect highly specialized knowledge with place-based knowledge—so that theory is ground-truthed in real life. It should connect the dots between issues and open conversations across divides of economic class, gender, and ethnic and cultural diversity. It must be sophisticated in multi-scalar analysis—able to move supply from the perspectives of local first responders to regional, national, and global levels. Lynne first introduced the term "first responders" in describing her grassroots organization. The rest of us picked it up, demonstrating the kind of infection of ideas that happened again and again in the synergisms of our ongoing conversations as we struggled to name important, emerging realities for which our language is inadequate.

It seems that our current knowledge and policy systems are crippled, unable to rise to these challenges. Why? In large part, the problem is barriers that separate the wisdom of communities from the resources of experts and government officials. These barriers have been a long time in the making—going back at least one hundred years to the formation of professional associations and the growth of government bureaucracies and universities vulnerable to being captured by corporate or other powers. Fundamental questions of power are revealed in the current movement to rebuild the connections among higher education, real life, community action, particular places, democratic public debate, and collective action.

Recognition of new opportunities for alliances makes this an exciting time. There are many different movements tending in the same direction. Service and action learning programs are growing explosively around the United States—getting college students off campus to volunteer for community action, learn civic skills, and develop values of service to others and to the public good. In many academic disciplines movements are growing for what some call "public scholarship"—research and teaching devoted to serving the public good. In addition to this, we join many who strive for "civic professionalism," or professional development that is immersed and engaged in civic life, the informal webs of everyday action and networking through which citizens communicate and act to take public responsibility. Perhaps most importantly, many citizen organizations are taking on scholarly tasks as they try to protect local communities and environments. For instance, there is a proliferation of citizen-driven "watches"—forest watches, watershed watches, bird watches, neighborhood watches, and so on. Such community-based knowledge systems have often arisen because of lack of government resources or academic care. Many of them are doing better work than so-called experts at monitoring community quality of life and helping communities get useful knowledge.

These movements point in the same direction, but they are not yet well enough connected. Adriana Kezar is right when she says that we urgently need to create a "meta movement" that brings community-based movements together with academic-based movements, opening the possibility of creating a "new vision for the public good" and a "more diverse democracy." If we cannot create this meta-movement, the social charter that has been the historical basis of our democracy might collapse. The UK Rockefeller Humanities Fellowship Program was itself designed to build bridges for this sort of meta-movement. We thought of it as something like building civic infrastructure, webs of civic networks, languages, skills, and mutual knowledge that transgress the barriers described above.[5]

Notes

1. H. G. Reid and B. Taylor, *Recovering the Commons: Democracy, Place, and Global Justice* (Urbana: University of Illinois Press, 2010).

2. C. Moraga and G. Anzaldúa, *This Bridge Called My Back: Writings by Radical Women of Color* (Berkeley, CA: Third Woman, 2002).

3. M. Mies, *Patriarchy and Accumulation on a World Scale: Women in the International Division of Labor* (London: Zed Books, 1998); M. Mies and V. Bennholdt-Thomsen, *The Subsistence Perspective: Beyond the Globalized Economy* (London: Zed Books, 1999); A. Salleh, "Nature, Women, Labor, Capital: Living in the Deepest Contradiction," in *Is Capitalism Sustainable? Political Economy and the Politics of Ecology,* ed. M. O'Connor (New York: Guilford, 1994), 106–24.

4. J. Castaneda, *Utopia Unarmed: The Latin American Left after the Cold War* (New York: Vintage Books, 1994); A. Isla, "Women and Biodiversity: New Areas for Capital Accumulation," *Socialist Studies* 69 (2003): 21–34; A. Isla, "An Environmental Feminist Analysis of Canada/Costa Rica Debt-for-Nature In-

vestment: A Case Study of Intensifying Commodification" (PhD diss., University of Toronto, 2000).

5. A. J. Kezar, "Creating a Meta Movement: A Vision toward Regaining the Public Social Charter," in *Higher Education for the Public Good: Emerging Voices from a National Movement,* ed. T. C. Chambers, J. C. Burkhardt, and A. J. Kezar (San Francisco: Jossey-Bass, 2005), 43–54.

Conclusion

Reflections on Public Scholarship in Appalachia and the South

Stephanie McSpirit, Lynne Faltraco, and Conner Bailey

In this volume we looked at partnerships that have formed across eleven separate cases where community and academic activists have joined forces to challenge corporations, the military, and government agencies. In the first chapter we met Sherry Cable as a young professor and read of her first meeting with the community group Yellow Creek Concerned Citizens, when she had to admit to the group that she could provide them nothing in return for their acceptance of her as a researcher in their midst. Her honesty at that moment went a long way toward winning the group's trust. In the next chapter Shaunna Scott described the process by which community leaders and academic researchers worked together to document land and mineral resources owned by absentee land interests within the Appalachian region. Initially, academic partners serving on the Appalachian Land Ownership Task Force tended to be analytically conservative, reluctant to make statements that could not be supported conclusively by the data. Community partners, in contrast, knew the real story behind the data and were more willing to make statements if the data were not statistically conclusive. Intense discussions led to shared understanding, mutual respect, and consensus. In talking about the partnerships that developed, Shaunna described the whole ALOF project as one that engendered trust and understanding among all partners.

The ability to build alliances based on trust among students, faculty, and people in communities struggling with environmental and public health issues is, we believe, a unifying theme across the chapters of this volume. Partnerships that have developed among faculty at Southeast Kentucky Community and Technical College, Eastern Kentucky University, Auburn University, the University of North Carolina at Chapel Hill, Jackson State University, and the University of Kentucky and with citizens from communities from across Appalachia and the South have been relationships based on trust, mutual respect, and honesty. The issues presented in this volume represent successful cases of community-based research and partnerships and thus stand as good cases of civic engagement that has bridged boundaries that often separate universities and communities.

Within this diversity of settings, actors, and experiences we see commonalities and differences. In most of this concluding chapter we focus on the experiences that bind the volume together. But we should also acknowledge that each case is unique and that none of the actors you have met entered an empty stage. No community is a blank slate and, as a corollary, there are no standard, cookie-cutter recommendations to be found herein, no cookbook full of recipes. What you have seen are challenges and partnerships embedded in the context of past historical events and current political and economic structures within each community and shaped by individuals who have their own histories and personalities.

Trust and Social Capital

Productive relationships of the type described in this volume come from mutual respect, honesty, and trust. In chapter 8 community resident Antoinnette Hudson reflected on the relationship that emerged between her and two university faculty, Suzanne Marshall and Rufus Kinney at Jackson State University. Antoinnette described how their help was very important for two reasons: first, they were able to gather and interpret the hard-to-find data that were needed to sustain protests against the chemical weapons incinerator and Monsanto Corporation; and second, these faculty, by being an equal part of the anti-incineration effort, increased local community residents' confidence in their cause and their own ability to lead. As Antoinnette said, "Most of the people directly affected by the PCBs and the incinerator in Anniston felt they were not alone in their fight, and a bond of trust grew between the community leaders and the academics of Jacksonville State University." For Antoinnette, the trust that developed was possible because both Suzanne and

Rufus let the people of the community know that whatever they had to say was important and worthy of consideration. They also regularly attended community and organizational meetings, whether they were in a public place or in someone's home. In short order, community leaders and activists, according to Antoinnette, saw Suzanne and Rufus as part of the prolonged struggle and as part of the community, not as faculty members from a university.

Steve Wing and Gary Grant (chapter 7) approached their partnership from a similar position of mutual respect and mutual engagement that likewise tended to erase any university versus community divide. When referring to his work with Gary and other community residents, Steve always used the term "we." This reference extended beyond polite words to include both Steve and Gary serving as "coprincipal investigators" on grants, reports, and publications and appearing jointly in public presentations.

The strong trust established between individuals and groups is the basis for what social scientists call "social capital." Social capital strengthens a community's ability to tackle social and environmental problems. This is an important resource to possess, yet it takes constant investment to build and maintain trust. Research has shown that some communities have a greater capacity to tackle environmental problems and crises due to the fact that they have a greater stock of social capital, allowing them to call upon individuals, groups, and organizations both within and outside of their community.[1]

Science and Power

In regulatory and legal settings, where scientific knowledge carries weight, corporations and other powerful outside interests are able to hire both private and university scientists to support their claims. As the chapters in this volume show, community activists have learned that mere expressions of local opposition often flounder on the rocks of what corporations and regulatory agencies are able to pass off as scientifically justified decisions. Many of the chapters in this volume reveal that there is a growing public distrust for the kind of junk science used to justify the continued local exploitation of natural resources and people. Community residents rightly have grown reluctant to trust the safety assurances of those actors who have caused the environmental problems plaguing their community in the first place. As a result of this loss in confidence in institutionalized forms of science and scientific risk assessment, and as demonstrated in these chapters, community residents and local activists have been building their own scientific expertise, working with sympathetic faculty and students to generate their own data to address their own questions about environmental health and safety in their communities.[2]

Development of such "counter science" is shown in the case of the deforestation of the southern Appalachian region from chip mills (chapter 6), and the public health impacts of industrial hog farming (chapter 7) and chemical weapons disposal (chapters 8 and 9). In other cases, citizens simply needed to document the fact that adequate scientific analysis was not, in fact, done to ensure public health after contamination of groundwater and surface waters (chapters 1 and 3). Assistance by knowledgeable university people may help disentangle the technical complexity of certain arguments and reports, but often what community activists need is simply a systematic way of collecting and presenting data, which university faculty and students can help provide. Sometimes the hard reality is that it is easier to challenge (or entirely dismiss) data collected by a community group than that collected by a college or university faculty member. Even if the data have been collected in partnership between the university and the community organization, involvement by faculty may help validate the report and scientific findings in the eyes of the general public, the media, and decision makers.

Trust Me, I'm from the University

Faculty at colleges and universities need to understand that they run the risk that community members will lump them into the same broad category of people coming from outside bureaucratic institutions that do not care about people, communities, and local concerns. As we said, communities are generally untrusting because they are facing big corporations with big money and often feel that they are fighting an uphill battle. The notion of outsiders versus insiders is very clear in environmental battles. University faculty coming into a community that is suffering from environmental harm are likely to be seen as outsiders, and it may take time for community members to fully trust sympathetic faculty and students. This lumping of university researchers into the same category as other institutional power holders is not surprising, since the public knows that universities and colleges rely on corporate and agency connections to fund their research through grants and contracts—indeed, university administrators proudly trumpet such accomplishments!

The interlocking relationships that one finds between corporations, governments, and universities have made many local people justifiably leery and suspicious of being involved with universities and their faculty members. Students and faculty need to realize that they represent powerful institutions within a constellation of powerful institutions, and this can create reluctance on the part of community partners to automatically trust even well-intentioned academics. Trust may have to be earned, and it probably will not be granted simply because you are from a college or university. In this volume we have heard stories from community residents about past experiences with university faculty. Sherry Cable (chapter 1) documented environmental justice advocates' bad experiences with university researchers, who too often were more interested in securing research dollars from a lucrative federal grant than assisting the community in its political struggles against a major polluter that was doing damage to the health of the local community.

One of the main ethical principles guiding research is to do no harm. Students and faculty must tread carefully in entering the troubled and vulnerable terrain of a community in trouble. If one looks honestly in the mirror and sees that one's motivations are guided by ulterior motives such as grant dollars and advancing a research agenda for career or other purposes, than one must also be honest with the community about these motivations. To do otherwise is ethically problematic. And, of course, to drain community resources, including time and energy, in support of a research agenda that distracts attention from the real problems a community faces would be a serious violation of ethical responsibilities.

For every relatively successful community-based partnership, there are likely others that have failed due to a lack of honesty and long-term commitment by faculty or students. These failures harm communities and make more difficult future collaborative efforts between communities and people at colleges and universities. One common source of failure occurs when members of community groups reach out to colleges and universities for help and are met with indifference or worse. Phone calls and e-mails that elicit no response are particularly discouraging in the context of widely publicized collaborations of colleges and universities with corporations and government agencies. Is it any wonder that communities struggling to understand the nature of ecological and public health threats feel abandoned, if not betrayed, when they are ignored?

Beyond the frustration involved, nonresponse to community pleas for help may mean an issue never attracts media attention or never comes to the attention of government agencies that have responsibility for dealing with the problems. It is hard enough to document events that occur, but it is far more difficult to identify something that has been kept from happening through subtle institutional mechanisms that quietly play out on a routine and daily basis and often prevent real problems from ever being acknowledged as real. Lynne Faltraco, the community activist fighting deforestation in the southern Appalachian region and one of the editors of this volume, recounted in chapter 6 her experiences with faculty in forestry departments of several universities. Her experiences were both negative and positive. Some faculty were willing to assist her community group in making their case about the damages and destruction the chip mill industry caused to local communities, economies, and forest resources, and other faculty, tied to the paper products industry, turned a blind eye. Lynne was fortunate to contact Conner Bailey at Auburn and other sympathetic faculty members at several other universities. Together, they worked to provide the documentation and justification that led to the state of North Carolina's forest management plan. Based on her experiences, and as a means to assist other activists in their struggles to bring local environmental issues to the table, Lynne went on to develop a citizens' guide to faculty at universities and colleges throughout the region who might be willing to work with local communities and activists (chapter 11). As one participant in this book project put it, "Whether communities should go to universities for help may depend more on finding sympathetic individuals than on basic institutional good will."[3]

This is all too true that partnerships are between individuals and not institutions, and it is therefore likely that there will always be a need for an up-to-date directory of individual university faculty willing to assist local residents in their environmental claims. As we have said, successful community-university partnerships are based on honesty and trust. One of the purposes behind this book has been to encourage faculty and their students to think more broadly about how knowledge and science can better serve the public good and how to incorporate such thinking into the public and institutional mission of colleges and universities.

Knowledge and Action

Embedded within universities and colleges is a set of conflicting messages about knowledge and action. Many cultures have long traditions of intellectuals leading contemplative lives of the mind rather than being engaged in political struggles for social change. As chapter 1 made clear, the emergence of modern scientific thinking tended to support this separation of knowledge and political action by placing great emphasis on scientific objectivity. It was argued that the intrusion of politics and values into scholars' work would violate the basic canons of the scientific method. Thomas Kuhn's classic work, *The Structure of Scientific Revolutions* (1962), challenged this notion of objectivity by demonstrating that scientists themselves are part of a social order, suggesting that the culture of this social order shapes the questions that they ask and the way that they interpret data.

Scientists and other technical specialists might operate within a culture where they might produce scientific models and projections that defy routine common sense. When the U.S. Army proposed incineration of its stockpile of chemical weapons (chapter 9), common sense told residents and local activists that it was probably not a good idea to burn a stockpile of lethal chemical weapons in the middle of a populated area, despite what the army and its team of scientists said. But as chapter 9 made clear, activists did not base their ensuing actions on gut reactions alone. They sought their own experts to clarify the risks and realities of incineration. Local activists consulted with professors from Eastern Kentucky University and Berea College and many other experts. These consultations gave backing to local claims that incineration was an unsafe and risky technology. As with other cases in this volume, local activists used hard-won scientific credibility as a driver in their continued fight by developing their own arsenal of counter expertise.[4]

Serving Whose Interests?

We should not forget that, despite the interlocking directorate between institutions of higher education, governments, and corporations that has unfolded since the early postwar period, colleges and universities historically have held a special place in our society as bastions of open inquiry and thought, repositories and generators of knowledge, and transmitters of values, culture, and knowledge to the next generation.

Colleges and universities frequently include in their mission statement recognition of their responsibilities to society as a whole. This is especially true of public colleges and universities, including land-grant universities, but even private institutions depend on public goodwill. Public support of higher education depends on the ability of colleges and universities to meet the needs of the taxpaying public. These needs include more than the traditional functions of teaching and research. Society expects colleges and universities to serve the public interest. When these institutions serve only the interests of corporations and government agencies, public trust is eroded.[5]

We recognize that universities and colleges must serve multiple publics and appease various interests. But we reject the idea that universities and colleges serve only institutional forms of power. Many large universities have research parks designed to serve as business incubators that draw on the talents of faculty and graduate students to develop cutting-edge technologies that support industrial production and state and corporate agendas of economic growth. These are natural alignments of technical and engineering interests at universities with corporate and military interests, yet this represents only a part of what colleges and universities have done in service to the public good. Readers of this volume have seen another side to university service. The work described in this volume did not generate substantial funding for university research parks or the bottom lines of university vice presidents for research, but it did make a difference in people's lives and did strongly validate the public mission and service of colleges and universities.

Civic Science

Challenging power can have serious consequences, both for people in communities who speak out and for academics. Despite this the tradition of the engaged scholar persists, perhaps nowhere as much as in Appalachia and the South, where faculty at community colleges and universities work closely with citizen-activists dealing with threats to local ecologies and human communities. This work has come to be known as "civic science," a term that describes a growing sense of responsibility among some scientists to use their talents in the service of society as a whole, not just institutional and corporate sources of power. The idea of civic science was a central theme in a 2002 volume of the *Journal of Appalachian Studies*. In that volume regional scholars advocated embracing and cultivating new partnerships between communities and colleges and universities to tackle the challenges of globalization, underdevelopment, and environmental degradation that face the Appalachian region. Rural sociologists have a long tradition of working with communities dealing with natural resource and environmental threats, and such work fits into the public service tradition of the land-grant university system where historically this discipline was centered. However, as Wendell Berry and Scott Peters tell us, increasing specialization has tended to separate land-grant university researchers from everyday concerns of citizens. Despite this, many scholars have called for more meaningful interaction with policy makers and the general public. In short, current trends of scientific and research engagement with communities are in keeping with strong intellectual traditions that have historically encouraged active political participation by scholars and intellectuals in promoting democratic and participatory social change.[6]

Apart from meeting the obligation to communities that universities and colleges serve, faculty and student involvement with communities facing environmental and other types of problems provides powerful learning opportunities and helps students and faculty draw out the connection between the classroom and real-world circumstances and conditions. This process of community involvement and engagement helps integrate knowledge that often is compartmentalized into separate disciplines within colleges and universities. In addition, students who are involved in or exposed to community projects come to appreciate the wider set of responsibilities that come with being part of a college or university. This understanding can influence their career choices and the paths that they follow into the future. Greater understanding of community needs can help shape research agendas, course designs, and curricular development and infuse the classroom with clear and powerful examples that make academic discussions come to life. Rufus Kinney eloquently took up this latter point in chapter 8, as he reminded us all that sharing ideas in the classroom is the cornerstone of a functioning democracy and that engaged discussion on topics of local and immediate importance draws students into more active learning to build a more vibrant form of democracy.

University and college policies and practices often have the effect of encouraging academics to retreat into the confines of their offices, to specialize, conduct research, and publish for narrow audiences of other academic specialists or to conduct research on behalf of corporate interests. Some of this book's contributors have spoken to these institutional currents and the tendency to separate colleges and universities from everyday democratic discourses about what constitutes a healthy community and a good society.[7]

Other currents challenge this separation of science from democracy by calling into question the notion that science and knowledge are the exclusive domains of experts. The chapters compiled for this volume have promoted the view that knowledge should serve shared and democratic values and that knowledge comes not only from institutional sources. Through civic science, civic engagement, and the emergence of public scholarship we can recognize that all citizens have an interest in knowledge production because such information is often used to justify decisions that affect each of our lives. Moreover, as has been argued and demonstrated throughout this book, citizens increasingly are able to see through the smoke and mirrors of industrial actions and regulatory decisions. Educated citizens have their own ability to set their own research questions and develop their own data to reach their own conclusions about what is good for them, their families, and their communities. Universities and colleges should be part of this education process, supporting students and faculty who want to offer their talents through an engaged civic science while simultaneously being open to what Betsy Taylor, Ana Isla, and Lynne Faltraco (chapter 11) refer to as "inreach"—the penetration of the university by the daily concerns of citizens rather than only the blandishments of institutional powers.

Notes

1. M. Aronoff and V. Gunter, "Defining Disaster: Local Constructions for Recovery in the Aftermath of Chemical Contamination," *Social Problems* 19, no. 4 (1992): 345–65; D. Gill, L. Clarke, M. Cohen, L. Ritchie, A. Ladd, S. Meinhold, and B. Marshall, "Post-Katrina Guiding Principles of Disaster Social Science Research," *Sociological Spectrum* 27 (2007): 789–92.

2. S. Couch, J. S. Kroll-Smith, and J. Kinder, "Discovering and Inventing Hazardous Environments: Sociological Knowledge and Publics at Risk," in *Risk in the Modern Age: Social Theory, Science and Environmental Decision-Making,* ed. M. Cohen (New York: Palgrave, 2000), 193–95; W. Freudenburg, "The 'Risk Society' Reconsidered: Recreancy, the Division of Labor and Risks to the Social Fabric," in Cohen, *Risk in the Modern Age,* 107–20; J. S. Kroll-Smith and S.

Couch, *The Real Disaster Is above the Ground: A Mine Fire and Social Conflict* (Lexington: University Press of Kentucky, 1990); S. McSpirit, S. Scott, S. Hardesty, and R. Welch, "EPA Actions in Post Disaster Martin County, Kentucky: An Analysis of Bureaucratic Slippage and Agency Recreancy," *Journal of Appalachian Studies* 11 (2005): 30–58; S. Scott, S. McSpirit, S. Hardesty, and R. Welch, "Post Disaster Interviews with Martin County Citizens: 'Grey Clouds' of Blame and Distrust," *Journal of Appalachian Studies* 11 (2005): 7–29.

3. J. Gaventa and A. Cornwall, "Power and Knowledge," in *Handbook of Action Research: Participatory Inquiry and Practice,* ed. P. Reason and H. Bradbury (London: Sage, 2001), 171–89; S. Wing, e-mail correspondence with S. McSpirit, 2003; S. Wing, "Social Responsibility and Research Ethics in Community Driven Studies of Industrialized Hog Production in North Carolina," *Environmental Health Perspectives* 110 (2002): 437–44.

4. Thomas Bender, *Intellect and Public Life: Essay on the Social History of Academic Intellectuals in the United States* (Baltimore, MD: John Hopkins University Press, 1993); Stephen T. Leonard, "A Genealogy of the Politicized Intellectual," in *Intellectuals and Public Life: Between Radicalism and Reform,* ed. Leon Fink, Stephen T. Leonard, and Donald M. Reid (Ithaca, NY: Cornell University Press, 1996), 1–25; Mark C. Smith, *Social Science in the Crucible* (Durham, NC: Duke University Press, 1994); Thomas Kuhn, *The Structure of Scientific Revolutions* (Chicago: University of Chicago Press, 1962).

5. Bender, *Intellect and Public Life;* Fink, Leonard, and Reid, *Intellectuals and Public Life;* C. Hale, *Engaging Contradictions: Theory, Politics and Methods in Activist Scholarship* (Berkeley: University of California Press, 2008); S. Peters, *Democracy and Higher Education: Traditions and Stories of Civic Engagement* (East Lansing: University of Michigan Press, 2010).

6. H. Reid and B. Taylor, "Appalachia as a Global Region: Toward Critical Regionalism and Civic Professionalism," *Journal of Appalachian Studies* 8, no. 1 (2002): 9–32; D. Billings, E. Pendarvis, and M. Thomas, "From the Editors," *Journal of Appalachian Studies* 8, no. 1 (2002): 3–8; A. Dirlik, "Civic Scholarship: Comments on 'Appalachia as a Global Region: Toward Critical Regionalism and Civic Professionalism,'" *Journal of Appalachian Studies* 8, no. 1 (2002): 33–41; B. E. Smith, "The Place of Appalachia," *Journal of Appalachian Studies* 8, no. 1 (2002): 42–49; J. Graham, S. Healy, and K. Byrne, "Constructing the Community Economy: Civic Professionalism and the Politics of Sustainable Regions," *Journal of Appalachian Studies* 8, no. 1 (2002): 50–61; J. Gaventa, "Appalachian Studies in Global Context: Reflections on the Beginnings—Challenges for the Future," *Journal of Appalachian Studies* 8, no. 1 (2002): 79–90; S. McSpirit, S. Hardesty, and R. Welch, "Researching Issues and Building Civic Capacity after an Environmental Disaster," *Journal of Appalachian Studies,* 8, no. 1 (2002): 132–43; S. Scott, "From the Sociology of Appalachia to Sociol-

ogy in Appalachia: Transforming SOC 534 into a Field Research Class," *Journal of Appalachian Studies* 8, no. 1 (2002): 144–63; A. Banks, A. Jones, and A. Blakeney, "Headwaters: A Student/Faculty Participatory Research Project in an Eastern Kentucky Community," *Journal of Appalachian Studies* 11 (2005): 104–32; Conner Bailey, "Natural Resource and Environmental Policy for the 1990s: The Relevance of Rural Sociology," *Rural Sociologist* 9, no. 2 (1989): 3–7; W. Berry, *The Unsettling of America: Culture and Agriculture* (New York: Avon Books, 1977); Peters, *Democracy and Higher Education;* Michael Burawoy, "For Public Sociology," *American Sociological Review* 70 (2005): 4–28; Jess Gilbert, "Democratizing States and the Use of History," *Rural Sociology* 74, no. 1 (2009): 3–24.

7. Berry, *Unsettling of America.*

Acknowledgments

In April 2005 we brought thirty-eight individuals to Auburn University. These individuals included university faculty and staff, community activists, and students, all of whom spoke of their collaborative organizing and research efforts in Appalachia and other parts of the South, aimed at protecting their local environment, human health, and the quality of life in their communities. Those discussions were a motivating force behind this book, and therefore we want to acknowledge the Office of Outreach at Auburn University for its generous contribution in underwriting the costs of that 2005 conference.

Roy Silver, the author of chapter 3, wishes to acknowledge that his chapter could not have been written without the assistance of Joan Robinett. Her leadership of the citizens' group and commitment to securing justice for victims of toxic exposure were critical. She reviewed many drafts and provided important insights. She and other members of the citizens' group have become not only allies, but, more important, lifelong friends.

Robert Futrell and Dick Futrell, the authors of chapter 9, wish to acknowledge that their chapter could not have been written without the extraordinary work of Craig Williams, John Capillo, Elizabeth Crowe, and Lois Kleffman. These four are the heart and soul of the citizens' efforts to push the U.S. Army to respond to the concerns of those who will live with chemical weapons disposal in their midst. Without their savvy, strategic, and committed activism, the outcomes of chemical weapons disposal for people and for the environment would have been very, very different.

Contributors

Conner Bailey is a professor of rural sociology at Auburn University, where he has worked since 1985. Bailey's work focuses on the sociology of natural resources and the environment, and he has been working on the connection between forestry and quality of life in the southeastern United States for twenty years. He also has been involved with citizen activist groups fighting solid and hazardous waste facilities in the region, which has led to research on environmental justice. Internationally, Bailey has had a long commitment to research on coastal aquaculture and marine fisheries. He has published in a variety of academic journals, including *Rural Sociology, Society and Natural Resources, Marine Policy,* the *Journal of Development Studies,* and *World Development.*

Alan Banks is a professor of sociology and director of the Center for Appalachian Studies at Eastern Kentucky University. He teaches courses in Appalachian studies and has written several essays about social change in Appalachia for regional journals and books. Alan lives near the Kentucky River in a house he built with his wife, Pat Banks.

Anne Blakeney is an Eastern Kentucky University professor emerita. For twenty-six years, until her retirement in 2009, she directed graduate students in research exploring the impact of environmental degradation on the health and daily lives of people in the coalfields. In 2005 the American Occupational Therapy Association recognized her work with the Lindy Boggs Award, for "significant contributions to occupational justice for the people of Appalachia."

Sherry Cable's primary research interests are environmental conflict, environmental inequalities, and environmental policy. Just published by Temple University Press is her book *Sustainable Failures: Environmental Policy and Democracy in a Petro-dependent World.* Recent articles include "Risk Society and Contested Illness: The Case of Nuclear Weapons

Workers" (*American Sociological Review*), with Tom Shriver and Tamara Mix, and "Mining for Conflict and Staking Claims: Contested Illness at the Tar Creek Superfund Site" (*Sociological Inquiry*), with Tom Shriver and Dennis Kennedy. Cable received the 2011 Allan Schnaiberg Outstanding Publication Award from the American Sociological Association. She is currently working with Donald W. Hastings on a book manuscript, "The Shaping of Pre-industrial Societies by Economic Activities: Classical Athens, Classical/Imperial Rome, and Medieval Britain."

Patrick Carter-North graduated from Eastern Kentucky University with a BA in sociology in 2003. His work with the Martin County project led him to Auburn University, where he completed his master's thesis on watershed management and received an MS in rural sociology in 2005. He currently resides in Portland, Oregon.

Lynne Faltraco's involvement as a community activist and organizer began in 1995. She has been the program coordinator for the Concerned Citizens of Rutherford County and was awarded a Rockefeller Humanities Fellowship to the University of Kentucky, where she completed "Bridging the Gap: A Resource Manual for Local Rural Communities." Her fellowship marked the beginning of this book project. She has spoken at public hearings, town hall meetings, and conferences such as the Southeast Rural Sociological Conference; conducted classes at various universities throughout the Southeast; and given presentations in local communities from Alabama to Pennsylvania. She has written and been featured in numerous articles, editorials, magazines, book reviews, and regulatory publications, such as the North Carolina Department of Environment and Natural Resources and EPA Region 4's performance partnership agreement.

Dick Futrell is professor emeritus from Eastern Kentucky University, where he taught sociology from 1974 to 2005. He now lives with his wife, Janet, at Egrets' Cove, a small eco-village east of Berea, Kentucky. He currently has two writing projects, one tentatively titled "Crossroads Classroom" and the other "Pragmatic Local Sociology, A Workbook." He spends much of his time on household projects, gardens, and projects around Egrets' Cove.

Robert Futrell is a professor of sociology at the University of Nevada,

Las Vegas. His research specialties cover social movements, environmental sociology, sociology of science and technology, and sustainability. He has published widely on science and technological controversy, chemical weapons activism, the U.S. white power movement, and environmental sustainability in the American Southwest. He is coauthor, with Pete Simi, of *American Swastika: Inside the White Power Movement's Hidden Spaces of Hate.*

Robert Gipe is a professor of humanities at Southeast Kentucky Community and Technical College, where he is director of the Appalachian Program. He coordinates a variety of community arts projects in Harlan County, Kentucky, and holds a master's in American studies from the University of Massachusetts at Amherst. He is originally from Kingsport, Tennessee, and formerly worked at Appalshop, a media arts center in Whitesburg, Kentucky.

Mark Grayson received his degree in political science from Eastern Kentucky University and taught social studies in Martin County, Kentucky, until his retirement. While teaching middle school Grayson also published and edited several weekly newspapers and was editor/publisher of the award-winning Martin County *SUN* from 1992 to 2001. Grayson was awarded an honorary doctor of law degree from Eastern Kentucky University in 2005 for his work in journalism and education as well as for protecting the environment. He continues to work as a journalist/editor and publisher of the now-online *Levisa Lazer.*

Sharon Hardesty is a lecturer in sociology at Eastern Kentucky University, where she teaches courses in introductory sociology, social problems, community, and research methods. She has worked on several student-faculty research projects in Kentucky and West Virginia.

Antoinnette Hudson has been an instructor of history at Jacksonville State University, Jacksonville, Alabama, since 2003; she teaches classes in American and Alabama history and is currently doing oral historical research on African American veterans of World War II. She has given speeches at conferences on topics ranging from "African-American Soldiers and the Civil War" to "The Endangerment of Chemical Waste on the African-American Community of Anniston, Alabama."

Ana Isla is an associate professor of sociology and women's studies at Brock University, Canada. She teaches courses on contemporary social theories, feminist theories, gender and society, and women and development. Isla is currently conducting research in two areas: an exploration of subsistence economies in the Peruvian rainforest, and Canadian mining in Latin America. She serves as a board member for the journals *Canadian Woman Studies* and *Capitalism Nature Socialism.*

Alice Jones is the director of the Eastern Kentucky Environmental Research Institute and a professor of geography at Eastern Kentucky University. Her decades of teaching, research, and applied community service have centered on the relationship between land use and water quality in both urban and rural landscapes. Since 2006 Jones has spearheaded and supervised the Big Dip community-based sampling project in Eastern Kentucky—a diagnostic sampling of dissolved oxygen, pH, conductivity, and iron from more than sixteen hundred first-order headwater streams in eastern Kentucky.

Rufus Kinney, a native of Birmingham, Alabama, attended Washington and Lee University and earned an MA in English from the University of Montevallo. He taught composition, literature, and speech at Jacksonville State University from 1984 until his retirement in 2008. He is a longtime activist in environmental issues and in 2002 received from the Alabama Chapter of the Sierra Club the Coosa Pit Bull Award "for outstanding work for environmental justice and human health." He has an abiding interest in, among other things, Celtic history and culture as well as Hinduism and Eastern philosophy.

Suzanne Marshall is an independent scholar, currently residing in Danville, Virginia. She previously was a professor of history at Jacksonville State University in Alabama, where she taught courses in environmental history. She was environmental justice chair for the Alabama Chapter of the Sierra Club, chair of Serving Alabama's Future Environment, and a member of the Chemical Weapons Working Group. She has published articles and a book, *We're Just Trying to Save Your Water, Lord,* an environmental history of the South.

Nina McCoy is a twenty-eight-year veteran biology teacher at Sheldon

Clark High School in Martin County, Kentucky. Her greatest passions are environmental justice and educating young people. She and her husband, Mickey, continue to lobby and protest against mountaintop removal coal mining and for environmental protection for the Appalachian Mountains she loves so dearly.

Stephanie McSpirit is a professor of sociology at Eastern Kentucky University, where she has been a faculty member since 1995. McSpirit teaches classes in statistics, introductory sociology, environmental sociology, animal studies, and community-based research methods. She has worked with teams of students on research projects related to environmental and water quality issues in Appalachia and throughout the state of Kentucky and has published her research in various academic journals, such as the *Journal of Appalachian Studies, Southern Rural Sociology,* and *Society and Natural Resources.*

Shaunna L. Scott is an associate professor of sociology at the University of Kentucky, where she has worked since 1990. She is the former president of the Appalachian Studies Association and director of Appalachian studies at UK. She currently serves as director of graduate studies in sociology. Her research, which focuses on class, gender, politics, and the environment in Appalachia, has been published in *American Ethnologist, Qualitative Sociology, Rural Sociology, Action Research, Appalachian Journal,* and *Journal of Appalachian Studies.*

Roy Silver has been a professor of sociology at Southeast Kentucky Community and Technical College since 1989. He teaches introductory sociology, sociology of the community, and modern social problems and works with students to develop community-based research projects. From his central Appalachian coalfields home in Harlan County, he continues to work in partnership with other members of his community on a number of community development initiatives and with many grassroots citizen groups.

Mansoureh Tajik is a faculty member in the School of Health and Environment, Department of Community Health and Sustainability, University of Massachusetts at Lowell. She focuses on environmental health and justice, geographic assessment, and media literacy. She has an integrated approach to teaching, research, and service through participatory student education and community-based participatory research.

Betsy Taylor is a cultural anthropologist who has worked on many projects for community-driven, integrated, sustainable development and participatory action research in Appalachia and India—including health, agriculture, forestry, culture, and environmental stewardship. She is coauthor (with Herbert Reid) of *Recovering the Commons: Democracy, Place, and Global Justice,* and is currently a research scientist in the Department of Religion and Culture at Virginia Tech. At the University of Kentucky she served as codirector of environmental studies and research director for the Appalachian Center and was on the faculty of the social theory program.

Index

Aberdeen (MD): chemical weapons disposal in, 156, 161

absentee landownership, 1, 39

academic-activist collaborations: in Anniston (AL) environmental justice activism, 15, 149–52, 167; benefits of, 5–6, 66–67, 110, 127–30, 233–34; in CCRC, 13, 110, 112–13, 114–17, 127–30; in CCT, 13–14, 132, 134–38, 141, 142–44; commonsense intuition legitimized in, 181–82; failed partnerships, 237–38; impact of, in universities, 6; in Madison County (KY) anti-incineration movement, 181–82, 190–91; models for, 229–31; power disparities in, 32, 218; public policy influenced by, 131–32; relationships in, 42–44, 234–35; social capital in, 235. *See also* participatory action research; *specific partnerships*

Ace Magazine, 102

ACENet, 220

Adams, Sandra, 100

Adkins, Lilly, 88

African Americans: in Anniston (AL), 14–15, 147–48, 150–51, 155–56, 162–63; and CCT, 133–34, 135, 137; chip mill jobs and, 111; industrial hog farm locations and, 13–14, 133, 138; land loss litigation by, 141–42; PCB contamination and, 14–15, 155–56. *See also* Anniston (AL) environmental justice movement; Concerned Citizens of Tillery (CCT)

Ahmadu Bello University (Nigeria), 220

air stripping, 69

Alabama: Appalachian Land Ownership Study in, 1, 39, 42; CCRC partnerships in, 121; landownership and taxation in, 47

Alabama Department of Environmental Management (ADEM), 159

Alexandria (AL), 157

American Land Forum Magazine, 47

American Social History Project, 51

Anniston (AL): chemical industry in, 147, 148, 150; CWWG group in, 149; location of, 147; media coverage of, 156–57; military facilities in, 147, 148, 151; PCB contamination in, 14–15, 148, 150, 151–52, 157, 234; poverty rate in, 151; racial/class divides in, 14–15, 147–48, 150–51, 155–56, 162–63

Anniston (AL) environmental justice movement: academic-activist collaboration in, 15, 149–52, 167; alliances of, 152–53, 154, 155–56, 160–62; chemical weapons disposal focus of, 5, 149–51, 154–57, 158–67; environmental justice focus of, 149, 152–53, 154, 164; march for environmental justice (2002), 163–68; media coverage of,

235–37, 240; historical role of, 17, 239–40; knowledge and action in, 239; participatory action research by, 17, 32–35; partnerships and "inreach" into, 6, 218–19, 242; publication motivations at, 7–8; public distrust of, 235–37; resource manual for working with, 227–28; resources of, 226. *See also* academic-activist collaborations; parasitic research; participatory action research; *specific institutions*

Colonialism in Modern America (Lewis, Johnson, and Askins), 40

Commission on Religion in Appalachia, 47

Common Ground, 176–77. *See also* Chemical Weapons Working Group (CWWG); KEF/CWWG; Kentucky Environmental Foundation (KEF)

commonsense intuition, 181–82

communities: government agencies distrusted in, 11–12; re-democratization of, 119–20, 221–22; resource manual for, 226–29. *See also* academic-activist collaborations; local environmental activism/activists

community activism/activists. *See* academic-activist collaborations; local environmental activism/ activists

Community Against Pollution (CAP), 151

community arts projects, 221

community-based scholarship, 234; barriers to, 222; models for, 39–40

community colleges, 67. *See also specific institutions*

community development model, 121–22

Community Environmental Legal Defense Fund, 124

Community Farm Alliance, 54

Community Health and Environmental Reawakening (CCT), 144

community service, 67

community surveys, 64–71

Concerned Citizens Against Toxic Waste (CCATW): affordable drinking water project of, 72; alliances of, 64, 65–67, 71, 72; blood lead testing by, 64; community survey initiated by, 64–71; formation of, 62; goals of, 62; government response to groundwater poisoning concerns of, 62–63; kidney study by, 71–72; participatory action research by, 11, 63–64, 66, 68, 72–73

Concerned Citizens of Madison County (CCMC), 174–77

Concerned Citizens of Rutherford County (CCRC): academic-activist collaboration in, 13, 110, 112–13, 114–17, 127–30, 238; alliances of, 120–23; awards received by, 119; community development model as basis of, 121–22; "counter science" developed by, 236; early activism of, 2–3, 13, 112–14; educational programs of, 117–20, 121, 128; expanded mission of, 117, 121–22; formation of, 2–3, 110, 112, 117; Good Logger Award given by, 118; impact of, 127; and UK Rockefeller fellowship, 220; publications of, 122–23; Willamette Industries sabotage and, 124–25

Concerned Citizens of Tillery (CCT): academic-activist collaboration in, 13–14, 132, 134–38, 141,

258   Index

North American Goldman Environmental Prize, 16; on PMCD, 179–80
Williams, Susan, 44, 49, 50
Wilson, Darlene, 96, 101
Wilson, Larry: alleged blacklisting of, 25; burnout suffered by, 22, 26; on EPA, 24; lay knowledge possessed by, 32; as YCCC president, 21–22, 24
Winfrey, Charles ("Boomer"), 43, 45–46, 49, 53–55
Wing, Steve, 14, 134, 136–37, 140–41, 142, 143–44, 235
Wirtz, Willard, 41
WMMT (radio station), 98
Wolf Creek, 75–76
Womersley, Michael, 78
Wood, Edward, 154
Woodard, Carlos, 167–68

Woods, Abraham, 163
World War II, 201
WYMT (TV station), 98

Yates, Evelyn, 150
Yellow Creek (Bell County, KY): location of, 22; pollution of, 22–26
Yellow Creek Concerned Citizens (YCCC): activist strategies of, 24–26; Sherry Cable's involvement with, 10, 21–22, 27, 32, 233; class action suit filed by, 26; formation of, 24
YMCA Blue Ridge Assembly (Black Mountain, NC), 120

Zaluski, Joseph, 104
Zimbardo, Philip, 29–30

CPSIA information can be obtained at www.ICGtesting.com
Printed in the USA
BVOW031450270612

293783BV00001B/13/P